THE
COMPLETE
FREELANCER
GUIDE

THE
COMPLETE
FREELANCER
GUIDE

Become Your Own Boss, Do What You Love, And Make Money Doing It

IAN BALINA
RAVNEET KAUR
ASWIN SATYANARAYANA

Dedication

I dedicate this book to my family—Charles, Vickie, Edmund, Charles Jr. and Queen. Thanks for inspiring me every single day. I love you more than I can put into words. You are my motivation, and my why. This book is merely the beginning; the best is yet to come.

Contents

Freelancing

Hustling And Finding Work

Sales And Marketing

Things To Avoid

Client Relationships

Hiring Or Working With Other Freelancers

Resources

Guides

Preface

This book is published by Peer Hustle, an on-demand local freelancer marketplace.

It comprises of compiled writings on freelancing from the staff at Peer Hustle. The book is divided into sections and can be read in order or out of order, so feel free to jump around if you like.

For more information on Peer Hustle, or to download the app, head to www.peerhustle.com. We can also be reached at info@peerhustle.com.

Hope you enjoy our writings on freelancing, and become the superhero freelancer you are capable of becoming.

Cheers,

Ian Balina
CEO of Peer Hustle

Freelancing

7 Vital Questions To Ask Yourself Before Becoming A Freelancer

Being your own boss is tempting, but switching your career from being a full-time employee to a freelancer can be a thought-provoking decision. Of course, the desire to bid good-bye to your steady job is more than likely the result of your feeling overworked and burned out, which seems to have taken a horrific toll on your physical and mental stamina. Add to it the brutal schedule, office politics, and psychological burden and the stress of not getting what you deserve for your hard work, perseverance, and commitment; you are almost certain to say it quits to your regular job.

This is exactly what I did seven years ago! But my decision didn't come out of the blue. I did introspect to ask myself if this was the best decision I could make and whether going for the magical world of freelancing was the right choice for me.

My self-confidence guided my way toward the freelancing route.

True, freelancing is a lucrative career opportunity, with the promise of autonomy, flexibility, and control, but getting success in the freelance field isn't a cakewalk. Quitting your 9 to 5 job for a freelancing career requires particular skills and the ability to work on your own and market yourself better than others to prospective clients. Doing so can help you outshine your competition and get a stream of clients to kick-start your career.

Here are 7 questions to ask yourself before making this life changing decision and giving up your status as a regular employee:

1. Can you work on your own?

Are you a self-motivated individual who can go it all alone? Do you have the confidence to work alone? Remember, working alone isn't everyone's cup of tea. It is not something that everyone can do, especially if you enjoy being in the company of others.

If you envision working for yourself in your company, freelancing is for you, with zero office drama and no coworkers to disturb you. But if you are someone who does best when there is a manager or senior to be accountable to, you are probably in the wrong boat.

True, freelancing offers you the autonomy to work the way you want, flexibility to work at your own pace and schedule, and control over what you do. But it does require good organization skills. Since you are your own boss and the entire burden is on your shoulders. As a freelance professional, you need market your services to sell your skills and also take care of invoicing and paperwork, besides working on the deliverable.

Not only this, you should be ready to give up your free time occasionally for timely completion of the flood of work coming your way. After all, you are working alone! Can you push yourself without anybody having to push you? Deadlines are always tight, and if you cannot meet them, you risk losing the client forever, as you will be seen as unreliable and undisciplined.

Remember, being your own boss doesn't mean you can be undisciplined. You have to be self-disciplined and sincere about your work to keep clients happy and coming back for more.

2. Do you have a marketable skill?

When your day job feels like hell, you are almost certain to entertain thoughts of switching over to freelancing. But this does not mean that you will immediately taste success in the freelance industry. Of course, you will need to pass through a lot of hurdles and spend time finding new clients. Unless you are well-established in the freelancing marketplace, you will need to look for work all the time.

So do you boast a skill that is in demand? If you're unsure whether you have skills that prospective clients would be willing to pay for, you may have to rethink your decision to choose freelancing as a career.

Introspect to find out what you are good at and how you will spread the news about your work and skills. Don't market yourself as a generalist; it is important to call yourself an expert in your industry. Peer Hustle is one platform where you can search clients that are looking for your services. Spread the word about yourself on these platforms, declaring your entrance into the freelancing marketplace and telling what unique value you bring to the table.

3. Do you have financial support?

Money doesn't fall from trees in the freelancing industry. It requires perseverance, commitment, and a lot of effort to succeed if you decide to choose freelance as a career. Of course, you have control over how much you earn in this industry. The greater the number of hours you put into each job, the more you can make!

But you need a strong portfolio to attract long-term clients and land big jobs, which can prove to be an income goldmine if you continue to keep clients happy with timely, quality submissions.

However, before quitting your regular job, make sure you have adequate financial support to take you through the initial dry period when you jump onto the freelancing bandwagon. Build your expenses rationally so that your savings are a savior when you hit a dry patch.

As a self-employed professional, you need to be able to keep at least 40% of your paycheck for retirement, health and life insurance, taxes, and vacations. Consider which perks you would like to keep and how they will be paid.

4. Do you have a network?

Do you have a strong network of professionals? Are you connected to other professionals in the industry? The most successful freelancers are those who are connected to others, as it is these connections that become an important source of business.

But this does not mean you need to feel distraught if you aren't part of an extensive network.

Attend conferences, webinars, reach out to professionals through social networks, and share your unique skill sets in an on-demand freelance marketplace, such as Peer Hustle. Spread the word what you are doing.

Encourage your friends, relatives, and neighbours to spread the word about your work specialization and skills. An important part of your network is a friend who is already freelancing has in-depth knowledge of the industry and can point you to resources. It will help to seek advice from those that have more experience in freelancing industry than you.

Or you may approach your previous employer to be your first client. If you enjoy a good rapport with your boss, do not hesitate to ask them if they would accept your plea to give you work on a freelance basis, so that you could continue your relationship with the company.

5. Do you have a strong portfolio?

What is it that brings clients to your doors? Of course, it is your strong portfolio that clearly details all the experience you have under your belt and talks about your specialization and skills with illustrations and samples.

Does your portfolio set you apart from the competition? Do you have something unique to offer clients? Or what unique value would you bring to your client's business? Does your portfolio walk clients through your expertise and skills?

Remember, it's your portfolio where everything starts, so you should have an impressive portfolio that leaves a lasting impression on prospective clients and pulls them toward your services. Tell them why you are different from others and how you can help solve client's problems.

Establish a connection between your skills and solutions and their problems and you are most likely to land a client and job!

6. Can you interact with clients?

Most freelancers are known to be introverts. Unless you've dealt with clients and customers in your office, you may have a tough time handling them when you take to freelancing. Of course, you'll have to learn to be polite, courteous, and responsive while interacting with clients.

True, in the freelancing industry, you are your own boss, but there is still a "big boss" on top of it all - the client you are working for. Treat your clients like your boss and keep them happy and impressed so that they keep coming back with more lucrative opportunities for you.

As an independent professional, you may find it challenging to negotiate a fair rate for your services with clients. There isn't anything wrong with starting your freelancing career with a low rate. Gradually, as you build your portfolio, reputation and sharpen your skills, you can raise your fee and keep it competitive. Remember, most clients are open to paying more for high-quality work.

Additionally, another prerequisite for a freelancer is to keep calm even in tiring situations and dealing with tough and difficult-to-please clients. The key is to stay cool and not let your emotions take over.

7. Do you have a dedicated space for working?

As a solopreneur, you are free to choose where you want to work. Whether it's your home, café, friend's place, or while moving in a train or by car, you are in full control when it comes to choosing the location of work.

However, this does not mean you do not need a dedicated workstation, especially if you are planning to jumpstart your freelancing career. If you aren't self-disciplined, it would be hard to taste success in the freelance industry.

Freelancing is just like setting up an office at home, with you as the team leader, employer, accountant, and boss. It is important that you create your daily work schedule and follow it holistically. Having a dedicated work space will help you focus better on the job and take things seriously.

Remember, freelancing is an income goldmine for the right professional, who can exhibit sheer dedication, commitment, confidence, and self discipline – the hallmarks of success in the freelance industry.

How Is Freelancing Better Than A Job?

So, what do freelancers really do? Do they really wear pajamas? Are they the hidden workforce that the world believes they are?

Alex Altman of Time.com believes that the future of work is like no one's ever seen before—it could be a bit of cloud computing, nanotechnology, or even Genomics.

While no one can predict the future accurately, the Internet has brought in a revolution of sorts, where the nature of work is concerned.

We now have freelancers, and there are a lot of them at that. Ever so slowly, there's been an up rise.

According to Jeff Wald, cofounder of WorkMarket—who wrote a guest post on Forbes.com—the number of freelance workers is expected to outpace full-time workers by 2020, worldwide.

Contingent, temporary, freelance, flexi-workers, and pay-as-you-go vendors are the new normal with more than 42 million independent workers in the U.S alone and that's up from 10.3 million workers in 2005.

As for the rest of the world, the numbers are a lot more but vague. Freelancers Movement puts up a few numbers. Italy and Germany have about 1.68 million workers and 1.53 million workers.

Australia has about 2.1 million people and counting. India and Philippines have no official count yet but the numbers are rising.

If freelancing is the future, and if so many people do it, does that make it a better choice than a full-time job? Is it really that good?

Yes, it is. This is how freelancing is better than a job:

Freelancing is semi-entrepreneurial

We call it semi-entrepreneurial only because there isn't any form of leverage in freelancing. This is where it's almost similar to a job. So, freelancing is all about a skillset you wield, and you get paid for that.

There's only so much time and effort you can expend to get paid in return, just like it is for a day job.

However, that's also where the similarity ends.

Everything a freelancer does is entrepreneurial.

For one, there's the question of figuring out what to do, deciding the scope of services to sell, packaging services, and setting up shop, then there's marketing 101.

Then, there's the daily hustle, the uncertainty, numerous pitches, getting things done all on your own, actual work, delivering work, and getting paid (and making sure the payments come through).

Full-time employees don't have to lift a finger in comparison. They just have to do their job.

Freelancing has no second chances

Employees are hired. They then go through rigorous onboarding sessions; training phases and continue with on-the-job training. All along the way, mistakes are treated as lessons and employees usually get mentors, coaching, and tons of opportunities for skill development and to get better at their job.

As a freelancer, you are on your own. Skill development is your prerogative. You don't get any onboarding sessions. You won't be trained. You won't have fancy meetings. Of course, you'll not have the privilege of making mistakes.

The best that you'll get is a project brief.

Freelancers have to hit the ground running. If you are a freelancer, clients presume that you know – and have the skills – for the job you are hired for.

You are your own mentor. You are your boss. You have no second chances.

Freelancing makes you an expert on handling uncertainty

Ever seen any of those forums where people complain endlessly about late salary payments? You do know that stress is a common ailment that the American workforce suffers from, don't you?

Full-time employees don't have to worry about the paycheck. In fact, they plan an entire lifetime around that paycheck.

As a freelancer, you don't get a chance to do that.

You can't whine. You can't complain. In fact, we'd be surprised you actually got the time to post a whining comment anywhere about how life treats you.

You'll wallow in uncertainty.

You thrive on the fear of non-payments, no shows, and occasional vanishing acts that clients do.

You become a pro in cash flow management. You handle uncertainty like most people handle breathing.

Freelancing can make you rich

A job is never the path to real riches. While freelancing also isn't the real path, at least it's better than working a full-time job and depending on a singular source of income.

You have windows of opportunity with every client you manage to source. You have a chance to work as hard as you like, charge as much as you like, work for as many hours as you like, upsell services, and experiment with alternative sources of income on top of all this.

You have a choice to make as much money as you want, given your own personal constraints.

Plus, you can claim expenses when paying taxes.

Freelancing prepares you for the Big Game

If you work hard at a day job, the best you get is to move up the ladder.

You get promoted.

Possibly, you get paid more your employer decides that.

If you do well with freelancing, however, you are in preparation for the big game. You understand business, you have an ever-growing list of contracts, and you are already in the throws of uncertainty. You manage hustle, sales, cash flow management, vendor management, customer relationships or client management, tax payments, and more.

This is the door to real entrepreneurship. You'll know how to build systems, start any business, and scale businesses the right way.

How do you find your freelancing stint to be? What's your take on freelancing?

Top 12 Paying Freelance Jobs And Careers

If you are fed up with the daily grind or are looking to make some extra dollars, you make a perfect candidate for a freelance career. Many freelancing opportunities are already up for grabs. With the available freelancing gigs, you can match your full-time income, if not make more than that. Of course, setting up for a freelancing career may not be as easy as you think, but there are some paths that can direct you to amazing freelancing opportunities. There are a few on-demand freelance marketplaces, such as Peer Hustle, where you can match your skills with an open gig and land in a freelance opportunity.

The perception that the traditional full-time job is secure no longer holds true. There is no guaranteed security for your so-called permanent job. Self-starting and the ability to pick projects of your interest gives you more ownership over your career, without having to be under the prying eyes of a boss. Freelancing offers you the flexibility of schedule and location as well as choosing a project that interests you.

What are the top paying freelance jobs

Long gone are the days when freelancing opportunities were available only in the writing, editing, and design fields. Today, there has been a broadening of freelance gigs across different industries and occupations. So you have an amazing range of freelance job openings in different niches – pick the niche you are passionate about and start working. However, make sure that you do not under-sell yourself as long as you have enough gigs to work on.

1. Writing

Freelance writing is one of the most common work from home opportunities available today. Writing takes plenty of research, but the best thing about choosing freelance writing is that you do not need a major investment or any special equipment to get started. You simply require a working computer and Internet connection, and of course, should know how to write clearly and without any grammatical mistakes.

From writing academic papers to CVS, reports, and ebooks, you can flood yourself with umpteen freelance writing opportunities. The key is mastering your writing skills on all subjects to make yourself more desirable. This is exactly what I did a few years back when I started my freelancing writing career. Give your best performance every time, and you will have clients for life.

2. Design

If you have been working as a web or graphic designer and are least interested in continuing with your boring 9 to 5 job, you can enjoy a great career as a freelance designer. The design field is growing by leaps and bounds, especially with the growth of the Internet marketplace. A large number of businesses are jumping on to the Internet bandwagon to find a place in the online market and spread the word about themselves. As such, they need an appealing website and logo design. They can leverage your skills to carve out a niche for themselves in the industry.

Join sites like Peer Hustle and announce to the world your entry into the freelance industry and get your designs seen by thousands of potential clients. Don't just wait for clients to approach you— adopt a proactive approach and make it possible for prospective clients to stumble upon your work in such on-demand platforms and come in contact with you.

3. Translation

The freelance translation industry is rising quickly, with the growth of the Internet. If you're fluent in a second language, chances are you can land in translation gigs. A certification from the American Translators Association can be a major plus and help you earn an average of $72,000 annually, compared to $53,000 for someone without that certification.

Of course, prices vary depending on what languages you are good at translating.

4. English tutor

English is the lingua franca – global language in demand everywhere. If you have excellent verbal and communication skills, you may choose to become an online English tutor of people who are non-native English speakers. Landing your first online teaching job may be difficult, especially if you do not have the experience to back your language skills. Nevertheless, you may start with offering a few free lectures and make an instant impression on prospective clients.

5. Programming

If you know a good deal of coding and scripts, you may look for freelancing gigs in the programming industry. Due to the significant development of software industry, there is a high demand of programmers. But simultaneously, an increasing number of people are choosing programming as a career, which has raised the competition. As companies are interested in hiring the best talent for their projects, you can impress them with your portfolio and services and get clients for life.

6. Search Engine Optimizer

Businesses of all sizes need the services of search engine optimizers to boost their online presence and get their websites ranked higher. It is here that an SEO can come to their rescue. This is a high paying gig and high-end freelancers even make as much as $300 and $500 per hour. At the entry level, you may make $50/hour.

Stay updated with the changing Google algorithms that have an impact on website ranking. This will ensure that your client's sites do not bear the brunt of algorithm changes. As businesses look for optimizers to improve their site ranking, many freelancing opportunities are up for grabs in the industry.

7. Marketing

The demand for online marketers is on the rise, as more and more businesses are looking for part-time professionals that can spread the word about their brand and services and take charge of their marketing campaigns.

If you understand branding, marketing, communication, engagement, advertising, targeting, and follow-up, and can help clients in marketing their brand through diverse promotion campaigns and strategies, this is a perfect freelancing career for you.

Prove your worth by marketing yourself first. If you can impress a prospective client through the way you sell your services, you can easily land in your first freelancing opportunity.

8. Mobile Development

Mobile developers make a good amount of money in the freelance industry. They can easily compare with web designers and developers. Some corporate clients are even ready to shell out thousands of dollars for having a single app developed. Mobile app development is the job of specialists, and if you can prove your worth to a potential client, the window to success will instantly open for you, and you can make a good income.

9. Social Media

Social media is everywhere. An increasing number of businesses are looking to harness the power of social networks to capture the vast majority of potential customers there. For this, they need the services of social media experts. While those new to the field may charge $15 per hour initially, the cost keeps going higher with experience, with a huge majority of social media experts charging as much as $250/hour.

10. Photography

Photography has become a much-desired profession today, and freelancers are no exception to it. In fact, clients are looking for freelance photographers that specialize in different forms of photography. To start with, you can charge anywhere between $1,500 and $2,000 per project, which involves a few hours of shooting and editing.

You may sell photos to a magazine or work for a client. Different photography specializations come with different price tags. It may help to start small, with little equipment investment. You can expand your equipment list as you grow.

11. Videography

Just like photography, doodling is becoming increasingly popular. More and more businesses are looking for ways to better spark creativity and interest in their target audience. Moreover, doodling is being seen as a way to share complex concepts in an easily comprehensible way.

If you have video animation skills and are proficient in Adobe Illustrator, Adobe Premiere, Adobe After Effects, Adobe Photoshop, Camtasia, jQuery, motion graphics, whiteboard animation, Flash animation, and illustration, you can become a freelance doodle video creator. Companies are interested in telling their stories in unique and engaging ways, and you can come to their rescue through your info-doodling skills.

12. Transcription

There has been an impressive growth in the transcription industry. As a result, it has seen a rise in demand for freelance transcriptionists. If you are good at converting speech, from the format of an audio or video file into text, you can take up the job of a transcriptionist. With the rise of webinars, digital boardrooms, and video conferencing, the demand for transcriptionists is rising rapidly. You can make as much as $12 per hour initially.

The freelance industry is fast growing. If you have creative skills, freelancing will be the right choice for you. Whether you are good at writing, designing, photography, doodling, marketing, optimization, networking, illustrating, music, application development, or have any other creative skills, you can find a range of high-paying gigs and start your freelance career.

How To Convert Your Freelance Hobby Into A Profitable Career

Freelancing may be your favorite hobby today, but have you considered turning this part-time activity into a viable career? Well, to me, it sounds like a great idea. Can anything be better than converting your freelancing hobby into a full-time career?

As a freelancer, you are living in your own paradise – away from the daily grind of the 9 to 5 job, where you have to deal with a boss looking over your shoulder all the time. On top of it, you have to deal with the stress of commuting everyday to your workplace! If your office is far off from your abode, you are only wasting time and energy on something that doesn't make you feel happy or fulfilled.

I quit my full-time job six years ago to kick-start my freelancing career with the hope of a better tomorrow. Yes, there was frustration and every day stress that would keep me from feeling happy and satisfied with my permanent job in a big corporate industry. It was more like having to pass through the grinding mill every day, without any significant benefits. If you add stress and frustration to my perseverance, I was only hurting myself more and more with every passing day.

That was the time I decided to hang up my boots to convert my freelance hobby into a career!

I have never looked back since I made the decision to say it quits because I have made it my dream career.

Though every day was full of challenges initially, I am glad all my efforts have paid off, and I am enjoying every moment living my dream.

Don't let early hiccups affect you

Without a doubt, starting your freelancing business comes with its own share of bells and whistles. That being said, you cannot ignore the efforts and time required for a successful transition. Add to it the risks and pitfalls along with the lack of financial security when you begin your freelance career, and your transition onyl gets harder.

It involves plenty of early morning wake-ups, no off-days, a heavy load of drudgery, emotional meltdowns, physical exhaustion, and whatever else! But those thoughts should not drag you down.

Yes, making a shift to a full-time freelancing career involves a steep learning curve. So when you finally decide to switch your after-hours passion into a viable business, ask yourself a few questions to see if you are ready for the transition.

- Will I enjoy doing my hobby with a time crunch?
- Will I keep finding pleasure in my hobby even when there is intense financial pressure to perform?
- Under these circumstances, will I derive the same kind of relaxation from my passion?
- Am I willing to market myself?
- Can I leverage my creative skills to make myself stand out?

Your field of dreams

Freelancing is one hobby that comes with immense benefits, and with huge potential to start your own business. Of course, it's a big decision, given the share of risks that come with relying on your passion as your only source of income. Moreover, when your hobby becomes your career, you are going to have to find something else to help you relax! But that's okay as long as your first passion continues to reap its rewards.

Initially, it can be scary if you do not have the stability of a regular income. But you can use the threat of failure to "fuel" your ambition. With the right amount of information, knowledge, preparation, and will-power, you will be all set to quit your full-time job and commit to a freelancing business.

Meet your market

Before making the decision to convert your freelance hobby into a full-time career, make sure you have done your market research to see what skills you have that your prospective employers would be willing to pay for. Is there a big market for your niche? Who are you going to sell your services to?

Remember, you need someone to buy what you wish to sell.

So how do you find your market?

Well, you can leverage the power of Internet and mobile apps to find your audience. Peer Hustle is a mobile app you can use to market your services.

Use these platforms to list specific skills that make you different from everyone else. Put your best foot forward while building your virtual re-sume with an appealing description that shows up in search engines.

Do anything and everything to make yourself attractive in the eyes of prospective clients so you can win business.

Draw up a business and action plan and stick to it. When you are confident enough you can turn your skills into services that people are willing to pay for. There's nothing to stop you then!

Create your portfolio

A portfolio accurately displays your work to prospective employers. Make sure you have quality work to showcase your target market. If you have none, wait to launch your freelancing business unless you have some quality samples to show off.

Do not hesitate to offer free services initially to create your portfo-lio – the quality and quantity of your portfolio will act as a magnet to attract clients.

You need to understand your customer's business and make sure your freelancing business is the perfect fit for them. If your services pro-vide results, clients will not hesitate to hire your services.

People have problems and are looking for solutions. They are least interested in what you are good at doing. They want solutions to their problems. If your portfolio can convince them and offer viable solutions, they will want to work with you.

Know your market value

What is your worth? How much should you charge for your services?

Step into the shoes of the client and ask yourself what you would be willing to pay someone with the same skills as you. Your answer will guide you to setting your work value. Of course, you may want to research online to make sure you get your worth and do not commit to anything less than that.

Once your general market value is established, it may help to undercut the market by at least 20-25 percent, since your freelancing business can survive with long-term engagements.

Deliver value to clients, create a positive perception about your business, maximize returns, and increase your chances of winning more business.

Remember, in freelancing business, initial contracts can help illustrate your value. So make all efforts to map yourself into the long-term success plan of the client and offer solutions to solve client problems.

When clients are happy, they will be more than willing to part with their money and reward you for your successful efforts. When they see you as a problem solver, they will gladly enter into long-lasting commitment.

Freelancing success is just a few clients away. When you convert your freelance hobby into business, your focus should be on winning and keeping a handful of clients. If you are able to keep them happy, you will never look back – winning repeat business and referrals!

What could be better than that?

Networking

Marketing your business may seem like a big challenge initially. One simple way to promote your creative skills is to carry your business cards at all times. You never know when you will meet a prospective client!

Additionally, innovative mobile applications like Peer Hustle give you a platform to promote your services to a wider audience and widen your network.

Social networking sites pack a powerful array of features to help you spread the word about your freelancing business. Leverage the power of social media platforms, such as Facebook, Twitter, LinkedIn, Instagram, Google Plus, and Pinterest, to announce your entry into the freelancing industry. There isn't a simpler way to declare your availability to prospective clients than social networks.

Start a blog and establish yourself as an expert in the industry. Your blog should be an ultimate recourse of information on your skills, offering valuable knowledge and solutions to the audience. Once your audience starts to see you as an expert in your industry, they will start to distinguish you from the competition and come back for more!

Initially, you may not feel comfortable with self-promotion, but that is the way to go in freelancing business, and all successful "solo-preneurs" do it.

Draw a line between your personal and professional space

Turning your passion into your career is a way to share your dreams with the world. You may be motivated to use your personal space for your freelancing business. But it's important to remember that you're a business. A lackadaisical approach will not help. There must be a dividing line between personal and professional engagements.

It's important that you do things that drive that point home. It will help to transform your home workspace into an area with an office-like atmosphere. Announce clearly to your loved ones that your "virtual door" is closed for personal engagements from 9 am to 5 pm or whatever schedule fits you. Discipline is critical to the success of your business.

If done correctly, freelancing offers tons of freedom, plenty of enjoyment and liberty, and thousands of opportunities to live your dream the way you want. Freelancing is a multi-billion dollar industry. Do it correctly with proper planning and execution, and you could go for a big slice of this multi-billion dollar pie!

So are you up for grabs and ready to go solo?

How To Start Freelancing In Style

There are two kinds of starts you can give yourself: the normal way and the fantastic way. You are reading this now, and that tells us that you'd obviously want to start the fantastic way. Since life is too short to be "normal" and since you obviously owe it to yourself, it is on you to make the most of what freelancing has to offer.

If you are looking for a great start to your freelancing career, you should aim to get away from the "run-of-the-mill" and "me too" strategies most freelancers commit.

Here's how you do it:

Where you look for work matters

First, join Peer Hustle and set yourself to work with some amazing clients.

Second, don't bother with content mills – you know, the kind of site that make you write and then you get a share of income from Google AdSense earnings.

Third, consider branching out to freelancing bidding sites. They are a great way to start your freelancing career. However, don't make that your bread and butter (you eventually need to move away from bidding and winning projects).

Reach out to the right influencers

Who you know matters in this business. Right from the start, aim to build your network with real relationships. You got to have friends in this industry.

Look for influencers of social media and other channels available to you and plan to reach out to them. You don't need to have an agenda.

You don't need to take help right away. Your intention is to build your network, and not to pitch.

Make a big bang with your portfolio

Although you might have to spend quite a bit of effort initially, setting up your portfolio right can do wonders to your pitching, the hustle, and the sales presentations.

- If you haven't worked with clients before or if you don't have clips you can claim rights to, start a blog.

- Since we are talking about a blog, a website would be great to go along with it. You'd typically need a portfolio-style website. Use Wordpress or other free domains and get started now.

- Apart from the blog, reach out to publications that can showcase your work. If you are a writer, start a portfolio on Contently. If you are a designer of any kind, host your work samples on Behance and Dribble.

- Make it a point to keep adding your latest work to your portfolio. Half-dead portfolios are as good as "no portfolios".

Keep the engine running

As a freelancer, you'd never know what you'd end up with this month and then the next. Pure hustle is that one thing you'd need to start your freelancing right, and to sustain it as you go along.

You just have to do the following:

- Get new clients

- Keep the old ones

- Deliver work on time, every time.

As long as you keep hustling and working to deliver beyond your clients' expectations, you'll stay on the course of freelancing success.

How To Run Your Freelancing Business Like A Real Business

The biggest problem with freelancing is that it's often a solo business, operated by just you. While there's nothing wrong with it, there could be a certain point in your freelancing career when it might seem natural for you to feel that you are overworked, stressed, and tired.

Real businesses have leverage built in. Business owners hire others or use technology, or both to make their respective businesses run. As a freelancer, you are limited by the time available to you and of course, other things such as motivation, determination, and commitment.

Your business is too precious just to depend on your moods, motivation, your ability to work, and your willingness to put in the time.

That's why it makes sense to run your freelancing business like a real business. Here's how you do it:

Change your frame of mind

Entrepreneurship starts with a particular frame of mind. It begins with an obsessive need to protect time, to make investments work for ROI, and delegation leadership.

To get off the "I'll do it all by myself" mentality to "Who is good at this thing?" mode, you need to change your frame of mind. You need to get comfortable with "investing" time and/or money to make it happen. You ought to be comfortable with taking calculated risks.

Do your one thing. Outsource the rest

As a freelancer, there's usually one thing that you are exceptionally good at. Say, writing, designing, coding, translation, etc. Or you may specialize in a particular subset of any of those broad ranges of skills. For instance, you could be a web designer exceptionally skilled at Wordpress.

Outsource everything else you do with your freelancing business. Find a virtual assistant, get a designer (if you are a writer), or find a writer (if you are a designer). Similarly, find someone else for invoicing or for keeping books.

Invest in technology

We live in an era that has so much technology around that you can probably find software or a web-based tool that can do the work of 2-3 others doing the same thing.

There are tools for keyword research, analytics, SEO work, ads management, project management, etc. Find what works for your business by signing up for a free trial and begin to invest in tools.

Develop processes

Everything you do as a part of freelancing should have a process in place. You'd do well to document every step you take for delivery of your actual work.

For instance, if you are a blogger, your processes could be as follows:

- How do you come up with topic ideas?
- Once you choose an idea, what's the exact process of building a blog post? Does it include getting quotes from others, linking to influencers, finding stock photos, etc.?
- After you write a blog post, what do you do?
- After a post is published, how do you promote it?

These are the basic steps to liberate your freelance career and run it more like a proper business.

How do you run your freelance business?

How To Grow From Freelancing To A Real Business Owner

So far we've written about the need to get away from the hourly pricing. Also look at the vast opportunities you can wade into, on top of your freelancing career. While you always have the option of keeping freelancing as a regular source of income and experiment with other opportunities, the need to constantly look out for opportunities is imperative.

The only trouble with freelancing is that you are limited by your time, energy, and your willingness to put in the work.

Real businesses have leverage – a little something that freelancers don't have in large supply.

Here's how you can at least begin to move into that direction and grow from freelancing to building a real business:

Experiment with outsourcing

No matter which line of freelancing you are into, there are countless tasks that don't require your involvement. These are tasks that you would do well to outsource. If you are a writer, outsource web design and development. If you are a designer, outsource writing. If you wanted, you could outsource everything and just choose to manage projects, clients, and your vendors (freelancers).

You don't have to throw everything into the outsourcing bag. Start small, experiment a little and strive to strike a balance.

Build a team

Efficient teams back up some of the most successful people. From movie directors to celebrities, sports players to business owners, everyone uses others' skills to bring in leverage, maximize time, and opportunities.

Building a team should be the first thing on your list. Strive to seek, train, and gain the trust of an amazing team full of bright and capable people you'd need for your business success.

It's not easy, but you have the time now.

Systems and processes

As a freelancer, everything you do must follow a process—from how you get clients to how you deliver projects. Following that, there must be a way for you to collect payments, invoice clients, track time, and more.

The more haphazard you are with these processes, the farther away you drift from your dream of running a real business.

Document everything. Build better ways to do each of the tasks, workflows, projects, and the other nitty-gritty that's usually a part of your business.

Prepare to invest

Finances are one of the most common roadblocks freelancers face while transitioning from the freelancer mode to the business mode. Running a business demands that you make investments into technology, people, and more.

That's why it's important to experiment first, build systems, and train your team in a way that's most conducive for your business.

Do you dream of being a real business owner? Do you have plans to hire a team? Tell us what's stopping you now.

How To Keep
Motivating Yourself To Work

How do you inspire yourself?

Studies show that how people think about themselves has lot to do with their success. We fail because we lack inspiration and motivation for success. If science has to be believed, it can be said that many professionals are unsuccessful because they don't feel that they can succeed.

They don't feel confident about themselves.

So, the fate of success and failure is nothing other than your own perceptions, beliefs and efforts. Until you feel happy about yourself, you can't be confident and inspired to do what you want to do. How can you feel happy and confident about ourselves? How can you keep motivating yourself to work?

Subscribe to motivational blogs

Start your day with a 5 minute reading to a motivational post. According to Time Magazine, you feel inspired when you feel positive and reward your achievements.

Reading an inspirational blog post can make you feel good in the morning. Science says early morning is the best time to give your mind a positivity boost. Therefore, subscribe to a motivational blog of your choice to get an early morning update. A nice motivational post will fill you with positivity and inspiration for the day.

So, this is one trick to start a day with a relaxed, positive and inspired mind. As a positive mind will help you be highly productivity, you will be able to better focus on your work and finish the work within targets. In return, this will improve your performance and self-satisfaction.

Spend some time with yourself

You know, sometimes it's really good to spend some time alone with yourself. And it's not a crazy thing to do. You need some time to know yourself, explore your strengths and weakness, identify and celebrate your accomplishments.

If there is no one to appreciate your hard work, take a little bit time to reward yourself. Stop dwelling on your past if you want to be happy. Spend some time with yourself and promise that you will let go of things that try to hold you back.

Everyday remember your achievements and celebrate them with no excuses. Your happiness should not depend on anyone. So, know yourself, love yourself, and pamper yourself to get inspiration.

Do what enormously successful people do

Everyday will be a challenge. But, you will be able to easily beat them if you can entirely focus only on the challenge of the present. Read about the successful and self-made entrepreneurs and millionaires daily.

Read Jamie Tardy's posts to know more about the world's successful people. Jamie Tardy is a business coach. She has interviewed over 250 self-made millionaires. She writes a lot about how successful people inspire themselves and get motivation.

Read more about stress-free productivity. Read books and blogs to learn how you can inspire yourself to work. Don't underestimate or devalue yourself. It can severely hurt your motivation. Be fearless and learn to take risks. This is how you gradually improve and get inspiration to work better every day.

How To Plan Your Finances As A Freelancer

A freelancer doesn't have a regular income. Even retainers don't seem like regular income since you never know when clients run out of budgets or stop projects.

Living paycheck to paycheck is exactly the thing you want to avoid. However, due to the nature of freelancing, it might just be what you end up doing. Leo Babauta of Zen Habits shows how to stop living paycheck to paycheck, and you should read that blog post first.

We'll wait.

While everyone should plan finances, save or invest money, freelancers have the greatest need for it.

Here's how to plan your finances as a freelancer:

Get out of debt and don't get into it again

It's a pain to get out of debt. It takes conviction, commitment, and complete dedication. It also takes sacrifices. It'll force you to take a minimalistic route.

First, use your credit card only when you know can pay off that loan immediately. Second, get extra gigs (or even a full-time/part-time job) just to close your debt accounts faster.

Being in debt sucks. Get out and never get into bad debt again.

Keep a stash of cash, always

You'll have emergencies. You'll run out of projects, and hence payments. However, you'll have your commitments such as unpaid bills, regular mortgages, investments, savings, and actual emergencies.

That's why it makes sense to stash at least 6 months worth of your average monthly earnings in a highly liquid savings account or a term-deposit.

Increase your rates, gradually

One of the biggest advantages you have over salaried employees is that you are in control of how much you make. While you have the disadvantage of unreliable income, you do have the advantage of increasing rates or work as hard as you'd like.

The folks at Freshbooks wrote on how to increase your prices without losing your clients. And they do have good points to make:

- Emphasize on value you provide, and stick by it.
- Expand the scope of your sale.
- Don't be apologetic about increasing rates reasonably.
- Increase your rates and test the market.

Automate your savings and Investments

Your finances will never be in order if you don't have a system in place. You should ideally be taking out about $100 per paycheck and reroute it into a savings account or any other investment you planned for short-term, mid-term, or long-term.

If you rely on yourself for writing out checks or doing online transfers, it's not going to happen. Also, relying on yourself is rarely a good idea as using an automated system.

Automate your investments and savings by giving mandates to your bank to make auto-debits off your savings bank. You'll be happy you did.

Stay insured

Since your emergency stash of money has to stay that way, you have your bills to pay, and you should also be saving for retirement and anything else in between, you have no way to spare cash for any unforeseen consequences. You can't afford to spend on a new laptop if it gets stolen (or you lose it), for instance.

Insure everything that's an asset, and that includes yourself.

How do you plan your finances? What are some tips you can share?

How To Survive As A Freelancer During Holidays and Downtimes

You've to make contingency plans for the slow times. There will be downtimes in every business. But, if you have a proper plan in place regarding how you want to use that time, you have nothing to worry about.

Why not productively use the free time during the holidays and downtimes? Freelancers will have slow business during the holidays and some unfortunate economic situations. But, why not see the situation with an optimistic perspective? As you will not have any heavy work burden during the downtime, you can use the free time to learn something new. Below you will find few amazing tips on how to survive as a freelancer during the holidays and downtimes.

Use holidays to re-energize yourself

Holidays are amazing opportunities to refresh the mind. You can plan some amazing traveling to free your spirit from all the stress and business targets. During this free time, practice mindfulness. Go to somewhere new and spend some time alone with yourself.

You need to do self-assessment. Are you really doing everything possible to make your freelancing career an amazing success? What are your ultimate goals? What have been your achievements in the past few years? Have you really improved?

You need to ask yourself all these questions. This will be the time when you will have ample amount of time to understand your goal. So, use it in your favor.

Use downtimes to learn new skills

Why not learn a new skill if you've got some free time in your hand? Depending on your professional expertise, you can choose to add helpful skills which will add value to your expertise. Even if you think you've interest in something really off the track, it doesn't really matter. What's important that you learn a new skill. Learn music, art, cooking, creative writing, coding, etc. Whatever you have an interest in.

Learning new skills improves cognitive abilities. Few things, like coding, video gaming, graphic designing are especially very helpful in improving mental health and resilience.

Study the mistakes committed in business

If you've not much work in hand due to downtime, you can do an in-depth analysis of your overall performance for the past few years. Find out the mistakes and accept them. Analyze what were the reasons when you had to lose some projects or couldn't deliver projects on time.

Try to see if there is any common professional mistake or personal problems which are causing the nuisance again and again. Use this free time to learn to get over your weaknesses.

Make a business plan

This will also be a great time to develop a business plan. Developing a business plan needs a huge amount of time. You certainly can't do this during the hectic days. You will need to sit down, have enough time on hand and seriously think and consider your future goals when developing the business plan.

Ideally, the free times during the holidays and downtimes will be great for this.

Read books on mind positivity

Improve your mindset, learn ways to build resilience by reading a lot about positive psychology and mind positivity. Give yourself a chance to improve.

Learning is never going to stop for a freelancer. So, use this time to learn more about mind development. Improve your mental stamina to perform better even in the toughest situation of the present.

How To Calculate
Your Hourly Rate As A Freelancer

If you are considering quitting your full-time job for a freelancing career, you are probably thinking about your freelance rate. What figure should you set in order to thrive in the industry and grow your business? Remember, it's not merely for survival!

Set your rate too low and you will be working harder and getting stuck with low paid projects, and set your freelancer rate too high and you risk scaring off new clients.

What is the best way to go about it?

Figuring out your hourly rate as a freelancer can be a pain. You may be wondering whether you're over-or undercharging and whether clients would be drawn toward you at that price. Then the next moment you start wondering whether your rate is sufficient enough to guarantee your survival, with a promise of good life.

True, calculating your hourly rate can be the most difficult of your tasks at hand!

Charging more than survival rate

When you are beginning your freelancing career, you may be tempted into charging as little as possible to net new clients and show up as a more attractive alternative. The thoughts of making up for your low rates by sheer volume start flooding your mind. Unfortunately, this kind of pricing is nothing more than a "survival rate."

When you are not sure of the ebb and flow of work in the future, working for low rates can be an extremely risky proposition. Of course, you don't want to be dealing with a disaster shortly after beginning your freelance career!

Low price has initial benefits in getting you a start. However, it has its own set of disadvantages. You may be classified as a cheap contractor, a name disproportionately seen to quality, and the worst of all, you run a risk of career stagnation. You may not be able to grow as you hope you may.

Since you would be struggling to meet your bare minimum needs with such a low freelance rate, there is no scope of business growth.

On the contrary, when you charge enough to survive and thrive, you are better placed to find good clients. It is as simple as that.

How much is enough

How do you find out how much is enough to survive and thrive?

Annual income

To begin with, it may help to start with your target annual salary. How much do you want to make annually? Have you thought of a figure yet?

As a self-employed person, you have got to deal with all of your overhead expenses on your own. When calculating your annual income, do not forget to factor in new and overhead expenses and tax obligations.

Cost of doing business

Now that you will be working from home or a makeshift workspace, you will have to bear all the expenses on your own. So do not forget to reflect upon the cost of working space, Internet charges, invoicing and accounting, marketing expenses, and project management tools, among other miscellaneous expenses. You don't want to leave any unaccounted expenses that would come up as a surprise later.

As a solopreneur, you are your own employer and thus will be responsible for meeting all of your cost of living expenses, including employment tax - half of which your employer would cover when you were working full-time.

Think of all the expenses that you expect to pay annually and work out your total expenses. Most professionals simply jump into freelancing hoping for better returns, without first assessing the overall cost of doing business. As a result, they end up with frustrations later!

Adjusting your new annual salary

Now that you have got an idea of all the expenses you would be covering working full-time as a freelancer, adjust your annual salary expectations accordingly.

You will see that your expectations have increased after including all the expenses. Now this is the figure you should be targeting in order to be a successful freelancer, who not only survives, but also thrives in the industry.

Moreover, you are turning to a freelancing career for more reasons than one. You have fallen for a freelance career with a hope for a flexible work schedule, more vacation time with loved ones, and more family time.

So now is the time to calculate your working hours per year. How much time do you plan to spend working annually?

While calculating your freelancer rate, keep 20% of your time for non-billable activities, such as making phone calls, signing new clients, emailing, performing administrative tasks, and marketing your services on different on-demand freelancer marketplaces. However, you can save some time promoting yourself on platforms like Peer Hustle, where it is easier to meet clients and land in jobs.

By dividing adjusted salary by billable hours, you will get an hourly rate. Congratulations, you have got an idea as to how to determine your freelancer rate!

Pricing your freelance services

When I jumped into the freelancing industry, I had no idea how to calculate freelance rate. Yes, I never wanted to portray myself as greedy, nor did I want to ask for too little to be underpaid or undervalued.

Then I realized that I had to see the bigger picture to set a rate that would keep both me and my clients happy! When it comes to setting an hourly rate for your freelance services, it will help to understand how your services fit into your client's budget.

In more cases than one, clients are looking for solutions to their problems, and budget comes second. While trying to find out the budget of the client, do not forget to consider their exact problem. How serious are they about solving the problem? Are they happy with substandard work? Or are they looking for a 5-star performance from a contractor?

Find answers to these questions before setting a rate for the project. Spend some time understanding and assessing your client's thought process. Doing so will add clarity to the value you wish to provide your clients and how much to bill. Remember, you need an hourly rate that will promise you a thriving career, besides helping build lasting engagements.

Your minimum acceptable rate

How much are you willing to let go off to ascertain the lowest equivalent hourly rate you can work for? However, setting a precise minimum acceptable rate will not help much, as you can expect too many variables to perfect the MAR anyway.

If you use the above calculation, it will be a good starting point when you are switching your career and transitioning into the freelance industry. But of course, there should always be some room for flexibility – all expectations will not remain the same, nor will the expenses! As you develop your career as a freelancer, your rate may increase, depending on your future expectations, as opposed to what you need.

Value your own time

You need an amount that will put you in the right mind-set and motivate you to produce exemplary work. Getting anything less will not inspire you to deliver quality work. You may not produce the highest quality work for clients that don't value your time. Unfortunately, this may not help your freelancing career, and you may end up damaging your reputation.

It is important to value your own time first in order to set a rate that keeps you motivated to produce high-value work that creates brand loyalty for your services. Don't feel tempted into the trap of undercharging for your services. You have jumped on to the freelance bandwagon to pursue your dream career and do what you are good at doing.

But this does not mean you should be overcharging clients. Doing so would be a wrong move, and you could end up with failures in the business. After all, why would clients come to you if you overcharge them for your services?

You need a balance between what you are willing to offer your services for and what the client expects to pay. It will help to see what other freelancers in your industry are willing to charge for the same services. But this does not mean you should base your quote on the market rates. Assessing competitors' rates will only help you determine your best rate, depending on your services, expertise, competence, and demand.

True, it is important to see your services as a high-value asset for your clients and your competence as an indispensable tool to help customers grow their business. Quote what your efforts and work are worth. This can have a huge impact on your bottom line and enjoy the fruits of your labor.

Switching careers can be tough. If you are looking for a start, you may be interested in Peer Hustle – where you can save marketing time and meet prospective clients who are happy to pay for your services and make long-lasting relationships. It was never so easy to share your unique skill sets! Use your saved time to earn some hourly dollars!

How To Ensure You Get Paid On Time, Everytime

Getting paid on time most of times might be even tougher for the new freelancers. If you're not much known or have no good credibility as a reputed freelancer, you might have to experience some hassles to get paid on time. This is why cash flow management can become a serious issue when you first start your freelancing career.

However, you'll gradually get to know how to complete all projects successfully, solve issues with clients and make sure payments are cleared on time. In the beginning, it will be difficult for you to understand what type of circumstances can delay the payments.

But, as you start to get more exposure, you will learn how to manage such situations and how to avoid occurrence of events, which can unnecessary delay the payment cycle. Here are few tips on how to ensure you get paid on time, everytime:

Don't commit to work without advance payment

If you're very new to freelancing, or you're working with a new client, make sure that you are paid for your project in advance. If your project and the payment is too large, then divide the payment in 3 or 4 equal parts.

What's more important that you talk to the client and mutually agree on the payment term. This is very important. If you talk about this clearly and make sure client agrees to it before you start working on the project, it will save both of yours and client's time. One rule to get paid on time is transparency.

You must explain to the client what you're going to deliver. If you think the price paid is inappropriate given the work expected from you, talk about this to the clients and ward off any chances of misunderstanding. This will also ensure that the client will releases the payment quickly without any dispute.

Be little flexible regarding payment

You'll have to be a little flexible regarding the payment mode. If the client prefers to pay you through wire transfer, as it helps the client save time, that should not be any problem. Only thing you should make sure that the client pays you in advance even if he/she prefers to pay in your bank account online.

Also, you might have to be little considerate regarding the freelancing price you decide. Sometimes, try to reduce the price a bit if the client offers you a very large project. This will also help the client pay you fast.

Earn your reputation to ensure on time payment

When you first start as a freelancer, you should be thinking about building reputation. Don't be too rigid about the price at this time. Be little flexible to charge a bit lower than the peers. This is the time when you've to work hard to prove your expertise.

And once you have a great portfolio to show to the client, you can then start charging what you deserve. This will also ensure that the client pays you on time.

Choose who to work with carefully

Some clients may have a natural tendency to delay the payments of the contractors. This is why it's very important that you choose to work with a client with a good reputation. This is not where you should worry about whether you're new as a professional or not.

Make sure you study the client's reputation as well before you start working with. It will reduce the scope of problems and ensure you get paid on time most of the time.

How Passion Fuels
Your Freelancing Business

When you started out with freelancing you had a purpose. No matter what your purpose was, you had it. But to make good of your purpose, you'd need a lot more.

You have a purpose and you now have a focus. Perhaps, you will need some Nitrous Oxide for that acceleration? How about a rush in the progress your business ought to make? Why not ensure that whatever you are doing, you will want to do more of that? How do you ensure that you will be at your best performing levels at all times?

Passion is the venerable answer. And here's how your Passion for Freelancing Business can play out:

Passion is the fuel for your focus. This is the engine that can drive your success to unimaginable levels. It can bring out the best in you, no matter what you choose to do. Passion is a renewable, ultra-clean, and an abundant source of energy which has been designed just to fuel you.

You don't get passion at staples.com. You don't get it in your neighborhood malls, and you certainly can't borrow it from anyone. It has to well up within you. It has to be borrowed from the extremely abundant reservoir of energy and power your mind possesses.

Delving into your inherent strengths and bringing out the very best in you is a direct affect of being passionate about what you do; that's where entrepreneurship, begins to make sense.

Freelancing is something you took up because you had to and you needed this paycheck at the end of every month; you have mouths to feed and bills to pay. But you aren't necessarily passionate about what you do at work, if you think of it as work.

Entrepreneurship has an underlying flavor of passion within, because it comes from a choice. When you start a business, it is always recommended that you start your business in spheres you are passionate about and know what you are doing and then you don't start for the money.

If you are a freelancer, you want to see how you provide value to your clients.

If you are a teacher, you love teaching and you would like to spread knowledge while helping other people achieve great things—starting a tutorial, e-tutoring or even consulting could all be great business for you to start.

Since you love what you do, you are focused enough on doing something very specific and well-defined and you have the passion to keep you going—money is waiting to be piled up in your bank accounts. You get the drift, don't you?

When you love what you do, passion comes automatically. When passion comes through, it is easy enough to stay focused and have a purpose. These are complex human dynamics and they are slated to remain that way. The best we can do is to try and understand that this strong interplay between these three traits makes for a great, show-stopping entrepreneurial material and is secret formula for roaring success.

These traits hold good for anyone who has got anything to do with wanting to be successful in any endeavor—sports, politics, Business, science and technology etc.

Obviously, those traits for your freelancing career too. How are you keeping up those passion levels? What gives?

Growing The Profitability Of Your Business In Four Simple Steps

Business owners from all walks of life are often idealistic and ambitious when it comes to the pursuit of success. These men and women relentlessly pursue their vision with determination and gusto, and this is especially true when first starting out in their market.

Unfortunately, the magic of opening a new startup eventually wears off and the initial rush of creative energy dies down to a dull roar. It's difficult for business owners to maintain consistency as far as profitability and growth are concerned. We always seem to get bogged down by the minutia of daily business practices and growth has a tendency to go by the wayside.

Are you ready to break the cycle? More profitability is waiting for you right around the corner. Follow our four-step plan and watch your company's growth begin to soar.

4 Steps to growth and profitability

Please use these steps in order to achieve the greatest levels of success. The four steps include:

Growth must become one of your biggest priorities – your company is never going to grow unless you prioritize it and make it part of your overall mission. Business owners often forget about growth when they are caught up in the daily tasks needed to run their business. Focus on making strategic and intelligent decisions that will help your company thrive. By planning in an actionable way, you'll put together a foolproof strategy that you can implement to grow your business.

How well do you know your organization? – It's time to get to know your company better. It's hard to know where to go without paying attention to where your company has been in the past. To implement an effective growth strategy, you have to look at your business objectively and determine your strengths, weaknesses, discover where improvements need to be made, and you must pay close attention to the competition. Once you know your organization from top to bottom, you'll be able to put a plan in place that will allow you to grow and prosper.

Always keep your eye on the numbers – how are you going to measure growth if you don't know your company's numbers? You have to crunch the numbers and continue to do so in order to measure profit margins. It's also necessary to crunch the numbers to find out where you are spending, where you might be overspending, employee pay as you calculate hours worked, and other vital facts that will give you a real understanding of your business metrics. By digging deep, you will become operationally efficient, and this will allow you to grow and expand in increments moving into the future.

Have a solid system in place – finally, having the right system in place is crucial to ensure that you can grow and keep up with the pace. If your system is faulty, not only will you struggle with growth, you'll even have a difficult time maintaining your current level of business success. Look at your system and make the necessary adjustments so that your company can operate at full tilt without stumbling.

Final thoughts

Growing your company and making it more profitable can seem quite challenging. If you follow our four step process, you'll have a much better chance at success. Put it to work today.

How These Successful Entrepreneurs Saved Money To Help Their Career

Freelancers who quit their day job to start working independently, must take a cautious and calculative approach to save the bucks during the initial years. Howard Lindzon is a solopreneur.

He is the co-founder and chief executive officer of StockTwits, a social media platform where investors, entrepreneurs and traders can interact for exchange of ideas and current information.

When he started working independently, he and his family decided to move from one city to another to reduce their overall family expenses and save some hard cash. He sold his house, took a house with much cheaper rent, became a one car family man and sacrificed many non-essential spendings.

This is to say that saving some good amount of money is a wise decision for the beginners. You can save money and set it aside as a fund to be used for the unpredictable expenses or as business investments. So, would you like to know how some of the most successful entrepreneurs saved money during the most crucial days of their life?

Smart money saving by Ali Wing

You don't always have to disappoint yourself or your family to save money. You can have many ideas to reduce the spendings. Ali Wing is the founder and CEO of Giggle—a very successful web portal for a wide range of baby products. But when she started the business on her own, she had to sacrifice many expenses to be able to invest the savings in her business.

When she had her baby, she had to decorate the baby's room. Ali Wing always believes that investing a bit more in quality long-lasting goods is a better choice. So she decided to buy only expensive industrial style adaptable long lasting furniture instead of the traditional furnitures which she had to replace in every two years. Her child, at the age of 8, still loves the room decoration and the furnitures. And this is how Wing saved a lot of money.

Christine Elia saves money with unconventional ideas

Christine Elia is the founder of Closet Couture, which is a successful fashion site. She needed people to help her spread words about her business. So she had to hire few interns to write content for her site. But she didn't have the money to invest in attractive salaries.

Christine doesn't pay any salary to her interns. But still she is their favorite, because Christine has amazing motivational ideas to make them happy at a very low cost. Besides the stipends that she pays to her interns, Christine also tries to make their job attractive by providing them perks such as attendance pass to an exclusive New York Fashion Week event. This is how Christine manages to retain her talented interns and also saves a lot of money.

Catherine Levene saves money by using opportunities

Catherine Levene founded artspace.com. She didn't have money to rent out as office space or pay to the staff. So she thought of using the modern day money saving ideas. She used LinkedIn and Facebook for smart marketing campaigns, which worked very well. She also used the inexpensive modern day apps to manage her emails and other important project work.

When you start as a freelancer, try to manage your expenses wisely so that you can invest in growing your business. What money saving ideas you would like to share?

How To Build Expertise As A Freelancer

Expertise is everything. It gives you confidence, it puts you ahead of the pack and it helps you make money in the end. However, it's not as easy as writing that line. For freelancers, expertise doesn't come easy. It's not handed over on a platter, and it's a lot harder than anyone wants to admit.

Here's how you build your expertise as a freelancer, a few other Tips for Freelancers, and doing things for free is not one of them:

Do performance oriented work

The difference between doing work for free and doing work for performance or results is this: you'd still get paid for results when you do performance related work. If you are a freelance marketer, you'd produce leads or sales and get paid for it.

If you were a freelance photographer, you could take photos, sell them online, and make money when sales happen. You get the idea. The best part about producing results and getting paid for it is that your confidence levels shoot up.

When clients do reach out to you, just name your price.

Give importance to relationships, not cash

It's understandable that you'd think of invoices, getting paid on time, and cash flow. Managing your finances is a huge responsibility you'd have to deal with. Because this is how it is normally, putting "people" ahead of "payments and cashflow" is understandably hard.

That's the point where successful freelancers take a different approach. It's at points like these that they start putting people first, thereby securing cashflows, establishing long-term contracts, and more.

Put in the work

As a freelancer, your work should speak for itself—be it your spec work, client list, your website, your blog, or your portfolio. Your portfolio or a visible presence on the web is the only way to prove your expertise. Where you hold the rights to your work and you are allowed to showcase, you should.

Show and tell, instead of talk and talk.

Facilitate social proof

The best way to build an expertise is when a few others can vouch for you. Provided you do everything you can to work hard, provide exceptional work, and prove your worth to your clients, they'd do all the "establishing" for you. But no one is going to put in the work without some facilitation from your end. You'd need to make it easy for your clients to give you reviews, testimonials, and more.

Setup your Google+ account and collect reviews, make it a habit for customers to share a good word on other social channels. You get the drift?

How are you building your expertise?

How Freelance Writers Can Ride The E-commerce Wave

According to Statista, worldwide B2B sales amounted to a whopping $1.2 trillion in the year 2013. More than 40% of worldwide Internet users have bought online and that's a eye-popping 1 billion online buyers and growing.

Wondering why we are talking about e-commerce for freelance writers? What does e-commerce has anything to do with freelance writing?

Everything.

Here's how e-commerce presents an amazing opportunity for freelance writers among others, and how you can leverage this phenomenon:

E-commerce stores are a goldmine

Think about it. When we are talking e-commerce, we are talking e-commerce stores. Each e-commerce store has an endless list of products, pages, and probably a blog. Stores also have social media accounts and at least one newsletter going out.

All of that is content – from blogging to copywriting, product descriptions to SEO, from guest blogging to social media management, from basic pages to email newsletters.

All that's called opportunity. Right there, in your face.

Ever wanted focus? You got it

One of the secrets to doing well with freelance writing is relentless focus. This laser-like focus not only pertains to the art and business of freelancing but also the niche you write on. So, you have bloggers, magazine writers, copywriters, and technical writers.

Like wise, you can choose to just work for e-commerce stores globally. Nothing else. You'd eventually find many such clients on PeerHustle, but you get the point, don't you?

Sell your services

It's a no-brainer but it'd be great if you can sell your services directly off your little e-commerce site.

With nothing more than a simple website and a Paypal button, you'd be well on your way to package and sell your services directly to clients all over the world.

Productize and sell your service

Online businesses are all writing businesses. Everything depends on copy and that's exactly what you provide. However, your freelancing is limited by the amount of time you have on your hands, your inclination, and your ability (physical and/or mental) to work.

You can productize your service, just like Dan Norris did it for Wordpress fixes at WPCurve.

This could very well be your little experiment with e-commerce yourself.

Start and launch your e-commerce store

Given all your freelance writing skills (and of course, a little bit of everything else), you are the perfect position to launch your own e-commerce store.

Whether you'd choose to write and develop copy yourself or hire others to do it for you, at least you'd know how to run the business well. Inbound marketing is your forte and that's what you need to make your e-commerce store successful.

E-commerce is here to stay. In the U.S and globally, it's just the beginning. Are you going to ride this huge phenomenon?

Freelancing Success: How To Build A Stable Life Around Freelancing

Freelancers trade time for money. While it's not the best way to make money, it's a definite starting point.

As Reid Hoffman and Ben Casnocha write in their popular book, The Startup of You, it makes sense to have three plans to do well in your career.

- **Plan A** – This is what you do, at this time, right now.

- **Plan B** – A slight pivot of what you can do. This includes anything experimental you might want to do. If you were a web designer, for instance, you'd want to try your hand at writing. Or develop a new web language.

- **Plan Z** – This is the ultimate backup for you. Whatever this plan is for you, it's built to hold your life together and give you ultimate security.

The book advocates these plans for everyone – including people who hold full-time jobs, freelancers, self-employed professionals, and entrepreneurs.

We believe that freelancers and self-employed professionals along with entrepreneurs need these plans more than anyone else.

Fickle, dicey, and unpredictable that your life as a freelancer can be, it makes sense to build plans that hold ground while other plans are likely to fail. Here's how you can ensure freelancing success:

Prepare. Embrace. Plan.

The moment you step into the world of freelancing or entrepreneurship, you'd meet Mr. Uncertainty. You have no way to deal with it without being prepared for it. You will have days when you wonder where your next paycheck is going to come from. You will often be tempted to drop everything and get a job instead.

All of these thoughts, however, are detrimental to the psyche you need so much for freelancing success.

That's why you need to prepare from the start. Build an MLP (Minimum Livability Plan) as startup culture likes to call it.

Make marketing a priority

Have what we like to call as the 15 x 10 rule. By the time it's ten O' clock on any given day, you should have sent out 15 applications, bids, cold emails, or pitches. These don't include follow-ups, by the way.

Your typical day should start with the hardest part of your day knocked off your to-do list first. This way, you'd have the rest of the day to focus on deadlines, tasks, and managing clients.

Get that cushion—A comfortable one

As a freelancer, you have no means to get a paycheck at the end of the month. You fight uncertainty. So, you need stability more than anyone else. The moment you get paid, for the next 6 months, route a part of that payment to another savings account to build for an emergency corpus. You may need to dig into this on any given month when you don't have any payments coming in or if your payments are delayed.

That's step 1.

After that, your goal is to build a short-term plan, and a long-term plan to ensure that your zigzag journey of freelancing doesn't derail your regular life – including paying for bills, insurance, mortgages, and covering your living expenses.

Devour opportunities. Make Deals.

Be on the lookout for opportunities while you hustle, get projects, work with clients, and manage your life. The moment you stop, you invite trouble.

Let's say you get a call from a prospective employer about a career opening they have. Don't just say no. Instead, arrange to meet up with the employer, have a casual chat, and see if you can compromise to get the job without having to work full-time, on-site.

You can negotiate your way to a remote working opportunity on retainer with that employer.

Or you could train, coach, or consult for a pay-as-you-go deal.

Never close doors on opportunities, but simultaneously work with adequate financial planning to ensure stability. Always work on marketing to ensure nothing stops you in your quest to freelancing stardom.

Freelancing Business: How To Manage Cash Flow Better

In business, it's all about cash flow. The more positive the cash flow is, the better off you are. It's also one of the most difficult things to attain thanks to pending receivables, due payments, and more. Managing your cash flow as a freelancer is not easy; but it's not impossible either.

Here are a few tips to manage your freelance business cash flow:

Build and present value better

It's not enough that you are skilled as a freelancer. It's about how you present yourself. It's all about the perceived quality of your service and how much value your service brings to the table.

Your first step then is to make sure you have that kind of quality to provide. Next, you'd have to present it that way.

This step you take has a direct bearing on your cash flow (we'll explain soon).

Get the numbers on your side

Once you know what you are capable of delivering having built up value and a way to present that value, it's important to hustle and do sales up to the point of abundance.

Build your pipeline and hence incoming business in such a way that cash flow remains positive, no matter what.

Keep expenses low

When you have money, it's tempting to spend it. But that's the reason why most people have unimpressive cash flows be it personal or with regards to businesses. As a freelancer, you don't have the luxury of getting paid each month on the exact same day. If anyone, it's you who should be spending frugally.

Reducing frivolous expenses is the best way – next only to making more money – to keep your cash flow in order.

Get into contracts

While you are free to experiment with one-off work and short-term work, the ideal situation for a freelancer is to get into a contract. If each contract you manage to enter spans more than a year or so, you'd have the comfort of incoming cash, steady business, and more room to grow.

After the initial run on a project, goad your clients into entering a long-term contract with them. If you have enough value to provide (see point 1 above), this arrangement with clients should just be a chat away.

Diversify

One of the most compelling reasons why you'd want to let go of a job and get into freelancing is because this move gives you the freedom to make as much as you need while doing work you love and that you are proud to do.

Since freelancing limits you by time available to you, experiment with "productization" of your services, other sources of income, completely different businesses, or even making money work for you (stocks, investments, dividends) by planning your finances properly.

How do you manage your cash flow? What tips can you give for our community here at peer hustle?

Top Rainmaker Habits
Every Freelancer Should Develop

Some habits are bad; some are good. Further, some habits die-hard. We sometimes wish we freelancers develop some strong, productive habits so that these habits don't die and we profit.

As freelancers, we basically manage everything ourselves. Every minute we don't use is a minute lost with a dollar tag attached to it. As such, it's imperative that we develop habits that help us achieve what we need.

Here are some Success Habits For Freelancers that we know will help:

The reading habit

Reading a must for everyone. Business owners, executives, students, and freelancers – everyone should read. It's that one habit that has the potential to make you money.

Invest in books or go for the digital versions. Use gadgets, if that helps, and read every waking moment of your life. It might be clichéd, but knowledge is power.

The marketing habit

If there's another skill that directly earns you money, it's the habit of marketing. We would like to call this a habit because for one, you'll need to do it every day.

You'll need to do this well, and you should be able to do it even when the days seem low, and when all you want to do is to leave everything behind and run. Whether you bid for new projects, send out new proposals, or perhaps place calls – do it every single day.

The habit of living with uncertainty

Projects are here today, gone tomorrow. Your clients will not do business with you forever. Nothing lasts forever. A freelancer's life is filled with uncertainty every single day. Can you live with it? Can you stomach the seemingly precarious, unstable, and an almost fluid calendar?

Make it a habit to lower your expectations and to go with the flow. Ensure that nothing ever affects you. Let projects and clients come and go. Let employees or contractors come and go. Just get into the habit of living with uncertainty; you'll be glad you did.

The habit of experimenting

Do you blog? Experiment with a new voice. Do you use web-based tools for running and managing your business? Begin to experiment with new tools.

If you have been working in one particular fashion, try out new newer methods. Consider experimenting with new businesses, new ways of doing your already existing businesses, etc. Experiment with everything but don't worry about making mistakes. Making mistakes is your ticket to premium learning and real-world experience.

What habits have you developed lately? What is that one habit that you are proud that you have?

What Does It Take To Succeed As A Freelancer?

It's the neo economy you are in, and it's time to disown anything to do with the old.

Freelancing is the new normal. It's the ultimate answer to an ever-growing need for many entrepreneurial souls to stand on their own feet and to start doing their own thing.

What was once a fancy job is a reality today. Millions, who were once a part of the regular workforce, now throng to the bright prospects of freelancing.

According to Quartz,

"In the EU, 14.5% of the workforce fell into the category "self-employed" in 2010. In the US, every 3rd person was self-employed in 2006, and forecasts predict this will increase to 40% by the year 2020."

However, freelancing is the same as anything entrepreneurial. It has its share of ups and downs. Freelancing can prove to be draining, exhaustive, and downright scary.

Though not if you know what it takes to succeed:

Have guts

Freelancing isn't for the faint-hearted. It's not for the meek. It's not for the lazy. It's also one of the worst ways to make "quick money".

Freelancing is everything entrepreneurial. You'd start with nothing but passion, a vision, and sheer tenacity. You have nothing but guts and skills. Glory follows only if you follow through.

Successful freelancing requires you to talk and pitch to complete strangers, network like there's no tomorrow, attend conferences you never knew about, and to generally stay on top of your game.

That isn't easy.

Be ready to say no

Success is more about saying "no" than it is about saying "yes." Saying yes to everything that comes your way, taking the plunge with every project offered to you, agreeing to work with every client, and not being selective with your projects generally puts a lot on your pretty little plate.

Too much on your plate leads to reduced efficiency, suffering productivity, and the possibility of working with clients from hell.

When you ever get into situations like these, you are facing an all-too-common burnout phase.

That's something you can avoid just by saying no. Remember, you are in complete control of how you feel by choosing what (and with whom) you work.

Upgrade skills. Upgrade skills. Upgrade skills.

Successful freelancing isn't so much about what you know than it is about what you are willing to learn. One of the common traits found among successful freelancers is their willingness — and speed - to pick on new skills.

Writers eventually learn some HTML5 and CSS3. Designers end up learning how to blog. Almost every freelancer learns a thing or two about digital marketing — and they should.

The ability to adapt

There's never a day in a freelancer's life that looks alike. Days change, clients come and go, and you never know when you are going to get paid. For some freelancers, you don't even know where you are going to work.

That's a stark contrast to regular workers and full-timers. Successful freelancers handle uncertainty well. They adapt quick. They make do with what they have, and they plan for unforeseen events that unfold anyway.

Do you have it in you to succeed? Are you already successful? Would you like to share your story with us?

1099 vs. W2 : Which Is Better?

Do tax rules confuse you? Wondering whether you are a 1099 contractor or a W2 employee? This is an important distinction for federal tax purposes.

Worker classification is done to differentiate between how you pay taxes and how you file returns. Whether you come under 1099 or W2 classification, this will affect your qualification for employer benefits, social security and Medicare benefits, and tax responsibilities.

If you are confused about your work status, this post can help you differentiate between 1099 and W-9 to establish your classification as a worker.

What is your work status?

Whether you are an employee or an independent contractor, it all depends on financial control, behavioral control, and relationship between parties, as defined by the IRS.

Behavioral Control

When a business has the right to give directions and extensive instructions and control the work process, in that case, a worker is an employee. On the other hand, if you receive less extensive instructions as to what needs to be done, you may be classified as an independent contractor.

Additionally, self-employed persons hardly receive training about the work procedures and methods, as opposed to an employee, who may get training from the employer to guarantee that the work is done in a specific way.

Financial Control

Employees do not make any investment to do work for the employer. Contrarily, an independent professional may require a significant investment in their work, though this is not a compulsion. If an employee makes an investment or business expenses, the employer is responsible to reimburse them. On the other hand, you may be an independent contractor if you are not reimbursed for the business expenses.

Relationship Between Parties

If you receive employee benefits, including paid leave, pension, and insurance, this is an indication that you share an employer-employee relationship. On the other hand, if you do not receive any such benefits, you could be an independent contractor. Ideally there is a continuing relationship between an employee and employer, though an independent contractor and a client may continue to work a long time, without any contractual agreement.

Are you an independent contractor?

A self-employed person is also known as a sole proprietor, independent contractor, freelancer, free agent, and subcontractor. In simple tax parlance, in order to be eligible for an independent contractor for taxation purpose, you must be able to show that you work as a self-employed person engaged in a business.

There is an increasing trend in the job market to move more and more toward independent contractors instead of hiring permanent employees on a payroll. But this has given rise to the confusion whether contractors are classified under 1099 or W-2 category. Well, independent contractors are always classified under IRS 1099 forms, whereas W-2 category is used for full-time employees. In simple words, an independent contractor is eligible to get a 1099 form, whereas a full-time employee gets an IRS W-2 form.

As an independent contractor, you are your own boss and

• Set your own schedule

- Work as per your own desire
- Use your own equipment to work
- Choose to work on projects as per your desire
- Can turn down work offers as you wish
- Work with more than one client

On the other hand, if you're an employee, you

- Work for and under someone else
- Have a set work schedule
- Are on a work schedule
- Are provided the necessary tools and materials for the task

There is a clear dividing line between self-employed workers and employees. Both are classified under different tax categories – 1099 and W-2.

Since independent contractors do not work under any employer, it is solely their responsibility to calculate and pay payroll taxes to the government on a quarterly basis. On the other hand, in the case of a W-2 employee, there is automatic deduction of payroll taxes from their paycheck by the employer.

Ideally 1099 employees are hired on a temporary basis or on contract to work on a specific project. Under work for hire contracts, independent contractors may be hired to provide temporary support in the absence of a W-2'd employee.

IRS Form 1099 Vs. W-2

Independent contractors get a flat fee per project and not a fixed or hourly salary, unlike full-time employees. As a self-employed professional, you are required to annually submit a 1099 form.

W-2 form documents the income, wages, commissions, and tips earned by employee. The earnings statement also includes the total amount of taxes, including social security, state, and federal, withheld by the employer throughout the year.

Contrarily, the 1099 form details the total amount of income or pay earned by freelance or temporary employees in a given year, without any social security, federal, or state taxes withheld at the time of payment. However, this income also includes dividends and interest earned.

The federal government expects independent contractors to pay appropriate taxes calculated on the basis of fee schedule established by the state tax commission and Internal Revenue Service (IRS) annually.

Contractors are eligible to deduct work-related expenses, including supplies or any other materials associated with work. However, the 1099 form must include all other sources of a contractor's income, including royalties or prize money.

Thus as a self-employed professional, you can avail certain tax benefits that a W-2 employee cannot. While a 1099 professional takes home the net income, W-2 people receive take-home pay, which is less than their gross wages, because of the employer withholding social security and taxes. Tax of an independent contractor is calculated on net income.

On the other hand, a freelancer or independent contractor pays twice the social security and Medicare taxes compared to an employee, because the employer is responsible for paying half of the Medicare and 12.4% social security tax for the latter. In the case of the self-employed professional, the client doesn't report withholding of income taxes, nor do they deduct Social Security/Medicare while making them payments.

In the case of 1099, unemployment and workers' compensation must be addressed independently. As a 1099 earner, you are responsible to make quarterly estimated tax payments, especially if you owe over $1,000 at tax time. As opposed to salaried employees whose employer withholds taxes at each paycheck, you make payments four times a year.

Self-employment tax deduction

As an independent contractor, you need to pay a tax of 15.3 percent on your net income if you earn over $400. This is almost double the amount of tax that W2 form people need to pay. Another difference between 1099 and W-9 is that self-employed people are eligible to deduct half of the self-employment tax paid from their income. This tends to lower their overall tax liability. All self-employed persons are responsible for paying Self-Employment Contributions Act – SECA.

Business Expenses

In the eyes of the IRS, a self-employed person is technically a small business, which makes you eligible to subtract business-related expenditure under Schedule C. The expenses may include the cost of professional services, like hiring an accountant for tax calculations, insurance premiums for business, and transportation expenses on business.

As an independent contractor, you will receive Form 1099- MISC (Miscellaneous Income) to report your income. To make estimated tax payments for the year, sole proprietorships may deduct business expenses on Schedule C of income tax return. Independent contractors are required to file a schedule C with tax return and receive a 1099 form for all incomes in excess of $600. All business expenses of an independent contractor are itemized on Schedule C. The expenses are then filed with the personal income tax return.

An incorporated contractor is a W-2 employee of the corporation and files a personal income tax return.

Bottom line

An increasing number of companies are interested to use independent contractors to save on their share of the tax payments, social security, workers or unemployment compensation. More and more people are choosing to become sole proprietors, given the benefits of working independently and the easy availability of gigs in on-demand marketplaces, such as Peer Hustle.

It is becoming increasingly important for employees, employers, and independent contractors to understand the clearly laid out IRS rules in determining the work classifications. Get the work classification correct upfront to avoid the hazards of misclassifications and save yourself on penalties later. This could even lead to jail time.

It is important for employees to know whether they are true employees or independent contractors so that they do not lose out on the benefits.

Whether to choose 1099 vs. W2 is a crucial decision that will impact your work status and ability to accept certain benefits, insurance, and assignments, besides affecting your tax liabilities. It is not simply a matter of choice, but a step further, which can have legal implications.

It is important to make the right choice and understand the IRS guidelines clearly so that you enjoy your dream career and get all the benefits you had expected.

3 Occasions When Freelancers Need Perseverance

Do you feel stuck, or sometimes, downhearted for not being able to manage your freelancing growth as expected? Almost all successful freelancers say that they dislike at least one aspect of freelancing. But, who says that being a freelancer means that you will have the easiest way to earn a living? Freelancing is hard. But, you will grow if you've perseverance.

As you will have the freedom to do anything you want to do to your business, you will certainly enjoy some unbeatable benefits over the people who work regular jobs. You will just need to stay cool, calm, be patient to adversities and stick to your faith during the difficult times. Here are the times when you will need perseverance for success.

When you have no jobs in hand

This will be one of the most difficult times. Sometimes, you may not even have right numbers of jobs to generate a convincing monthly income. It will be easier to lose interest at that time. It might seem your struggle is never going to end. But, this is the time when you should hold onto perseverance. Carrier Smith was in $14, 000 debt when she started her freelancing career. But, she decided to stick to freelancing and thought out ways to increase income and pay her debt off.

Therefore, instead of giving yourself to dark thoughts, use your time to learn more about how to grow a freelance business.

When you feel your freelancing career shows no signs of progress

If you didn't experience such moments yet, you will have during the downtimes. Freelancing or consulting, they never assure stable and consistent flow of opportunities. There will be some good times with lots of great projects and great income. And sometimes, you will feel like your luck has turned its back on you.

What you should do? You should remember that you need perseverance. Stay calm and figure out what can be done to handle the situation. Learn more about freelancing skills and ways to grow a business. Read how successful people find out creative means to increase their income. For example, a freelance expert described how she earned thousands of dollars with a single blog.

When you're afraid to ask for a fair price

Experts say one of the biggest mistakes that most freelancers make during the initial years is being too afraid to ask for a fair price. You can't grow being too afraid. It's normal to fear, but, if you want growth, you've to learn to manage fear. When you're in freelancing, you will have to continue to work hard and ask for price you deserve. If you think you're not getting quick response, be patient and stick it out. You will have to get over the fear of losing clients. If you have to let some business go for a while, let it be. By that time, learn what can be done to improve the charm of your portfolio, how to market your skills or improve the scope of earnings.

Freelancing has many challenges and threats that not many professionals would like to deal with. Most of the times, you'll be alone when you'll have to manage bundle of responsibilities. But, as mentioned earlier, your growth will be unavoidable if you correctly work on self development and can maintain perseverance.

3 Productivity Tips
For Busy Freelancers

World Health Organization (WHO) says that our eating habit directly impacts our productivity level. WHO claims that adequate intake of nutritious food can improve national productivity almost by 20 percent.

Therefore, healthy eating habit is something which you should definitely take into consideration, if you're concerned about how to improve productivity.

But, this is one of many important factors that can help in increasing your concentration, focus, attention, mental health and work turnaround. You also need to develop helpful habits. Below you will find few productivity tips for the busy freelancers -

Happiness leads to better productivity

Shawn Achor is a positive psychology expert. He has been studying how human personality and mental health condition impact success for many years. After years of research, he has come up with an excellent unconventional perspective to improve productivity and success.

Shawn Achor says that people should try to be happy to be successful, which is quite the opposite to our conventional belief. We think that success can make us happy. But, it's not. Several research findings have conclude that it's happiness that leads people to success. Happy and mentally satisfied people are smart, highly productive, and therefore, successful. Read Shawn Achor's article about how to be happy during the working hours and at workplace.

According to Shawn, simple things like making the working environment interesting, changing the color of the wall, being with people and changing your mindset can be extremely helpful for improving productivity.

Refrain from extreme visualization of success to improve productivity

Extreme visualizations of success don't work. Science has discovered that imagining success too much can actually work against productivity.

You definitely should have a goal and be optimistic. But, thinking too much about it will not be helpful. Your brain will gradually start to think that imagining success will be enough to produce result and no real hard work and effort will be needed.

Therefore, constant visualization of success can actually affect your productivity. You should set a goal. But, additional efforts are also necessary if you want to accomplish your goal. Stop thinking too much, and start taking actions to improve productivity and end results.

Say no to multitasking to improve productivity

It has been proved long back that multitasking is a myth. For example, a study conducted by the National Bureau of Economic Research has found that employees who tried to multitask produced extremely poor quality of work. However, employees who tried to focus on one task at a time produced a much better outcome.

If you're thinking that multitasking can save your time, you're wrong. It's time to understand that multitasking is not a thing to be proud of. Multitasking actually wastes time and declines productivity. So, never be too tempted to work on several things simultaneously.

It's better that you try to improve focus and concentration instead. Try out tools and techniques to improve attention. It will dramatically improve your productivity.

Each person has his/her unique reason to be happy. Find out what makes you feel confident and improves your self-esteem. If you feel happy when you read books, help others, are with friends, or frequently shopping, try all these to help yourself and improve productivity.

3 Ways B2B Freelancers Can Grow Their Business

Freelancers must do market research to understand who are their prospective clients and where they come from. Entrepreneur.com listed 8 most successful online entrepreneurs who had excellent individual strategies to attract the target customers and grow their businesses.

Freelancers can't expect to increase their earnings simply registering to an online freelancing platform and waiting to grab a job. You'll have to spread your wings. Go to places where clients will notice your talent, understand your ability and your offerings. Hence, little bit of market research will be required to ensure consistent business growth.

You will have to spread words, talk to interested people, and sometimes, create demand for your skills and services. Here are the 3 ways every freelancer should try to ensure consistent earnings and business growth.

Market research

There are many quick market research tools available. You can start with keyword research, which will perhaps be one of the easiest ways to understand the target audience. Understand what people are looking for in your niche.

Market research also involves getting insight of the current competition. If you want to understand who will be willing to buy your services, you will have to understand the market competition and competitors. That is why it's also very important for you to understand what your competitors are doing, how they are better from you, how much they are charging to offer the same kind of service, etc.

Next, read blogs. Find out the most reputed blogs in your niche and try to track what people are talking about and asking for.

Build an audience on LinkedIn

LinkedIn is an excellent social media platform for B2B freelancers. According to hubspot.com, LinkedIn is 277 percent more effective in generating business leads than any other social media platforms.

B2B freelancers should build a nice profile on this excellent platform and try get connected to industry people. Try to get connected to experts and influencers in your niche and build groups of like minded people.

Always participate in blog post discussions and publish your own posts to get attention. It's a very effective platform for freelancers trying to build reputation and their own brand. Socialmediaexaminer explains how you can attract more prospective leads on LinkedIn.

Build a blog for branding

Build a blog of your own to show your brand. Also, if your blog gets popular, you can use it several other ways to earn handsome monthly income. You can earn via advertising, affiliate marketing or selling other things like market research reports and ebooks.

Entrepreneurs-journey compiles quite a few fascinating case studies that show how few bloggers make around $4000 - $8000 a month via their blogs.

You can follow famous internet marketers to learn about viral marketing through blogging. Blogging can actually help you bring organic traffic from various sources, build reputation, generate leads and make money. However, this is not easy. You will need to try seriously and consistently.

Build your reputation to increase your income as a freelancer. You need to gain trust of the clients. And for that, you'll have to show how you can become a potential asset to them.

4 Freelancing Strategies To Win Better Clients

Freelancing has turned out to be a vast landscape with a huge income potential. It is one evolving platform to live your entrepreneurial dream with little or no monetary investment. But unless you have years of experience as a professional or a long list of loyal clients, sailing through the drought of work could be difficult.

So what should you be doing to win clients and give your drowning ship a rudder to sail through safely in turbulent waters?

A well-designed freelance strategy can come to your rescue and become a light in darkness to guide you through the work famine you are experiencing in the world of freelancing.

Focus on the popular saying in the business world that it's easier to sell to existing businesses than find new ones. Of course, this does not mean you do not need to plan how to gain new customers. But it is important to ensure that you are paying greater attention to your present customers. Remember, it costs more to gain a new customer than to retain an existing one, so always think long term!

Unless you get a steady stream of long-term customers, keep exploring all options.

The bottom line is that a steady stream of freelance gigs is all that is needed to stay afloat in this vast ocean of freelancing!

If you think that simply being good at what you do is enough to attract clients, you may be up for a surprise and end up with no clients. Your freelance strategy should be designed to get attention.

So how should you go about it?

1 - Get into the head of prospective clients

Yes, the phrase may seem odd, but it has no comparison in terms of getting eyeballs. So what should you be doing to get into the head of your target market?

The first baby step is to register with reputable on-demand freelance bidding sites, such as Peer Hustle, which offer you a platform to connect with potential clients and market your skills. Of course, you don't want to be a victim of online scams. Trust leading names in the business and start spreading the word about yourself.

Start with offering solutions to problems of potential clients, instead of boasting about your skills.

Use the briefcase technique to impress a potential client. When you're pitching a client, do not forget to prepare notes as to how you plan to make their business better. Most clients are impressed with freelancers who have done their homework.

Further, it may help to look for successful freelancers and reach out to their clients to find answers to a few questions that could help you know what you are doing wrong:

- What drew them toward that particular independent contractor?
- What problems were they facing before hiring a freelancer and what results were they expecting?
- What skills they were expecting in a freelancing professional?
- Has the freelancer helped solve their problem?

Do not expect response to all the messages you send to these clients, though a few would not hesitate to reply you back with answers, as this gives them an opportunity to show their expertise in the niche. Your best chance to get a response is by uttering a few words of praise and being brief yet specific about what you want from them.

When you finally get a few responses, analyze them closely to find the common points raised by all. This will also give you an idea as to what exactly your market hears of offerings in your niche and how you can grab attention with laser-like precision. This will help you to target your market more accurately.

What's more, you can use the critical information shared by clients to describe your skills to prospective clients. Besides, you may find the most important thing a potential client may be expecting from you. Certainly, this will help you redesign your profile and pitch your skills in an interesting way that can attract prospective clients.

When a potential customer sees you as someone with the skills they have been looking for, chances are that you will land in a project. Deliver value from the first interaction and create a positive perception about yourself. This will be your master stroke to win long-term business from them.

2 - Say yes to short-term projects

Of course, not getting too many opportunities for long-term work can be frustrating. But this does not mean you should lose hope and waste time in remorse. Rather, use this time to leverage your skills and attract short-term gigs. Some short-term projects do translate into long-term business opportunities.

My freelancing experience has shown that a few of my long-term alliances began as small projects. True, a small gig is least attractive, but it has the potential to turn big. I have been working with some clients that started small with me, but have become my permanent business alliances for over four years.

So worry not, and put on your freelancing hat and start with small engagements that come your way. You never know which clients would turn into your long-term business partners.

After all, it's better to have some work in hand than to idle away your time, waiting for long-term projects.

Remember, some clients like to start small. Of course, they don't want to take the risk of doing business with a freelancer without testing their skills. So take this opportunity as a test and illustrate your value, showing clients how you fit in their long-term plan best and why they should choose you over others.

My advice - Grab the opportunity and get going!

3 - Meet them regularly

Most freelancers prefer to stay behind the curtains and not interact much with customers. However, this strategy does them no good. Avoiding client contact gradually translates into a lost long-term work opportunity with the client.

Unless you meet your customers regularly, you cannot truly know and understand their problems. If you do not know their problems, how can you consistently offer them solutions?

Remember, everyone is out there to enhance their business and make money. Solving client problems that could be hampering their business prospects would make you indispensable to meeting their goals.

When you interact more often and offer proven solutions, clients would be more than willing to part with their money and prefer to keep you with them for long.

Weekly meetings are beneficial for both sides. Each meeting with customers is a golden opportunity to highlight your USP and renew relationships, which is critically important to the viability of your career in the freelance industry.

Do not forget – a happy customer has the potential to translate into more business in the form of referral.

So keep your customers happy and they would not hesitate to retain your services and spread the word about you.

4 - Position yourself as a strategic consultant

Some clients are skeptical of hiring services of freelancers. After all, they do not want to hand over the responsibility of managing a crucial aspect of their business to an unreliable contractor. If they have had a bad experience, they are bound to be distrustful.

But more often than not, these clients are looking for reliable, long-term alliances that would take the burden off their shoulders.

Who would want to rely on an unreliable contractor?

So what should be your freelance strategy to deal with such clients?

When you see a potential client overpowered with clouds of mistrust and distrust, it is important to sell yourself carefully. Start by positioning yourself as a strategic consultant and improving your value proposition in the eyes of prospective clients.

Show them that you are unlike other freelancers that are expendable. Tell them what makes you different.

It will certainly help to put their needs before your own. Make it a point to make new recommendations regularly. This will ensure that customers gain value from your approach. When customers are happy, they will keep you busy and prefer long-term engagements.

Doing so will help create a more magnetic business for you. Remember, long-term clients are looking for contractors that can provide them with consistent quality work. As a result, such clients want freelancers that can fuel their marketing efforts and are thus not hesitant to pay more to make that happen.

All in all, good freelancers are always in demand. If you have got the skills, passion, and commitment to live your dream career, then do not hesitate to make the aforementioned freelance strategies a part of your greater freelance plan. These proven tips and tricks will help you pick up more business and land in more jobs and long-term engagements with clients.

Remember, the key to winning pitches lies with showing potential clients that you care about their business and have solutions and ideas to make it better. Who will not want to work with you if you can prove your acumen?

4 Life Hacks Every Freelancer Should Embrace

The best way to learn life hacks is to read what successful people have to say about it.

Leonardo da Vinci always believed that a man would be successful only when he would be able to smile during the troubles, collect strength from the odds and grow brave with experiences. The point is pretty simple - you'll succeed if you know how to survive the life troubles.

People, who were homeless, later became multimillionaires. So, when you're a freelancer, things may seem a bit hard, but, you can succeed if you can figure out which life hacks make you the best performer. Here are 4 life hacks for freelancers:

You need a never give up attitude: Suze Orman

A lot of people are there who became very successful despite unbelievable odds. To be successful as a freelancer, you must learn to become a survivor.

For example, Suze Omran is now a financial advisor, a television host, a successful author and motivational speaker. But, there was a time when she was homeless. She used to earn only $3.5 per hour and live in her friend's truck.

But, she knew that she had to get over that situation and become successful. She worked hard and raised $50,000 through donations to open a restaurant. But, she lost all of the money when a broker mishandled her savings.

She lost all of it in three months. But then, Suze developed a curiosity for how the brokers work. She studied Wall Street and learned all she could. Soon after that she bagged a job as broker in Merrill Lynch. From there, she never stopped and grew as a successful individual.

Decide a day free of interventions: Dustin Moskovitz

Dustin Moskovit founded Asana. He also cofounded Facebook. He likes to keep a day in the middle of the week free of any meetings to solely concentrate on his work. That one day of the week he likes to use productively to complete all of his important and pending tasks.

You can also decide a free weekday this way if you think it works for you. That day you should only focus on planning for next weeks work, tracking the performance of the last week and learning from your mistakes. This is how you can make great improvements in your freelancing career.

Get some fresh air in between work: Mark Slater

This may work to increase your productivity. This works a lot for Mark Slater, CEO of Pingup. Slater leaves his office for half an hour every day to clear his mind and get some exercise. For him, it works as a productivity booster. He loves to spend some quick time outside which actually gives him fresh ideas.

Make time to exercise no matter how much busy you are. Invest time in walking. Set aside some time for meditation to make your brain productive and focused.

You decide when to do the toughest job: Lucas Donat

If you think you work most productively during a particular time of the day, try to complete the most important and the toughest job during that time. Lucas Donat, a successful businessman, loves to get the most important job done before his family wakes up.

Similarly, Ellevate Network, the former president of the wealth and investment management division of Bank of America likes to do her most important task during dawn, at about 4 a.m. She thinks she works most productively during that time.

These can be few of the most successful life hacks to follow as a freelancer. You can come out something which works the best for you. So, what you would like to advise?

5 Morning Routines For Freelancers And How They Help

Few brain engaging morning activities can help us work with the highest level of efficiency. However, these habits and preferences may differ from one person to another. Have you been able to figure out your preferential early morning habits that can make the days productive and meaningful?

Ideally, you should dedicate at least the first 30 minutes of every morning for your personal sake. You can use these 30 minutes numbers of ways to feel good, focused and sharp the brain. We all know the importance of eating right and doing exercise in the morning.

But besides them, you can make your brain do some interesting tasks, which ultimately will make you feel confident and more goal oriented. Would you like to know the morning routines for freelancers and how they can help? Below you'll find few expert recommended ideas:

Disengagement is necessary for personal renewal

Do you tend to overburden yourself with unending work? If so, you've to stop doing it. You can't work with an optimum efficiency level if you stress yourself by overestimating your work capacity. Practice disengagement to make yourself the most productive.

This habit will need you to disengage from all kind of electronic device when you wake up. You should stay away from everything which can fill your head up with tensions and worries in the early morning.

You should practice disengagement in the night before going to bed also. You should take a small walk after you finish the work, go to bed and read a book which can help you start the next day in an exiting way.

Practice 24 minutes morning routine to start an excellent day

Some experts recommend practicing 24 minutes routine to start an amazing day. How can this help? Well, after you wake up, manage your time to develop some very healthy and energizing habits. You don't need to give much time for this.

The 24 minute routine will need your 2 minutes for brushing the teeth, 1 minute to drink water, 7 minutes for meditation, 5 minutes for developing focus, 7 minutes for exercise and 2 minutes to do stretching.

Try these fun brain workouts

After you wake up in the morning, get a couple of minutes to relax. And then try some of these brain workouts. These are some amazing ways to engage the brain in some fun and powerful habits.

Sudoku, Wikipedia random, simple maths, reading an inspirational story, meditation, luminosity are few very helpful things you can try. Making these early morning habits and practicing these exercises will help you develop a very clear vision, focus and attention going forward.

Find out secret brain empowerment habits of experts

You can even try something like making a list of top to do things for the day, writing about something you like, asking yourself what's most important task you would like to complete that day, recalling the biggest achievement of the previous day, etc.

Making them your morning routine will help you feel confident, energized and attentive.

Sleep on your right side

This is a scientifically proven method to energize and improvise the brain and the mind. Eating on the right side influences good dreams and fills up a person with emotions of love, peace and compassion. If you want to help yourself start a great day and make a good use of a day, then try develop this habit.

These are some of the tips and tricks to revitalize the brain. You need to develop habits which can make you highly motivated. Also, some experts say you need to manage your energy to start a good day. So, you must know how to balance your energy so that you can use it for the right purpose and goal of the day.

4 Ways For Freelancers To Break Out Of Comfort Zone

The very idea to renegade a regular way of life was to live it. Wasn't that the reason why you went freelance? Command your days and earn the way you want. No harking of instructions and rigid corporate cultures. Deep within the comfort of your home, you work. Till you slowly spiral into a low-risk, neutral state. Freelancers, especially the ones who have created a space for themselves and have a sparkling portfolio to boot, more often than not become entrapped in the coziness of the virtual world. Providers like Elance, Freelancer and quite a few others surely bring work to you, but for growth and continuity it is absolutely necessary to move beyond your zone. The Comfort Zone.

So how do we get out?

Brake the train and go for a hike

Well for too long you have ambled along monotonous writing assignments. You are sheltered within the idea of a comfortable pay writing the way you are. Break the trend. Your writing is becoming too predictable, even for you. Take a risk by changing genres. The biggest one was already taken, that of you changing careers. So this one will be puny in comparison. Shake things up. Go for assignments which pull you towards the edge of your imagination. How about a sci-fi write up or, let's say, a travel blog. Chances are, you would have to move your derriere to write one. Good for you.

Han Solo

I wondered for too long how that could be a name before I realized it could be because this guy operated solo. Singularly. For you to get your feet moving, get off from Elance and ODesk. They are wonderful platforms for freelancers and almost feed you with a golden spoon. But then the joys of life were never meant to be suppressed within the confines of your study. Go solo. Create your website, meet clients, visit live events and take part in gigs. Transform that awkwardness into positive creative energy. Even in the virtual age, a real person to talk to is always worth more. And the virtue of promoting oneself in person will never go out of fashion.

It's an advertisement of your confidence.

Beyond commitment

Never over-commit but at times to get you out of a slumber it is necessary to overstep that boundary. Your 7 days deadline is pretty easy. You have been maintaining it all your life. How about a 3 days thunder? Amaze your clients with the infinite possibilities a new and changed freelancer can provide. You not only can deliver quickly but have now increased your repertoire to fulfill most genres.

Be true and be you

Bringing out the persona that really defines you is what a comfort zone does not exactly do. It creates a facade of timelessness where everything tends to infinity. Snap out of it. Be the real you. That energetic self-motivated freelancer out to beat the odds. That's you. Be You.

Freelancing Lessons From The Avengers: Are You A Superhero Or What?

If you've had enough of watching The Avengers and the sequels, the interviews, and burnt enough cash on the Marvel's Merchandise, it's time to do something else with it.

Let's start with this, from IMDB summary of The Avengers: "Earth's mightiest heroes must come together and learn to fight as a team if they are to stop the mischievous Loki and his alien army from enslaving humanity."

Guess what? There are lessons for everyone from the movie series. That includes hardworking, worried-about-that-elusive-paycheck, and industrious freelancers just like you.

If you thought you had nothing more to learn from the likes of the blue evil guys, from the delusional Loki, from the smashingly handsome guy who wields the hammer, The Hulk, The Black Widow, The Iron Man, Captain America, and all others, you are wrong.

You are a freelancer. You are an entrepreneur. You run a business.

You are, in effect, a superhero.

Even superheroes can pick a lesson or two. Here are a few freelancing lessons from The Avengers for you:

You have power. Use it well.

Thor is from another planet with a hammer that only he can lift. Captain America has everything he must have to save America from bad guys.

The Iron Man has a suit. You don't want to mess with the Hulk, and he doesn't need a suit.

What do you have, you think? To start with, you have guts. You have the tenacity to keep it going with projects, deal with clients (sometimes crappy ones), you pick lessons fast, and you are productive.

You are a wonder freelancer who does marketing, packages, produces, sends out invoices, manages time, manages yourself, and then does some more marketing.

Plus, you have infinite potential to be anyone you want to be and do anything you set your heart to.

Use it wisely. Use it well.

When questioned or when in doubt, you have the answers

Hulk goes off hiding somewhere in Kolakata, India until The Black Widow comes to retrieve him. The Iron man is always questioned for his brash nature and his occasional frivolous nature. Thor temporarily loses his hammer power because his dad deploys a curse. Captain America is unsure of himself when confronted by the absolute disinterest his superhero team shows at some point.

As a freelancer, you'll hit the bottom of the barrel. You'll run out of cash with $2 in the bank. You'll starve. You'll even cry when no one's watching.

Yet, you'll get back to your hustle the next day. You'll do the hustle. You won't give up.

You have all the answers you need. You'll eventually find those answers.

Don't be at war all the time

You'll notice that the superheroes aren't always fighting. They aren't always at war. They discuss, plan, strategize, and often take a step back only to lurch forward. They get away from the scene to find someone they love, they visit someone important, and they often talk to a mentor. They work as a team. They sometimes vanish altogether.

As a freelancer, you think it's normal to work all days of the week. You think it's almost blasphemous to say "no" to a client. Chances are that you don't discuss work with your family.

Change that. Step back. Wait for the right time, every time, to get back into action.

Know what to do with the evil

The Avengers know what to do with their enemies. As a team, they decide the best course of action to take to tackle all sorts of evil their enemies come in – huge, ugly, flying ships? Funny semi-robots? Or just a good guy turned bad thanks to Loki's spear?

For you, the evil could be clients who have "scope creep" as their middle name, or those that don't pay you (or on time), or those that question everything you do and act like they own your soul just because they paid that last invoice.

Or, the evil could be all others who suck your time out of the day, your team, other vendors, other businesses, and more.

Don't get aggressive. Cut your losses. Just be strategic.

What lessons are you going to run with?

Freelancing Productivity: 5 Ways You Are Probably Wasting Time

As if your days as a freelancer were hard enough, there are those everyday things you'd have to deal with just like everyone else. Since there's only so much time in a day for everyone, you'd have to be careful about how and where you apportion your time.

Chances are that you are probably wasting tons of time (and effort) on tasks that you shouldn't have and things you don't have to do.

Here are some ways to stop wasting time and boost your freelancing productivity:

Not waking up early

Mornings are the most productive time for many freelancers, business owners, busy executives, and many others. Yet, it's surprising how some people never take the effort to wake up early and get some serious work done. It's understandable that it's supposed to be "your freedom," but all that freedom won't play out if you are not productive in the first place.

Wake. Up. Early.

Sleeping too early

We won't get into the big debate of when you should be sleeping or when you should wake up. But sleeping too early, like 8:30 or 9 PM, for instance, is ridiculous.

As we mentioned, we won't question your choices. However, sleeping too early is just as bad as waking up too late. Enough said.

Stop working with cheap clients

We've written about it a lot, but it's worth mentioning another million times. Never work for cheap clients. Look at it this way: clients who pay way less than your market rate not only pay you less but are also the most troublesome of the clients you'd ever get to handle. They'd eat you alive and then pay you peanuts.

All that time spent agonizing over this kind of work, or with clients, or taking the trouble to find them – all that is a drain on your life.

To learn, when you don't have to

First, it's a good thing to keep learning. It's chic to upgrade your skills, and it also makes tremendous business sense for you as a freelancer. However, not all learning is built equal.

Allow us to explain: if you are a freelance writer and if you wanted to learn HTML code and CSS3, go ahead; it's good for you. If you wanted to learn HTML5, CSS3, Ruby, Python, and all other technologies out there just because you thought being a designer or developer was cool, that's something that might not work for your benefit.

To do everything yourself

Usually, you'd start off treating freelancing like a business, but rarely do they really treat it that way. Eventually, it tends to become a fancy job and you'd feel that you got yourself a fancy job.

It won't that much fun as it was once. Stop yourself from feeling this way and avoid the temptation of doing all the tasks yourself. There's plenty of help (virtual assistants and even full-fledged companies) available for you online.

Where does your time go?

4 Types Of Freelancers Who Are Not Easy To Beat

You will be surprised to know that around 65 percent of entrepreneurs have been found to be driven by their heart. This kind of entrepreneurs are influenced by their own rock hard sense of purpose.

So, being a freelancer, you must be working hard to increase the number of clientele. You must be craving to improve your personal or business credibility, and get more numbers of well-paid contracts. But, before you dream of that, ask yourself this: which type of freelancer are you?

Here are four types of freelancers who are not only successful, but extremely hard to replace or surpass. Would you like to know them?

Freelancers who diversify skills and expertise

You can't grow your business sticking to a limited number of specialization. You have to embrace versatility. A 2013 study conducted on a wide number of businessmen and employees found that successful entrepreneurs never restrict their skills and expertise.

They always find out ways to grow and diversify. Entrepreneurs need to handle a huge range of services to manage their business. There is no way they can survive being restricted themselves only to a handful of work and responsibilities.

So, to become an unbeatable freelancer, you'll have to think of increasing your skills and expertise. You've to grow beyond your obvious capabilities.

Freelancers with no shortage of confidence

Successful freelancers are incredibly self confident. This is not to say that you're not confident, but, it signifies that you should be well aware of your own strengths and weaknesses. And this is not something new. Lots of research have already been done on this. A Purdue University study conducted in 1988 found that around 33 per cent of the successful entrepreneurs thought their business had 100 percent chance of success.

Additionally, to be a successful freelancer, you should be concentrating on your strengths, not on your weaknesses. Self-awareness of strengths will help you build confidence.

Freelancers who dare to disagree

People with an entrepreneurship spirit are found to be disagreeable. Innovators and entrepreneurs, who are successful in their business, are often found to have the spirit to go against the willingness of the society. They don't wait for social approval. They believe in their dreams and capabilities.

So, what you learn from this? If you love your passion and your career dream, you should stick to it, no matter what. Survival is not easy. There is no place for weakness. You've to be strong and confident to believe your own abilities. And then follow your passion and dream. You don't have to seek approval of people around you to chase your vision. If you have faith in your dream, you should dare to disagree.

Freelancers who are conscientiousness

Research data points at the fact that professionals and students with conscientiousness have higher chances of success. Conscientiousness is the personality trait which makes one organized, eager to perform better, careful, efficient and vigilant. So, if you want to grow as an efficient, remarkable and popular freelancer in your niche, you've to develop this personality trait.

According to a National Institute of Mental Health Study, professionals with conscientiousness earn better salaries. These types of people have higher self-satisfaction and perform better in the professional life.

So, now you know how these types of freelancer differ from the average? Tell us how do you plan to improve today.

5 Irrefutable Freelancing Laws You Should Obey, While Starting Out

Freelancing is hard, as it is and you don't have to make it harder than it already is.

"I wish I knew better."

"You only learn from experience."

"God, how did I not see through this?"

"I didn't realize it'd turn out to be this way."

Statements like these are common, but you don't have to go through this if you knew better. As it is for every kind of business, freelancing has some irrefutable laws you should obey.

Note that you don't have to agree, like, or see the point with these laws. Some of them might make sense to you, and some won't. In fact, some of these rules could be counter-intuitive to what you know. Yet, these are laws. They exist to make you a happy, rich freelancer.

Here are some of those irrefutable freelancing laws from our experience:

Know what your clients really want

Stop being a "freelancer", a "vendor", and a "service provider". The world has enough of those. Your clients really need problems to their solutions and they are looking for "partners".

They want you to look in their eye and tell them when they go wrong, or help them with their strategy, or solve their problem for them. They don't want you to go ad nauseam about your skills, your Behance portfolio, or how many of those 10,000 hours you spent perfecting your art.

Always hustle

Yeah, we have thing for the word "Hustle", as you can see, our company is also called Peer Hustle.

We love hustle because it's what makes money. It's the only thing a business or an individual does that brings in the cash. Everything else you do is to "support" your business.

Hustle is the only thing you do that "gets you business".

You could be a caricature artist, painter, writer, developer, designer, sports coach, or even a doctor. You'd still have to hustle—every single day.

Never do free work

The web is awash with advice on how and why you should start for free, build up a portfolio, and then start charging clients. We all know how hard it is to do just that.

You have the skills, and the entrepreneurial mojo. There's no question about the fact that you'd not have thought of freelancing if you didn't have the requisite skills or at least the hunger and drive to learn on the job.

This alone disqualifies you to do any kind of free work for clients. When you go looking for work, state your price.

Stop doing free samples, free work, and wait for the world to come to you. Instead, experiment with paid trials. Even if it's a dollar, charge your client that dollar.

Value your skills and time

Don't sell yourself short. Don't devalue your own work. It's one thing to be awesome for clients by doing little things they didn't even ask for – that's called "Value Added".

However, setting yourself up for failure by giving away unlimited revisions, letting go of unpaid invoices, and letting clients get away with "scope creep" are not tolerated.

From the start, work to get deliverables, milestones, and results clear. Set the right expectations with your client and work towards awesomeness.

Cut your losses

If you've experienced Clients From Hell, welcome to the club. Sooner or later, you'd end up walking hand in hand with monster clients who'd want you to be on Skype all day long, call you multiple times in day, and expect you to slave for them without even bothering to pay you enough or on time.

There's only one rule when you deal with clients from hell: fire them.

Don't be afraid to cut your losses and move. Chances are that you'd end up making more money and retain your sanity without those clients around.

What are some of those irrefutable freelancing laws you abide by?

Examples Of Freelancers Who Learned New Skills and Made It Big

Passions for new skills are born anytime in life. And if you can use the skill you're passionate about the right way, you can make big money and lots of visibility for your expertise. New skills not only will help you get many attractive jobs, they also can help you meet new professionals from other backgrounds, ideas and expertise.

The whole process will help you become a part of a larger community. The more you will learn new skills, your brain will become stronger in critical thinking. Eventually, it will give you the ability to learn fast, shift your focus on more positive things and help you grow as a freelancer.

Chase Jarvis's photography skills helped him establish a company

Jarvis never knew about his passion for photography until one day he actually thought of using the camera left by his grandfather. When Chase Jarvis was planning to apply to a medical school after completing his graduation, he was informed about his grandfather's unfortunate death. His grandfather was a photographer.

Jarvis one day suddenly found one of the cameras his grandfather used. So when Jarvis planned for a Europe trip with his girlfriend after graduation, he decided to take the camera with him just to capture some trip photographs. During that time, he immediately realized that he was in love with photography.

After they returned from their Europe trip, Jarvis decided to go to Steamboat Springs to get some photographs of the snowboarders and skiers. He did an amazing work. He was able to license some of his great photos at $500.

Eventually with time, he earned so much money with his few licensed photographs that he could open his own shop. After being associated with several big brands (Apple, Red Bull and Nike) as a freelance photographer, Jarvis opened his own company called Creative Live. It educates students about how to cultivate creative skills.

Aline Brosh Mckenna became a screenwriter from a freelance Writer

She used to be a freelance writer. But now, she is a famous screenwriter. It's amazing to see how she turned her dream into a successful profession. Aline didn't have screenwriting skills from the beginning. She took a six week screenwriting course when she was working as freelance writer for women's magazine. She got a big chance when she got to write for a film. She wrote many scripts for films including *The Devil Wears Prada* and also *27 Dresses*. She advises everyone to chase their dreams.

According to Aline, persistence is the key to success. You'll have to keep on trying. And if you are one of them who never stop learning, or always love to develop interest in new skills, you're the luckiest.

Learning new skills is an amazing thing. It's never right to say that you should be expert in only one thing. Also, it's your thoughts and efforts that count. No one is interested to know what your educational background is. What really matters is that how you can help people. New skills can help you develop abilities to solve complex problems. You just need to figure out what makes you happy and confident.

6 Lessons From Sharktank For Freelancers

So by now most of us have become ardent fans of Kevin O'Leary and his merry band of Sharks as they go about searching for the next big entrepreneur. ABC's Shark Tank has caught the imagination of the world, basking in its dog eat dog world of entrepreneurial indulgence and competitions.

So what have you as a freelancer, hell bent on creating legacy, your legacy, learned from Shark Tank?

Passion

And nothing kicks you harder than your passion. It is all that you have to climb up the perilous steps of success. Now you can also use the words "Determination" and "Urge", but without passion the rest just falls flat. Have passion, show it. Simple.

Know thy home

So if left alone in the dark, blindfolded, will you be able to walk back home? Ideally, you should. If not, look around. Probably, you are in the wrong neighborhood. It's the same with your business, skills, and ideas. If you aren't thorough with it, how do you expect to pitch it to your client? Your idea needs to be drilled down to the last atom inside your mind. Become your idea. That's the mantra.

Pitch it well

Mold your net correctly. It is this with which you are going to fish. Your pitch is your first advertisement for work. Neither too detailed nor too shallow, make your pitch similar to something you would want on your epitaph. Unique. Clients, investors, and financiers are clearly looking out for the next quirk to surface. Be the one.

Superman, think thee not

You aren't Clark Kent disguised as a freelancer. Do not over-commit. Stay within your limits of perseverance. But definitely over-perform. Go beyond your client's expectations. Though that comes much later.

Kill Bill

You couldn't have killed Bill had you been pondering over your next project. Killing him should be your full-time job. So is building up on your passion. Nothing below 100% should be given. This is what you intend to do. So go do it.

Telescope

Use it. You need to be see far ahead. For freelancers planning ahead is very important. You are not in a regular job to cushion you. You are also in a very competitive market. So reinventing yourself is more important than reinventing the wheel. Look ahead. Beyond today and tomorrow, the future needs to be nurtured.

Freelancing is indeed an adventure, provided you are able to rough it out. Nothing gives you more satisfaction than seeing your work getting appreciated and your client base expanding. SharkTank gives you the lessons but the reader is always you.

Hustling And Finding Work

How To Hustle: 5 Ways To Make Money With A Side Hustle

Staying financially afloat in these tough economic times can be challenging. If you seek more ways to make extra income, you aren't alone. A large number of people are finding fortune in side hustle while pursuing what they are most interested in.

No, side hustling cannot be dubbed as a get-rich-quick scheme. Hustle is more about being resourceful and accomplishing a lot without too much qualification or investment. A majority of side hustles require sweat equity, that is, dedicated time and energy, self-discipline, and no fear of failure. If you can commit your time and energy and practice self-discipline, no stopping you!

Like you, I knew that it would be challenging to figure out how to support myself while doing something I loved. However, since childhood, I wanted to find something that would motivate and challenge me for an entire career. I truly believed that life was too short to be wasted doing anything that didn't give me satisfaction.

Fortunately, I struck gold while doing my first and only full-time job! I found a way out to give wings to my dreams and do better at the financial front with my love for creativity. Yes, it revolved around creative writing!

That was the beginning of my blogging journey.

My write-ups focused on exactly what my readers wanted to read. Voila! My blog became a hit with readers soon.

So while I started to live my dream, my passion for writing turned into a goldmine for me. The fast-growing popularity of the Internet helped my cause further. What more could I ask? Six years on, I feel satisfied and happy that I ventured into side hustling for good!

In fact, a number of people prefer to give up on earning more in their steady jobs and rather focus on bringing in multiple income streams. Cultivating a side job instead of a permanent job gives you the opportunity to earn extra money on top of all that you already bring home from your full-time work.

But how do you get started?

Make money on the side

Starting out a side hustle isn't all that difficult, especially with a number of virtual on-demand marketplaces, including Peer Hustle, which offer you umpteen gigs for extra income.

Optimize Your Time

You will learn time management skills more speedily while doing a side hustle than anything else, since you have to manage your permanent job while prioritizing everything else on your plate. With a side hustle, you learn how to leverage every second that ticks by. So the busier you are, the more balanced and organized you tend to become.

When you have a side hustle, you have more than one job to work on, besides giving your 100 percent to your day job. This can be challenging in the beginning but with a cool mind and a good bit of planning, you can seamlessly manage your priorities and give everything the best attention.

With scheduled hours, productivity expectations, and readiness to sacrifice extras, you can ensure that your professional and personal lives sail smoothly despite turbulent waters. Mastering challenges is one thing, and growing your business is another. You can't build a business alone, so you need to be smart enough to automate and outsource tasks that others can do easily, saving you time and without costing you much.

5 Ways to make money with a side hustle

If your income isn't much, you might want to do a side hustle to make some extra income. While side hustling may include pet sitting, baby sitting, tutoring, selling your old stock, it can also get broader to include more specialized things, such as coaching, writing, consulting, being a virtual assistant, freelancing, designing, sketching, or selling your art work.

When you focus on side hustling, your attention is on earning more, rather than penny pinching, to reach your long-term financial goals. Side hustling has proved to be a game changer for me, helping me diversify my income stream, increase my income, fund my passions, do more fun things in life, and pay off debts.

When you are starting out, ask yourself what skills you bring to the table. Why will people pay for your skills? What value your skills and efforts will bring to your audience? How much time are you willing to devote to side hustle? How much do you expect to earn?

Answers to these questions will help you choose the right path that you can tread to live your dream life.

Freelancing

Whether you love writing, editing, designing, or more creative things in life, you might want to try your hands at freelancing. Working as a freelance writer or graphic/web designer can bring you fortune while also enhancing your reputation. A number of people are jumping onto the freelancing bandwagon to live their dreams and make their dream career.

If you are into app development, you might want to develop interactive apps for clients online, offering virtual services and making good money. With graphic design skills, you can make extra income designing websites, book covers, invitations, posters, and marketing collateral for individuals and companies.

As a writer, you may want to start with blogging and build an audience that cares to read your written word. Blogging is a great way to make more money, as you can do it at your own pace. Sell advertising on your blog or become an affiliate to earn extra income.

Ghost-writing offers another lucrative side hustle for writers. Writing for other busy writers who are getting paid for the work you do can help you hone and establish your writing skills.

On-demand mobile platforms, such as Peer Hustle, can help you spread the word about your skills and land in a side hustle relevant to your skills. So get your creativity into play and enjoy making good money from your passion.

Focus groups/volunteer studies

Marketing firms are always on the lookout for people to test out products and services. If giving opinions and rating products is something that interests you, get in touch with such focus groups to give wings to your passion. Aggregate opinions are then sold to companies that need the information to create new products. This is a great way to pick up money while doing something that interests you.

You can check your local newspaper for research studies being organized in your area. You can find help online as well. Many medical labs look for volunteers to be part of medical research on certain ailments. You can earn several hundred or even thousand dollars being a guinea pig. However, try to find studies that are non-drug testing, so you do not end up with lab tests that are harmful.

Virtual assistant

Most entrepreneurs find it taxing to handle everything at the same time. While they have to focus on their core competencies, they are willing to delegate smaller tasks to skilled professionals. So if this is something that appeals to you, you would be thrilled to find multiple such gigs in the virtual marketplace.

Look for on-demand platforms, like Peer Hustle, for clients interested in getting some of their load off their shoulders. In order to progress and expand their business, such entrepreneurs seek external help, so they can focus all of their energies on core business. A virtual assistant works remotely as a personal secretary, responsible for overseeing project progress, email management, task delegation, document management, and content management.

Sell your stuff online

Yes, you can make extra income selling your collectibles, art, or craft online. Whether you have CDs, DVDs, books, art or craft, you can consider selling them on Etsy, eBay, Fiverr, or Amazon. If you are creative, you can bring your creativity into play and start selling your crafts online. You may want to start small initially, and as you build your audience looking for unique products, you can expand and even turn your side hustle into a full-time gig.

Pet-sitting/baby-sitting

Whether you love kids or wish to be swarmed by pets, take your passion to the next level by offering to take care of pets or toddlers of friends or neighbors while they are busy elsewhere. This is one side hustle you would want to continue doing while earning excellent rewards. You can start with baby sitting or pet sitting as early as in high school. While you live your passion, you give yourself the opportunity to make some good income. What more could you ask for?

No matter what you choose to do, side hustle offers you an amazing opportunity to earn extra cash to live the life you have always wanted. Do something you love and get paid for living your passion while still being tied to a traditional job.

Choose your dream side hustle today and take the plunge into your dream world! As soon as you start making money, there won't be any regrets whatsoever.

The Death Of The Full-Time Job

The world has gone crazy about freelancing. An increasing number of professionals are making the switch to a freelancing career, quitting their permanent jobs for more freedom, better perks, and being their own boss. After all, who wants to work 40 hours a week under an aggressive employer who is always standing over your head and dictating terms?

So does it mean death for the full-time job and birth of the freelance industry?

In the past, the 9 to 5 job was the centerpiece of work life. Today, more and more individuals are preparing their move from the job-centric system to the information-powered individual economy.

Professionals are keen on taking the plunge into the world of freelancing as a multi-faceted free agent and are happy to refer to their full-time job as "ancient history"!

When you aren't happy with your permanent job, there can't be a better option than freelancing.

As someone who has been working as a solopreneur for over 8 years, I have seen it all – witnessed the decline in interest in full-time jobs and arousal of interest in part-time gigs. When I quit my steady job, the feeling was more like "mission accomplished." Today, I am happy to announce that I have never been happier at work ever before. I stayed at a dissatisfying job for years before finally hanging up my boots.

I am glad I made the decision to quit my boring 9 to 5 job and to start on an exhilarating journey, full of rewards and excitement. The journey isn't over yet, and I am enjoying every bit of it!

Of course, you can't make the decision all of a sudden and need time to introspect and assess the job market before saying good-bye to permanent employment. Moreover, a career transition to freelancing means giving up paid sick time, health insurance, and vacation time.

These are some issues that reflect in the minds of all those who decide to take the plunge into the freelance industry. Nobody dreams of being a temporary worker, but it seems to be the best option in today's economy and job situation!

A world without jobs

A permanent job is a contract between a worker and an employer, wherein the former agrees to devote their valuable skills to the latter at agreed upon terms in return for regular income, which include working hours, time, place, and schedule.

It's more about expectations and responsibilities of the position and interrelationships with co-workers and employers, not to mention the explicit-implicit agreements about how to conduct yourself, how to dress, and when to show up and when to leave. Then there is the question of overtime and related issues. It keeps getting complex.

On the contrary, freelance industry, though in its embryonic stages, is focused on simple, hands-on work, with no long-term commitments or contracts to stick to. You enter into a short-term contract with a client, do their work to satisfaction, and get paid, with no issues of having to deal with difficult co-workers or commuting long distances to reach the workplace. Choose your own place of work, set things up that make your task easier, and you are all set to take a pleasant journey.

An increasing number of companies are shifting focus to contracting out work to cheaper markets, instead of hiring permanent teams that are more expensive. This sends positive signals to professionals wanting to bid good-bye to their permanent jobs.

As a worker, you may find freelancing as a lucrative opportunity to transform yourself into a "nano-company," without requiring any expensive capital equipment or infrastructure. You are your own boss with easy visibility and access to some of the most powerful freelancing platforms that promise to bridge the gap between you and your potential clients. One such on-demand freelancing marketplace is Power Hustle, where it is seamless to set up your account and start receiving job invitations from potential clients.

With unemployment rates rising in the United States, more people see hope in a freelancing career as a path out of joblessness. There is no dearth of work in the freelancing industry. With very little capital, you can kick-start your business and create your unique selling point and stand out from the crowd, offering extraordinarily valuable services.

The search dynamic lets you find the focused audiences that need exactly what you have to offer as an individual economic actor. There is no shortage of audience in need for your talent, creativity, and insights. Digital evolution has ensured that the market for your economic value lies in your hands.

It is this economic revolution that threatens to slowly wash away permanent jobs and make way for the growth of the freelance industry.

Full-time job: The most expensive box on the shelf

Imagine visiting an imaginary store to buy labor solutions for getting your tasks done. You will be amazed to find an astonishing array of choices – full-time, part-time, outsourcing, crowdsourcing, and freelancing, among others.

In this age of economic flux and uncertainty, the largest, the most expensive, and the least flexible and competitive box, that is, the full-time job box, will be seen as the riskiest alternative. Sane customers might want to try other economical and less risky alternatives first.

With the full-time job being the most expensive option for companies, businesses are looking to leverage the talent of independent professionals to take care of their projects as they come, that too, without the headache of hiring permanent employees and making expensive infrastructural arrangements.

The transition from full-time to part-time or freelancing jobs is gradually picking up momentum. It won't be a surprise if it soon takes the form of an avalanche and threatens a majority of steady jobs. As more and more individuals make a career transition, the steady rise in part-time jobs is accelerating the pace of erosion of breadwinner jobs.

What's more, the information-driven movement toward collaborating independent economic actors is proving to be a big drag on full-time jobs. With the advent of technology, collaboration has become seamless, costless, and frictionless, giving independent contractors the best platform to showcase their skills and land in gigs that interest them and keep their work spirits high.

This only signals toward the emergence of an individual economy where professionals are unwilling to spend a majority of their lives working under someone as employees.

Good-bye full-time jobs

Freelancing seems to be the best way forward, with just a handful of businesses showing readiness to commit to hiring full-time employees.

The present situation points toward a structural shift, wherein there will be a noticeable increase in the use of temporary help. More industries are shifting focus to using contract workers. With a lot of perverse incentives for businesses to hire part-time labor, industries beyond verticals are using more contract workers.

Outsourcing to independent contractors allows businesses the flexibility to increase or reduce their workforce as and when desired and thus save big on cost.

Innovative, intuitive, and interactive freelancing platforms, such as Power Hustle, are making it cheap and simple to start an independent venture, allowing professionals to be solopreneurs and set up their standalone business.

On the other hand, professionals see freelancing as a lifetime opportunity to enjoy a flexible work schedule, spend more family time, and work under less pressure, as opposed to steady jobs. Freelancing is seen more as a lucrative work opportunity to live your dream career and work independently, putting as many hours into working as you may wish.

Long-term employment is unequivocally dead, and doesn't have a chance to come back. Access to opportunities is no longer limited to location. Thanks to the advent of digital technology, you can sit in New York and work for a Birmingham-based client. It's as simple as that.

The road to freelancing

When you need no one's permission to be yourself, you can self motivate to perform better and live the life true to yourself. Freelancing offers you this freedom to be yourself both at work and home. No one who takes a road to self-employment wants to return to full-time work.

Freelancing affords you more work opportunities and access to clients all across the globe, so you have more freedom and a sense of autonomy and less restrictions and loyalty to a specific organization. You may work for as many companies and clients as you desire and set a goal as to how much money you will make every week.

The demographics of workers are changing. With it, employee attitude, expectations, and values are undergoing a dramatic change. The mind-set of permanent employment doesn't exist for a number of young employees. Many aren't even aware of the notion of pension. In all totality, professionals simply expect to work at flexible hours at will, spend time with family, enjoy vacation time, and strike a harmonious work-life balance, without having to be loyal to a single employer.

The writing is on the wall – full-time jobs face death and are slowly but steadily going to meet their dead end. The freelance industry is flourishing, and it is time to join the bandwagon of self-employment and make a switch to a thriving freelancing career.

Reasons For The Rising Freelancer Economy

Who would have thought just a few years ago that the freelance economy would balloon to become one of the fastest growing global workforce sectors? Indeed this certainly gives some food for thought to those who are still wondering whether to jump onto the freelance bandwagon and join the ever-growing freelancing industry. Latest statistics reveal that one in three American workers work part-time or full-time as a freelancer, and the share is expected to increase to become 50 percent of the national workforce by the end of the decade.

According to a recent survey conducted by independent research firm Edelman Berland and sponsored by Elance-Odesk, over 53 million Americans do freelance work, contributing about $715 billion to the economy. Almost 80% of non-freelancers are interested to work outside their regular job as freelancers to make more money. The biggest motivation and driving force for non-freelancers is the freedom, flexibility, and an additional source of income.

Contrastingly, those who are still not confident to take the plunge are concerned about the difficulty in finding work as a freelancer and income instability. True, the fear of not finding the next project can cause you sleepless nights and be a big hurdle for anyone willing to go freelance.

When I opted for a freelancing career, these scary thoughts would reflect in my mind often. But when you have the skills and urge to go big in your life, you can easily overcome such distressing thoughts and take a step in the right direction.

When I quit my regular job, the freelance industry was still experiencing birth pains. But never did I let the scary thoughts impact my determination or kill my desire to join the freelancing bandwagon. What helped my growth as a freelancer were the online platforms where I could easily spread the word about my services and connect with clients, both local and global.

What more could I ask?

Peer Hustle is one such intuitive application where you can set up your online presence without the need for a website and make money working for clients from all over the world.

Sounds interesting indeed!

Freelancing industry is here to stay

Freelancing is seen as a highly rewarding and lucrative career opportunity, with 77% of freelancers believing that the industry's best days are yet to come. This only goes to show that the freelance industry is here to stay.

One of the most satisfying aspects of being a solopreneur is choosing the kind of work that suits your taste and skills. Additionally, the flexibility to take time off to do something you have always wanted to adds to the impetus and drives your liberated thoughts as a freelancer.

To me, freelancing is certainly the key to your dream career.

I love being my own boss and channeling my thoughts toward building a dream career, without having to work under an aggressive employer or in a sucking environment where everyone is out there to drag you down!

The best thing about freelancing is you can be selective if you are good at what you do, without having to bother about working on a project that is least interesting to you!

The opportunity to work on a range of projects and across different industry verticals is both appealing and interesting. So you never have to be stuck in a low-paying job working on a boring project that does not challenge you, nor offers you any growth prospects.

I contrast, in the freelance field, you have ample choice to make when it comes to working on a project. If something interests you, it's your decision to make a choice.

This is one reason that attracts most non-freelancers to take to freelancing as an opportunity.

Almost 38% of respondents in the Freelance Union-Elance survey say that the diversity of projects is a significant pull for them to choose freelancing career.

While 68 percent of respondents in the survey prefer to choose freelancing to earn extra money, 42 percent want to go freelance for flexible work schedules.

New freelancing platforms

When I made the switch to the freelancing career, there were a handful of platforms that connected clients and independent contractors. Surviving as a freelancer in those days was a struggle in itself. Fortunately, I was able to sail through and carve out a niche for myself in the industry!

On the other hand, today, there are an increasing number of platforms to work remotely, from mobile apps to devices to online applications, which pair talent with businesses. These platforms are designed to facilitate communication among independent professionals and clients from virtually everywhere.

On-demand freelance marketplaces, such as Peer Hustle, let businesses connect with professionals with work profiles that correspond with their needs, making these applications a flexible option to find talent and qualified independent workers.

Co-working spaces

Co-working space is for you if you feel isolated working alone and are willing to break the isolation. The advent of co-working spaces only points toward the growing freelance economy, since the concept of such hubs is specifically constructed for freelancers. With more and more people preferring to become solopreneurs, an increasing number of such work hubs are coming up.

For independent contractors that feel isolated, the advent of co-working spaces is sheer bliss, offering freelancers a sense of community and social connect. The collaborative environment offers solopreneurs unprecedented support as well as resources to maximize their potential while working as per their schedule and pace.

If you are more of a social soul, co-working spaces can prove to be a blessing in disguise, helping you live your dream career amid the buzz of an office while operating on your own. What's more, there is an opportunity to mingle and interact with like-minded people, working side by side and creating an ultimate office ambience, without being under the watchful and prying eyes of a boss.

Working in such environments has umpteen benefits. You can you show your clients that you are an independent professional working in an innovative creative space, where there are no distractions and nobody gets too involved in others' work.

Not only this, it is a free marketing space where you meet with other independent professionals that might be looking for your services.

The rise of the freelance economy

There are reasons galore why freelancing is on the rise. Corporate downsizing, shifting economic conditions, frustrations at work, and employee dissatisfaction are just a few reasons why professionals find freelance industry as a goldmine of opportunities. Independent contracting has thus become the top choice for professionals looking to live a life of their dreams while working at their pace.

The need for contingent labor is being felt in all industrial sectors. Research indicates that at least 30 percent of organizations are making strategies to attract freelance talent. The freelance industry is driven by creative, innovative work, which not only delivers diversity, but also economic and strategic gains. The shared economy is benefiting one and all!

The advent of new technologies, work independence, self-controlled work schedules, altered work habits, and changing tastes are prompting workers from different sectors to opt out of the traditional work arrangement to independently design their career course.

Additionally, the rising acceptance of freelance work is contributing to a surge in the number of freelancers, which is expected to grow by almost 25 percent in the coming decade. According to the labor research firm Economic Modeling Specialists, there was a significant surge in the number of job categories populated mostly by freelancer from 20 million in 2001 to 32 million in 2014.

The rising freelance economy is encouraging and empowering highly skilled and efficient workers to choose their dream careers that dovetail with their choices.

Besides, it is giving a ray of hope to baby boomers and the millennial generation who have survived the toughest situation posed by the economic downturn to extend their earning horizon. The rise of independent contractor has brought about a transformation in the economy, helping it become more flexible and adaptable.

Affordable for clients, lucrative for workforce

The growing freelance economy is raising hopes for millions of workers to choose career paths that could have never materialized without the advent of freelance industry. With more and more experienced professionals and workers taking to freelancing, it is proving to be a blessing for many organizations that lack funds for hiring a full-time employee.

Today, companies can hire highly skilled workers through an online job portal for a fraction of what they would pay to bring in a full-time worker. Thus freelancing promises to be an affordable alternative that provides high-quality value for businesses.

As the world of technology grows, clients need occasional help of specialists. This is where freelancers can prove to be an invaluable resource for such organizations that need specialized skills on a temporary basis, without the need to hire a permanent employee for a higher price. Independent contractors can easily fit in at a much cheaper rate.

The global shift toward getting work done via a freelance model has afforded economic and strategic advantages for businesses and resulted in an incredible ecosystem of skilled workers that create innovative, responsive work.

Yes, freelance economy is constantly growing, and the trend shows no signs of abating any soon. There is no reason the freelance balloon could burst in the recent times.

The Definitive Guide
On The Sharing Economy

What's the buzz about the sharing economy? Well, in simple words, it refers to sharing ideas, values, and materials through the Internet. Freelancing is a form of sharing economy that fits well within the preferred work structure of the future, with 34 percent of the American workforce working in the freelancing industry and the figure is rising speedily. Statistics reveal that more than 50 percent of Americans would choose sharing economy by 2020.

Of course, with the freedom to pursue your dream career without committing too heavily to a client, freelancing economy is slowly becoming the charm of the job market. From renting cars to babysitting to skill-based gigs and what not, peer economy is taking everyone by storm.

No doubt, it is here to stay, expand, and become bigger, with a larger workforce willing to commit to the gig economy.

Sharing economy jobs – a more lucrative alternative to fixed price gigs

With the promise of work and workplace flexibility, sharing economy seems to be the magic wand for professionals to supplement their stable income. A vast majority are even ready to take the plunge into making a full-time job out of their part-time gigs.

Not a bad idea.

I, too, joined the freelancing bandwagon a few years back after quitting my steady job and have never looked back. Yes, I have no regrets whatsoever!

The flexibility and freedom to be my own boss while pursuing my dream career has kept me going! The work satisfaction you get from working for yourself does not have a match.

So now you must be wondering what's so special about collaborative consumption that every other person seems interested in today.

Well, a freelancer enjoys the freedom to set their own work hours, choose their place of work, enjoy more off days, spend ample time with family, and still make a reasonable income. Yes, independent contractors can do pretty much whatever they want outside of work, and it is this work flexibility that is attracting skilled and non-skilled workforce to the sharing economy.

Peer to peer lending

As technology makes it easier for people to connect with each other and share ideas, values, and items, sharing economy is evolving at a fast pace. Collaborative consumption ensures that people are open to renting or sharing their stuff with others, which may be tangible or intangible.

Receiving someone's services, with no product involvement, is an intangible form of sharing. For example, guest blogging, freelance web designing, and working as a virtual assistant are all forms of peer economy. Simultaneously, you have the opportunity to divulge in different arenas.

It's time for independent-minded workers to steer the new marketplace, which seems to be becoming a top choice for work opportunities for professionals and non-professional workforce.

According to the American Psychological Association, a quarter of Americans do not trust their employers and seek the right opportunity to make the switch to a more fulfilling career. Another report states that there has been a significant increase in the number of independent workers since 2011, which only points toward the rising popularity of sharing economy among the masses.

Since a number of people aren't happy with the current system, collaborative economy could prove to be a better model for such people, including those looking for a job transition, the unemployed, part-time workers, and stay-at-home parents and even those in their retiring years.

Working in a sharing economy affords the best opportunity to baby boomers, who do not have enough to do, to stay engaged while making some income as well and the aspiring Millennial generation to pursue more entrepreneurial paths and live their dream careers.

Additionally, the new collaborative economy allows people to share their underused assets to make some money. According to a Forbes report, the sharing economy revenue will grow by 25 percent to surpass $3.5 billion this year.

Collaborative consumption – way to go

The gig economy is an interesting way to challenge the way we live and work. There isn't anything better than working for yourself under your own banner, unlike a full-time job where you work like a machine and are always under the scrutinizing eyes of your boss. Gig-based work gives you the freedom to craft your own schedule and liberate yourself from the burden of the stable job responsibilities.

Collaborative marketplaces allow people to monetize their assets, skills, time, and enjoy the life they have always dreamed. It also provides the platform to connect with like-minded people, who share common interests.

Sharing economy is revolutionizing the way people think about entrepreneurship and ownership, and a lot many are waiting for the right opportunity to get their share in the new economic system. Independent contractors are seizing all opportunities to reach customers and clients that were once thought inaccessible. In doing so, they are adding value to the nation's economy as well as local communities while increasing their work satisfaction experience.

The sharing economy isn't just a way to supplement sagging paychecks; it's much more than that. A good number of people are using peer-to-peer platforms, such as Peer Hustle, to live their dream careers and turn them into their primary sources of income.

Today, freelancers are in almost every industry. They are micro-entrepreneurs, powering the sharing economy by building brands and small businesses. They are turning garages into manufacturing units, apartments into hotels, and what not! A string of small gigs is the new normal. And an increasing number of people are happy to switch over to gig-based work to earn work satisfaction and contribute to a sustainable peer economy.

Research predicts that the ranks of freelancers will rise to 40% of the American workforce by the end of the decade.

The changing working landscape

Self-employment is not new, though it is recently getting widely recognized as a lucrative work opportunity by a wider audience. Moreover, as organizations continue to cut jobs, replacing permanent staff by freelancers, the entire job landscape is undergoing a dramatic shift. The new contract between an employer and worker is in the form of a series of transactions and not an "enduring relationship."

The growth of technology platforms and on-demand marketplaces, such as Peer Hustle, has given the much-needed support for independent-minded workers to switch over to their dream careers. As a result, self-employment has undergone a technological makeover, giving a new lexicon to freelancing – the sharing economy.

With the emergence of gig economy, the very notion of what freelancing is all about is undergoing a change. In the new economic landscape, freelancing is no longer gig-based; rather, the peer economy is transforming it to become more diversified, flexible, and anchored. Now freelancers offer more diversified services, not only in their professional fields, but also in other areas. Renting space, furniture, or digital equipment are a few examples.

Collaborative workspace

The concept of shared workspace is also raising its head with the growth of peer economy. In today's fragile economic situation, there isn't anything like a job for life, since there is a high risk of redundancy in steady jobs. With a high risk of growing unemployment, concepts like sharing economy promise to power new job creation. Gradually, this new work concept is taking the world by storm.

Trust is critical for all peer-to-peer businesses. With the growth of sharing economy, the focus is now on online reputation and image. All those involved in this new form of economy need to trust the people they are connecting to work with and the online platform they are using. Using reliable and reputable peer-to-peer platforms is critical to the growth of the peer economy. An increasing number of sharing economy platforms are strengthening their security to stay in demand.

Peer economy is here to stay

Creative entrepreneurship, solopreneurship, sharepreneurship, and disruptive innovation are the key features of the sharing economy, with freelancers being at the heart of the gig economy. Sharing is a form of caring, and it supports people to deeply engage in communities and become active citizens

As digital innovation creates exciting ways to connect and do business, the future of sharing economy is bright. Collaborative consumption platforms are unlocking a new generation of solopreneurs, who are willing to make money with their skills and assets. Obviously, the route to self-employment was never so simple.

The new array of sharing economy platforms are easily accessible digitally, which makes it easier for freelancers and independent contractors to connect through like-minded people online or through smartphone apps.

True, sharing economy is transforming different sectors and changing the way we do business. It allows you to share things you own with people you have never met but are connected to online. A number of people are happy to embrace the shift and be part of the growing gig economy. After all, self-employment is liberating.

Who would mind connecting to a trusted marketplace that can offer the best prices for their services? Yes, a sharing economy gives you this freedom!

Freelance Hustle: Smart And Bold Ways To Get Business

Hustling for your freelancing business doesn't have to be as hard as the world would like you to believe. In fact, sales are easy or as hard as you'd like it to be. While there are normal ways to hustling and getting more clients for your freelancing business, there are also riskier, bolder, and smarter ways to get your clients.

Just what are they?

Build a platform

Writers need to have a platform. So do illustrators, designers, voice-over specialists, caricaturists, artists, and virtual assistants. In fact, we believe that everyone should have a platform. It's the era of self-branding and you are who you brand yourself to be.

Using an encompassing set of tools such as blogs, social media, and emails, it's only a matter of proper execution, consistent work, and tenacity.

Doing this gets you branding, impressions, a community to rave about, and of course inbound business.

Are you ready?

Just ask

Let's say you are a freelance writer. What's stopping you from reaching out to an online publication, magazine, or a blogger to ask if you can write? If you are a designer or a developer, you could reach out to small businesses and prove that you can change the way their website works for them.

Most freelancers freeze at the thought of "asking" But ask, and you shall get.

Give away a free trial

Did you ever see how some SaaS companies, startups, web-based tools, and software companies do business? They give away a free trial—be it a week, 2 weeks, a month, three months at a time, or for as long as you want. The free trial helps users familiarize themselves with the products, ask questions, poke around, experiment, and see how the products work without any inherent risk.

Although it's trickier to do this with services, can you imagine how many clients you can onboard just by giving away your services for free, for maybe a week?

Challenge potential clients

This act is several notches above the act of just "asking", but it can go a long way to get you clients who'd love you for your guts. What would happen if you were to call, email, or meet prospective clients and challenge them?

You could say things like:

"I bet your website copy sucks and it isn't doing anything for you sitting there. I propose new copy and if it brings in customers for you, we'll talk cash"

"I'll get you leads. What'll you give me?"

"The way you are doing digital marketing is all wrong. If I show you a better way, and if it works, we'll sign a contract."

You see where we are going with this?

Have we missed out any smart ways to get freelancing business? Tell us all about it.

4 Tips To Make More Money As A College Student

To make money as a college student, you need to explore your own interests, and know how to make a great use of it. Lele Pons is a 19 year old teen who has an ability to create 6 second comedy sketch. She knew what to do with it. She is now the most-watched person on Vine. She has 3.4 million Instagram followers and around 384 thousand Twitter followers.

Similarly, Sean Belnick was barely a 14 year old child when he first launched bizchair.com, a site that sells different types of furnitures.

He initially invested just 500 dollar to get started. And by 2010, his site had a sales turnover of more than $58 million. Who said you can't do it? Here are few ideas of ways to make more money as a college student:

Start your own youtube channel

The sky is the limit in today's world. Why not start your own YouTube channel? You can make a good amount of money via advertisements if you can develop and post popular videos. Although here the income is not instant, it works, and it can be a good long term source of money.

Jordan Maron has a great interest in video making. He is only 23 years old and has already made millions. He became a frontline news when he launched his first YouTube channel named Captain Sparklez at the age of 18. His channel features different videos of Jordan playing Minecraft.

Build your own tutorial website

Ideas need to be well executed. What you can do most efficiently? You must have an expertise, right? You can build a website where you can post DIY videos. Or, you can write and publish tutorials which explain how to become an expert graphic designer.

Heard about Ashley Qualls? She is now an American entrepreneur. But when she started her first website, she was only 14 years old. Yes, she started whateverlife.com that provides HTML tutorials.

She had incredible success with the site as she could generate 7 million visitors for her site monthly. Her major source of earning is advertising revenue.

You can sell what you can make

Are you a good arts and crafts person? Are you a good photographer? If you can create something good, you can sell it online via your website locally. There are ample numbers of opportunities available for people who really want to make a good use of their skills.

Moziah Bridges is a kid who runs his own $150,000 business. He started his business at the age of 9. He sells Bow ties on his site.

He even supplies bow ties to basket ball players. He has created his own collections of amazing ties. He has huge followers on Facebook and sells his products on Etsy. Do you now understand how having a skill, expertise or interest can help you make some extra money?

Why not become a trainer?

There is nothing odd about that. You can become a fitness or sports trainer. If you don't have a certification, it's ok. You don't always need to be a certified professional to begin with. You can start teaching exercises or sports to people close to you.

And once you start earning money and gain popularity, you can gradually use that money to get certification and become a professional. You can also make it a long term profession if you have an interest in it. You can make your own fitness videos and sell them online.

This is how you can earn a good amount of money when you're a college student. Any new idea you would like to share?

Stay-At-Home Mom Jobs: 10 Ways To Make Money Working From Home

In these tough economic times, as a stay-at-home mom, you may want to contribute to the family income and are thus looking for legitimate work-from-home opportunities to make money while also staying closer to your kids. When every dollar counts, you cannot waste your time on deceptive opportunities that promise you the sky but are big time frauds.

After kids, your responsibilities have doubled as a parent. If a work-from-home opportunity promises to change the world for you and is up for grabs, would you not pounce on it? But the moot question is what can you do to get your share of the work-from-home pipe?

Let's see!

Like many other parents, you have sacrificed financial security in order to stay with your children. But in one corner of your heart, you want to earn extra money by doing something flexible and home-based, so you can contribute to your family finances while simultaneously having a mommy magic time.

Starting your career as a stay-at-home mom can be a big hassle, because you are unsure whether the opportunity knocking at your door is legitimate or not. But there are genuine opportunities as well that can open the doors of a dream life for you.

1. Writer/Editor

You can supplement your husband's income by working as a freelance writer for a few hours a day while the child is napping or there is downtime around the house. If you have sharp English writing and language skills and are confident you can write good content, freelance writing can prove to be a golden opportunity for you. It's easier to find freelance writing work in on-demand freelance platforms, such as Peer Hustle, where you can connect with potential clients and start working immediately. What's more, you can also write blogs, articles, web content, and marketing collateral for clients and kick-start your freelancing career.

When I started as a freelance writer, there weren't many opportunities, as the field of freelancing was still new. However, my self-confidence to sell my words kept me going and my persistence and commitment to produce the best quality content for clients has helped me stand apart from the competition.

If you have proofreading or editing skills, then you may be a highly sought-after independent contractor for companies seeking your experience to provide final touches to their content.

2. Designer

Use your creative skills to create beautiful things and make some serious income from home. Vintage and homemade products are trending these days. So if you are creative, leverage the well-known online stores to sell your stuff and make money doing something you are passionate about. Can you design appealing totes, bags, mugs, T-shirts, posters, and other printables?

Research a little about your competitors. What are they selling and how can you be different from them to make an impact in the market? Give potential customers a visual feel for your products by clicking appealing photographs that add 5 stars to your product and convince them to click the buy button. Remember, one happy customer can easily translate into a customer for life. Additionally, they can spread the word about your products and make you widely popular!

3. Consultant

There are specialized online consultant jobs available for skilled and knowledgeable people like you. Whether you have knowledge of marketing, accounting, finance, or numbers, you can offer your advice for a fee and make a good income from home. Some clients may be interested enough to visit you personally to get consultation. It may help to keep your home office ambiance clean and welcoming.

When you are working as a stay-at-home marketing consultant, package yourself in a way that the potential clients do not hesitate to trust you. Join groups online to connect with people from the industry. You may use a marketing brochure, sales letter, or portfolio to spread the word about your services and impress prospective audience to do business with you.

4. Transcriptionist

You may choose to be a medical transcriptionist if you have a good ear and can type quickly. From patient medical histories to electronic medical records, physical exam reports, and referral letters, there is a lot to transcribe in the health industry. Same is the case with the legal industry. With the advent of digitalization, medical and legal facilities have to get an electronic version of all records. If you can quickly type the audio and video words into secure written files, you may choose to work as a medical or legal transcriptionist.

Additionally, there are people that record podcasts, webinars, and teleconferences. They often need a transcriptionist to transcribe their audio/video files, so that they can share the written copies of the discussion with their audience.

You can make a decent income as a work-from home transcriptionist.

5. Bookkeeping

If you have good money management skills, use them to work as an online bookkeeper and manage a company's books. As a bookkeeper, your responsibility is to track client accounts and keep a record of receivables and expenditures.

A number of handy software tools are available with support applications that can make your job easier and help you work with the financial information of clients.

6. Virtual Assistant

If you are organized, you might want to consider a virtual assistant gig coming your way. Clients could include a business looking to save money by hiring a virtual assistant to handle e-mail, data entry, scheduling, transcription, and travel arrangements. In order to be a virtual assistant, it would help to have excellent organizational, administrative, and time-management skills. If you are good at organizing things and can relieve your client of a multitude of everyday tasks, you can make money working from home as a virtual assistant. As a VA, you will either have to refer complex issues to the client after reviewing them closely or deal with all customer issues yourself.

7. Translator

An increasing number of businesses are on the lookout for translators as they expand their global reach. This is certainly good news for people who know more than one language. If you have the ability to read, speak, and write fluently a non-native language, such as Spanish, Mandarin, French, you can make good money as a stay-at-home translator.

There is a lot of translation work in Spanish, followed by French, Korean, Japanese, and Mandarin. Sign up for an on-demand freelance marketplace, like Peer Hustle, where linguists and clients meet and start getting translation assignments right away.

8. Data Entry

There is a lot of data entry work online. If you are good at typing and enjoy a high speed, then many companies are looking for you. Though it may not be the flashiest of jobs, it certainly ensures that dollars keep trickling in while you provide ample time for kids.

Data entry requires simple tasks – sourcing and collecting information for the client's business – to ensure smooth processing of bulk data. As a data entry specialist, you should be able to read and type and enter data into the client's system. The freelance industry is brimming with data entry jobs for the right person. If you are a right fit, you'll be flooded with data entry gigs.

9. Babysitting

Do you love children and can run after them here and there? Can you look after their needs to entertain them and keep them happy? Have you decided to quit your 9 to 5 job to raise your kids and spend more time with them? You could think of starting a home daycare center. As a babysitter, you're responsible for ensuring that the kids follow their meal and nap time and stay healthy and happy with you.

The best thing about opening a daycare center at home is that you get enough time to spend with your kids. Additionally, your kids will have other children to play with, which will help in building their social and relationship-building skills and boost their cognitive development as they grow up.

10. Online Tutor

Online tutoring is a wonderful work from home opportunity for stay at home moms who have good knowledge of a subject, passion to share with others, and positive attitude. You can utilize your skills and knowledge to tutor students online.

Starting an online tutoring business does not require any major investment. As an online tutor, all you need to do is have a high-speed Internet connection and webcam, so you are available at the right time for students. You can have a successful home-based career working as an online tutor while sparing a good time for your children.

At the end of the day, you will have no grudges, since you have done your best to raise kids while doing your bit to add to the financial income stream! Work from home is a blessing in disguise for stay at home moms, fathers, single parents, or anyone that wants to work independently and make money without the worries and hassles of a steady job.

The list of online home-based jobs is endless. So what are you still thinking? Explore all the options and jump-start a flourishing freelancing career as a stay-at-home mom!

How To Use A Temp Agency To Find A Job

If you are looking for a job and are unable to find one in these tough economic times, it can get quite stressful and overwhelming. Worry not! I have sailed in the same boat. Keep your mood upbeat and morale high and you will find one way or the other to jump-start on your dream career.

Whether you are a new graduate, a career-changer, or somebody looking to make the switch to freelancing and part-time work, a temp agency can come to your rescue and give you something to cheer about.

Since finding a permanent job may be difficult in this economy, you may want to consider temporary jobs to ensure money keeps trickling in. Something is better than nothing.

Tapping into the world of talent, temporary agencies provide an option for those worrying about the growing gaps in their resumes. Temping could make a big difference to your resumes and, of course, careers. Who would not want their resume to shine in front of potential employers?

Fill in the gaps

A growing gap in your resume can do your career a lot of damage. Of course, if you have a blank-slate resume, it will keep getting harder to find a job. Temp or employment agencies provide a way to fill in those gaps in employment dates. The temp agency is more like your advocate that represents you before a potential client and raises chances of your being hired, though for a temporary gig most of the time.

Temp jobs provide an excellent alternative to unemployment to those completing a degree without a job. Temp agencies open the door to a stream of temporary jobs that can give you money without the commitment of a full-time job.

McKinsey Quarterly portrays a greener picture for temp agencies, referring hiring temps as the third top business technology trend to look out for, with more and more companies increasingly becoming interested to assign "more work to specialists, free agents, and talent networks."

How to get started

Companies looking for temporary workers enter a contract with the temp agency, seeking to fill jobs with workers with appropriate skills. Temp agencies often deal with a specific niche or profession, such as accounting, information technology, health care, or office administration.

Candidates may be required to complete tests when applying to a temp agency, so that they can match you to relevant jobs. You'll also likely need to submit a resume and a list of your skills and proficiencies so the temp agency can get a sense of which jobs you will succeed in.

Contact a good staffing firm with your resume. They will set up an interview to learn about your skills and the type of job you are looking for. A good recruiter has in-depth information about the job you are applying for. Additionally, recruiting or temp agencies also have jobs that aren't posted, which means you could be a potential candidate for such jobs, provided your skill sets match with the job requirement. The temp agency may recommend you for something you didn't even know existed.

As more and more businesses are looking to tap into the world of talent, statistics reveal that contract and temporary staffing agencies employ millions of jobless each day.

Yes, temping is your best way to build your resume and add valuable experience to your list while keeping paychecks coming. Of course, you are free to continue job hunting, seeking permanent work in your field.

Temping offers college students and career changers the advantage of facilitating career exploration. It can be a godsend for students looking for flexible work hours, giving them the flexibility to work around their academic schedule while making some money for tuition expenses. Additionally, it is a good work opportunity for someone with uncertainty about making career moves.

Getting a foot in your career field

If you get an opportunity to work on a temporary assignment for a company you wish to work for, grab it with both hands. Of course, it is an opportunity to prove your skills to the company.

Who knows the company you temp for may want to hire you as a permanent employee when a permanent position opens, with the temp staffing agency assisting in the process?

Yes, you have heard it right, if the company you are working with as a temporary employee is impressed with your skills, you may be lucky enough to get a permanent job there.

Their human resources staff would contact the temp agency you are employed with and inform that they are interested to hire your services. The temp agency would release you from its employment, so you may feel liberated to work for the new employer.

Meet an array of people

Temping is a perfect networking opportunity, which allows you to work with more than one company. Not only this, when you work as a temporary worker for different companies at a time, you rub elbows with numerous influential people in client companies, who get to see your skills. Yes, this is your opportunity to dazzle and leave an impression.

When working on temp assignments, you can grab the opportunity to show to potential employers that you are the best fit for their vacant position.

You might get a job offer

A number of employers are looking for not only hard skills, but also soft skills in a prospective employee. Doing your best work and being personable can help you present yourself as a good fit for the position a in their office. Who knows the company that uses your services as a temporary employer enjoys working with you and may get interested to consider you the next time there is an empty slot in their office.

Exposure to new skills

The best thing about working with a temp agency is the freedom to choose the work of your choice. Working for temporary positions gives you the best way to polish typical office skills while providing you with a perfect opportunity to improve soft skills, such as organizational, socialization, and interaction skills. Temping is a great platform to learn a thing or two about business etiquette and handling difficult personalities at work.

Besides, the companies where you work temp offer you the possibility of gaining referrals. Some employers may even want to hire you for a long term. According to temp agency statistics, 75 percent of people temping are offered full-time jobs.

Broad experience

Temping is certainly the way to go for people who enjoy variety and new situations. As a temp worker, you will experience different types of environments, situations, and work with a variety of people. So you may use this experience to determine which environment best suits you.

Moreover, when you enroll for temp work, you can have a lot to learn about different job types specific to your niche, without a long commitment. Of course, this experience and knowledge can work wonders for your career when you decide to go for a permanent or full-time job.

The right temp agency will take the opportunity to help with your resume and offer career counseling. Besides, it gives you the opportunity to learn and unlearn a few things and using the client feedback can help you improve yourself all the way and become a better full-time employee. This makes it easier for you to tread your intended career path and accomplish your overall goals.

Get training

May be you are taking that first step toward building your career and thus have no work experience under your belt. You may be lacking some job skills when you approach a temp agency. Worry not! Training is available at most temp agencies, which can help you learn work skills that are new to you. Some companies also offer on-the-job training to temps. You can use the training to gain practical work experience in your chosen industry.

Temping enhances your knowledge in your work area more than you can learn in the classroom. Besides, you get to work with some prestigious companies that have always topped your list of prospective employers. Not only this, proving your worth and acumen to such companies can get you a permanent position there.

No doubt, joining a temp agency can open up the door to a happy career.

Getting started

To get on to your temping journey, come in touch with some of the leading names in the industry. Once the recruiter has a rough idea of the types of work that will be befitting your skills, you'll be ready to start getting the required work experience. Temping also offers you the best way to explore the industry you want to build your career in. You also get to access hidden job opportunities working with a temp agency and take a career journey you have always envisioned embarking upon.

Peer Hustle is one such agency with which you may want to get connected with. Such mobile on-demand marketplaces are designed to connect you with temp gigs matching your skill set. Get access to a variety of gigs that interest you and kick-start your dream career.

How To Work And Freelance While In College

Your college life is not just about studying and attending classes, but it is also the time to learn how to become self sufficient. Being on your own without being dependent on anyone is a liberating feeling. However, including a part-time job into your college schedule requires better planning and coordination so that you do justice to all of your obligations.

With a part-time job in addition to class work, you tend to become more organized and disciplined. When you start earning at a young age, you learn to spend wisely, since it is your hard-earned money. This goes a long way toward building a strong work ethic and rational spending behavior. Not only this, the sense of accomplishment that you get out of it is matchless.

How to work while in college

Having a job while studying in college has more benefits than one – it gives you financial freedom and helps enhance your time management skills. Additionally, it helps you become financially empowered to pay the ever-rising cost of attending college. But it can be difficult to balance work-school schedule.

Fortunately, freelancing affords students the best opportunity to earn while attending college. The level of flexibility associated with work from home gigs does not have a match. In fact, the beauty of freelance work lies in the freedom to choose your hours and capacity. This is exactly what benefits students the most, who do not have much time to commit to work, apart from their studies. Undoubtedly, freelancing gives you a golden opportunity to be on your own and set your work hours to make money.

However, landing your first gig may be little difficult. Fortunately, with on-demand marketplaces, such as Peer Hustle, you can kick-start your freelancing career and set yourself up for a satisfying career while still attending college. Such places bring freelancers and clients together and can be a boon for both – while clients get talented minds at work, students get the much-needed experience and money.

As a college student looking for some part-time work, you may want to turn to such mobile platforms to meet clients, market your services, and make some money.

As an added bonus, work from home gigs typically pay a higher rate than the average minimum wage, with more than half of students making between $20 and $59 per hour. However, this is certainly not enough to pay off your entire tuition fee, but it does contribute significantly to your career.

Working students tend to borrow less than those who do not. Hands-on knowledge gained through working part-time while pursuing your education is an obvious plus on your resume, particularly if it relates to your field of choice. Even if it doesn't, the experience gained can benefit you in more ways than one, helping you learn highly desirable professional skills, enhance the ability to meet deadlines, improve time management skills, and work under pressure.

Working while in college instills a sense of responsibility, discipline while enhancing your ability to effectively structure time blocks.

Perks of joining an on-demand marketplace

It is hard to trust just anyone on the Internet. You may be wondering whether to look for work online, fearing fraudulent activities. Of course, you do not want your hard work to go waste. As a student, you are working hard to take some time off studies, and losing your hard-earned money to fraud can be devastating.

Fortunately, there are some reputable on-demand platforms that ensure you get your time's worth and are paid for your services. These sites are responsible for collection of payments from clients and depositing of the funds into your account, thus minimizing the risk involved in working with a range of people on a short-term basis.

Working on online platforms gives you an opportunity to hone your skills, lighten your debt burden, gain work experience, make money, and attract a stream of clients who could turn into your loyal clients in the long run.

With the flexibility and freedom to set your own work hours and be your own boss, you can be selective in choosing jobs that appeal to you while managing your full course load. Working while in college gives you the benefit of building a portfolio that can be your star attraction or a showcase of your skills and talent in finding permanent work in the future.

Freelancing gives you more flexibility and control over what you do to make money, so taking a few days off from work to prepare for tests or midterms won't be a hassle. This would give you ample time for preparation and a confidence boost.

As college enrollment and tuition have increased, you may be interested in the following careers to earn some cash while attending school.

Content writer

If writing interests you, there isn't a better freelancing career than freelance writing. It requires you to custom create well-researched, engaging, and informative content according to client's specifications. Since the content is ghostwritten, the writer will not get a credit for the work, except their fee. If you can produce an impressive paper, take to freelance writing and kick-start your freelancing career.

The idea of writing seems daunting to some people. Even I had never dreamed I would be working as a full-time freelance writer some day. However, some reliable online resources made it really easy for me to get started. Peer Hustle and similar on-demand marketplaces are the best platform to look for writing gigs.

Do a self-assessment of your writing skills and look for gigs that require quality writing. If your skills fit in with the requirements, you could soon join the ranks of the college students who launch their freelancing career as writers.

Virtual assistant

A number of work from home professionals take up virtual assistant gigs. As a student, you may want to join the freelancing bandwagon and become an administrative assistant who works remotely to provide services in proofreading reports, compiling data, arranging client meetings, handling communication and collaboration, and troubleshooting technical issues. However, working as a virtual assistant may be a challenge, as you need to match your client's schedule. Fortunately, many clients are quite considerate and happy to accommodate a student's needs.

Online tutoring

Use your knowledge or subject expertise to work part-time as an online tutor. This is a great option for students. Help other students understand their homework and class work through chat or video messaging. It is a rewarding opportunity for students who want to make money while leveraging their knowledge to gain some work experience. This will help you gain better understanding of the subject and sharpen your skills.

Programmer

If you have taken higher level computer training, programming offers you the best freelancing opportunity as a student. Students with some experience in writing apps or knowledge in a programming language can easily find freelance programming gigs. If you have a good understanding of how the Internet works and know common computing languages, such as CSS, HTML, JavaScript, and appreciate good design, you could become a freelance programmer. Programming experience can be a star attraction on your resume.

Internet marketer

Of course, a majority of students use social media for fun. But Internet marketing can be a lucrative career opportunity as a student. Creative minds that can help drive traffic to client websites by deploying social media campaigns and creating ads can find good part-time while in school. If you can prove yourself as worthwhile to clients, you can make a good income working as an Internet marketer.

Data entry

This may include data mining, researching, copying, and pasting from one source to another. Most students prefer data entry for part-time work, as it is easy to start and requires little to no training. Though it does not always pay a lot, it is tuncomplicated and does not require specific skills. If you know how to use a computer and the Internet search feature, you will find data entry as a simple work that you can speedily do in your spare time to make some income.

Survey

Taking surveys online is the easiest way to make money and working while in college. The work is best left for side income and does not pay much. If you want a quick-money making gig, take online surveys. Answer questions honestly and you can earn some extra cash.

Explore all your options and choose the one that interests you. Of course, you don't want to be doing something that sucks. Choosing the wrong part-time job option can make your work-study job less desirable. Undoubtedly getting started and building a portfolio can be a challenge. It will get better as you keep trying.

Working while in college gives a fillip to your resume and boosts your chances of getting a better job upon completion of your studies. This could help you stand out from the crowd and land in a job of your dreams.

How Traveling The World Makes You A Better Freelancer

A **solopreneur's mind** needs lots of fresh ideas, inspiration, energy, focus and willpower to confront the endless challenges. You can train your mind to focus and concentrate effectively. But, traveling does a lot more good to you besides just re-energizing the brain.

The world needs people who can understand and solve critical problems. If you're a freelancer, your expertise and hard work are going to help someone, or an organization in the end. However, you will have to keep some of your personality aspects always alive to be able to do that. You should be creative, adaptable, develop amazing communication and research skills, and be a great learner.

Traveling can help you with all these. Would you like to know how traveling inspired many people to come up with new ideas, learn how to be happy and solve practical problems? Here are some amazing stories which tell how traveling the world makes you a better freelancer:

Nature can be inspirational

Being out in nature alone can be highly inspirational. A lot of people agree to the fact that simply traveling to the countryside, or a walk in the neighborhood areas inspire them to think differently, or think out of the box.

For example, Jessica Swift is an artist and surface pattern designer. She needs lots of creative ideas to add flavor to her work. She loves to take long walks in the nature. The color of the plants, leaves, shapes of flowers, and trees help her produce beautiful designs.

People say her artwork is very inspirational and positive. Jessica believes her love for traveling and nature helps her put that flow of inspirational energy into her work.

Entrepreneur found business idea when traveling

When you travel, you get to see and know real life situations and problems. Chris and Will Haughey were on their business trip when they felt inspired to start a business to help provide employment to the poor people. They initially didn't know what to do. But soon they found an amazing idea when traveling to Germany for their usual business meets.

They came up with the idea of manufacturing magnetic wooden blocks for children. This manufacturing process needed local people who knew the work and so could help them. They hired locals with fair wages to manufacture the wooden blocks. Additionally, they also train their employees about leadership, manufacturing and professional skills.

Entrepreneur shares how traveling makes him incredibly productive

Jay Meistrich is the CEO and co-founder of Moo.do. He traveled to 45 cities in 20 countries. He did this, leaving everything behind. He sold everything he owned and started his journey with just a 40 litre backpack. He believes he works most productively when he is traveling.

According to him, when he was not traveling and was just working sitting in front of the computer screen for 12 hours a day, he was never so productive.

During his journey to different places, he was able to come up with better ideas. He loved his whole journey because it made him feel alive, healthier, and creative. Traveling is very important to him now because it helps him manage his working hours. This is why now he is able to spend his personal and family time better than ever.

Traveling is important for the mind. Also, you need it because you get to become more cultural, learn time management, develop better communication skill, learn to face problems and become more flexible to different life situations.

Part-time Jobs For Teens And Students

Finding a part-time job while studying can be a daunting task for a teen or student, but doing so does give you some amount of financial freedom. Of course, balancing work with classes makes you more disciplined and provides you with much-needed autonomy. Additionally, you learn how to be more responsible and handle responsibility, manage money and time, and deal with people.

Whether you choose traditional part-time jobs for teens, such as babysitting or lawn care, or wish to tread a professional or entrepreneurial path, such as computer repair services, there are a lot many options to explore. A less intensive temporary job can be a great learning experience that can help you learn useful life skills.

I started working during my teens babysitting my younger siblings, toddlers of relatives, and neighborhood kids. I thought this was the best part-time opportunity for me at that age, as I didn't have to travel far and wide to make some money. The best part is I learned how to handle toddlers while staying calm and not losing my temper. True, managing small children can be a big challenge, and this experience has certainly helped me control my temper even in distressing times.

Part-time jobs for students

Working part-time while studying gives you the green signal that you are stepping into adulthood, so you should start to earn money to pay for your interests and favorite activities. The type of part-time job you choose should be based upon your skill set and ultimate career goals, which will ensure that you gain experience as an experienced professional. Peer Hustle is an on-demand marketplace for students, teens, and professionals to look for gigs and meet prospective clients that can provide you the work of your interest.

Lawn Care

You could make easy money by offering to do yard work for your busy neighbors. If lawn care interests you and are prepared to rake the yard, mow lawns, cut grass, and trim hedges, you could make good money for your efforts. Not only this, you also get to enjoy the sunshine on a cold winter day! Your family's lawnmower can come in handy and make lawn care a real part-time money-making opportunity for you.

Pet care

Animal care jobs are some of the most sought-after part-time jobs for students and teens. If are a pet lover, this could be an opportunity to make some income while doing something that interests you the most. In fact, you could make money during summer holidays when families plan holiday travel, providing potentially lucrative opportunities for students and teens to care for their pets in their absence. Pet walking services can be offered all through the year! Teens can also offer pet waste removal services and earn money cleaning out animal cages. Get some hands-on experience as an animal shelter worker if you want to become a veterinarian.

Tutoring

Tutoring is big business now. Parents are ready to pay good money for tutoring their kids. If you have a good grasp of a subject, use your knowledge to help other kids. You could offer to help an elementary school student with reading, or a junior get those calculus questions right. Register yourself in the Peer Hustle platform and start looking for tutoring gigs. As a private tutor, you can set your own schedule with clients and enjoy helping others learn.

Retail

Many students and teens find retail jobs interesting, which comes with diverse work options. You can expect to make anywhere between $11 and $13 per hour in a retail outlet. The pay depends upon the duties involved, which may include product demonstrations, standing behind a counter, stocking shelves, offering customer service, handing out samples in grocery outlets, or operating a cash register. Retail jobs are perfect for teens that are sociable and have no problem interacting with customers. This type of part-time job for teens offers you experience to deal with clients and customers. Additionally, you will learn time management, money management, responsibility, and customer service.

Babysitting

You may have a relative or neighbor who is looking for a babysitter. Grab that opportunity to make some money. Ideally babysitters work Friday and Saturday, so you have the entire week to complete homework, participate in school-related activities, or do some other part-time work. Parents are ready to pay more when they are crunched for time.

Golf Caddy

A perfect part-time work activity for teenagers who enjoy spending time in the outdoors, caddying requires an understanding of the game. Of course, you got to have some physical endurance, since this requires a lot of walking and carrying a weighty bag. However, the pay is good, and you can expect to earn $50-$100 for working for about four hours.

Personal assistant

Working as a personal assistant is a lucrative part-time job opportunity for teens. Let the adults know that you can help them with personal assistant services. As customers start to trust your services, you will get more responsibilities, which may be sporadic initially. More responsibilities mean more money. This type of part-time job could help you become more responsible and organized. You could start with $10 per hour and go up with expanded services.

Document and photograph archival

A number of people do not have time to get their old photos and documents scanned, archived, and stored. Many of them have thousands of photos clicked in the pre-digital camera era and would love to digitize them to scan and safely store them online or offline. Of course, they don't have time for this time-consuming task. Announce to your parents and their friends that you are available for document and photo digitizing services and can help them scan, store, and archive their old photos and documents. It may help to set a price per item, depending on the amount of time it will take you to complete the tasks. The work can be tedious, and you must ensure that the documents and photos are handled carefully.

Restaurant employee

You could choose to work as a line cook, busser, or server in a restaurant? Spread the word about your availability for work as a restaurant employee and ask restaurant owners in your community if they need any help. Working in a restaurant is a great way to interact with people and hone your social skills. This could go a long way in helping you become a better customer services staff member. Or you could also choose a full-time career as a chef when you grow up.

Movie theater employee

You have always been fascinated by movies. So why not choose a part-time job in a movie theater? Working in a theater may involve working as an usher, cashier, cook, busser, dishwasher, booth crew member, ticket sales staff, or server. As an employee, you will learn to work together to meet the needs of a busy movie crowd. If the world of cinema interests you, this is the job for you.

Housekeeping

Do you love to keep your house and surroundings neat and tidy? If yes, this job is for you. You could start with $10 per hour in a housekeeping job. You will learn responsibility and develop your organizational skills. Often hotels look for extra housekeeping staff during the rush season. This could be a lucrative opportunity to do what you love and make some cash. Even malls and parks also look for people to help keep public areas organized and clean. Simply grab the opportunity!

Warehouse

If you don't mind using some muscle for loading and unloading inventory to and from containers and shelves, you could do well working in a warehouse. This type of job could be little monotonous but it's okay as long as you are making money from it. Stay focused and keep moving to enjoy your work.

Car wash attendant

If you live in a warm area, you are almost guaranteed to stay busy washing cars. People are often looking for car wash attendants to get the job done. If you don't mind wetting or ruining your clothing and enjoy working outdoors, you will enjoy doing this kind of part-time work. Not only this, you will learn to keep your car shiny and clean, without any cost.

When looking for part-time work for students, you can take advantage of your unique abilities and skills to start off. If word of mouth marketing doesn't help, you can always find online mobile marketplaces, such as Peer Hustle, as one of the best platforms to find part-time work and keep yourself busy during holidays while making some money. Do not forget work experience learned at this stage of your life will make life much easier in adulthood, when you actually need to do something and make your career. No doubt, working part-time can help you become a better student and enjoy a better future.

Small Habits, Huge Gains: How Little Things Push You To Succeed With Freelancing?

Small is underestimated.

Our society looks up to the "big". Bigger is usually better. Big is flashy, gets us attention, and big is preferred.

Anything big starts with small though.

So, it goes like this in reality:

Small gives way to big.

Simplicity is hard to achieve.

The power of compounding helps your saving corpus grow huge despite small sums of money invested periodically.

In freelancing too, you can achieve humongous gains by doing those hundred little things you never thought were "that" important.

Here are some of those small things that give you huge gains and the path to succeed with freelancing:

The speed of hitting "reply"

How long do you take to reply to your clients? Is it something like 24 hours?

Did you know that the chances of a client hiring you shoot absurdly northwards when you respond quickly?

Let's take customer service as a benchmark: According to Jennifer Beese of SproutSocial.com, a 2012 study points out that over 32% of customers expect a response within 30 minutes.

Customer service comes in "after" products or services are sold. Can you imagine how quick you'd have to be to respond "before" products or services are sold?

Being yourself

Too many freelancers make the mistake of being too clammed up, "professional", and almost stuck up.

Clients aren't just looking for help with their projects; they are also looking for real people. They need humans to work with them; not machines.

Stop being a bore. Be who you are, complete with the smileys, occasional jokes, and dare to even poke your clients.

Life is fun that way.

Respect. Respect some more

Freelancers want to be respected for their work.

You, we are sure of this, obviously want to provide value through your work. You clients get it. They ask for it. They pay you for it.

But often, this respect is lost somewhere. Clients tend to disrespect your time, for instance, and you'd revert back with a couple of emails trying to train clients on how this or that shouldn't happen.

You'd do well to respect yourself first. What does that mean for freelancing, you ask?

- Don't let "scope creep" happen.
- Don't ever do anything for free.
- Stop being the "vendor". Be a consultant.
- Try to become a partner instead of being a freelancer.

Walk those extra 10 miles

Walking the extra mile is out. It's now time to walk at least 10 miles more for your clients. If you do web design, give your clients a heads-up on how to use their website for better conversions. If you are a PPC market-er, give your clients a couple of free landing pages.

You get the drift, don't you?

What are some of those little things you do to make freelancing work for you?

Sales And Marketing

How To Promote Your Freelance Business, The Smart Way

Freelancing isn't going to work for you without marketing. Irrespective of the skill-set you posses, marketing is a mandatory skill-set you ought to possess.

Simply put, marketing puts food on the table. It helps you keep the lights on. It allows you to pay the bills, and is the main pillar of support for your freelancing business.

If you embrace marketing, you will never have to go through the usual peak and valley cycles most freelancers have to put up with. Also, you will learn precious lessons, which enable you to handle any kind of business tomorrow.

Whether you are a veteran freelancer or a rookie, you'd need to promote your freelance business. Here's how:

Cold-calling and cold-emailing

Meeting clients offline is fine, and you'd still do well doing it. However, reaching out to potential prospects using cold-emails and -calls is still a great way to land your initial clients. Although most people frown at the thought of having to call strangers, it's still the good way to add a few good clients at least when you are starting.

The blogging thing

Whether you are a designer, a writer, or an illustrator, starting a blog is mandatory. It's a direct way for the world to see what you are capable of and it's a great window for your clients to peep into your work. Apart from enhancing the appeal of your offering, acting as a portfolio of your work, and helping you to network, it's also a great way for you to establish your credibility and build authority.

Your social/community presence

The trouble with your blog is that almost no one knows about it, unless it's already popular. Assuming that your blog is popular, most people just forget that it exists.

That's where your social media presence along with your constant presence in forums, groups, and communities helps.

Strategic partnerships

Chances are that you could partner with businesses selling products and services are related to your offerings but don't directly compete with your services. For instance, web designers or developers can't form strategic partnerships with digital marketing agencies. Marketers can tie up with web designers. You get the drift?

Finding creative ways to market

We know a fashion designer who was struggling to find high-quality, profitable e-commerce and traditional businesses that deal with fashion goods and accessories. She realized how hard it was to find new clients for her freelancing business and so she went looking for these businesses off affiliate networks such as Commission Junction, Share-a-Sale, and others.

Normally, these affiliate networks are frequented by merchants and their affiliates. We just don't realize that those same networks are also niche directories with contact information that freelancers can use to directly reach out to those companies.

5 Sales Principles Every Freelancer Should Follow

You are a freelancer, an entrepreneur, and a sales person – all rolled into one. There's no escaping the fact that the onus of responsibility of getting more business is in your hands. Now, that's a huge responsibility and it takes a lot to make it happen.

Since doing sales is a huge part of your everyday marketing equation, you'd spend more time and energy in sales apart from your actual freelancing work.

It's a responsibility, yes. But the act of making sales demands that you adhere to a few rules. Here are a few sales principles every freelancer should follow:

Do sales like religion

You are in business, and doing the act of sales is religion for any business. It isn't something that you do when the well goes dry or when you aspire to do more. The act of sales – along with the act of marketing – is a relentless, continuous, and the only profitable endeavor in business

You avoid sales and you will have no revenue.

You shall follow up

The difference between success and failure in sales is the act of follow up. The simple rule is this: follow up until you get a response such as "Yes, But I need more time" or "No, I am not Interested".

The number of times you have to follow up is immaterial for the reason that your prospects can take as long as they like to actually decide to work with you.

Always put time at a premium

Do you find yourself waiting on clients to get back to you? Even worse, do you end up waiting before and during meetings? Stop that.

Even before clients learn to respect your work, they have to respect your time. Look for little clues right from the start about how your potential clients deal with you.

As for anything else before, during or after the sale (unless it's got to do with customer service) charge hourly. This also discourages any possibility of scope creep.

Qualify leads and prospects

Not every client who comes asking for your services is an ideal client. You'd have to qualify leads as they come to differentiate between good clients and the bad ones. How do you decide between good or bad? It's up to you.

The point is that you'd have a qualification mechanism or system in place. Your leads can move further along the sales cycle only if they qualify, so to speak.

You will not tolerate value erosion

If you'd like to give discounts, make a few changes to your usual work policy, or amend contracts to fit the scope of projects, it's all your choice. What you'll not do is to let anyone devalue the core service you provide.

If clients tell you that you are expensive, or that there are others who can work for less, or if your clients believe that your Turn Around Time is a little too long, it's their problem.

Which of these sales principles do you follow?

How To Master Sales
And Follow Up For Freelancing

Freelancers have a role – among many others – in sales (for themselves), much like sales-people work everyday to build a pipeline, manage their sales process, and bring in the cash.

Your sales management prowess puts the food on the table. It's the only way to make sure you get clients. It's exactly what keeps the lights, pays the bills, and helps you survive.

Being that important, it's surprising that most freelancers don't do it as often as they should. If they do, they don't bring themselves to do it right.

Here's how to bring in a semblance of a system to your sales and follow up for freelancing business:

Pitch everyday

Here's how a typical freelancer does sales: call up, email, or meet prospects. Close deals. Get busy with the mountain-loads of work that you now need to do to meet deadlines.

As a result, your sales activity will now see a slow death while you spend the entire day on actual work.

The trouble comes when any of your clients leave (for any reason). When that happens, you are back to square one. You have to start looking for work again.

That's why it's critical to keep the sales engine going, whether or not you have clients.

Use a CRM

The CRM market is crowded, and that's good news for us freelancers. You have a ton of options to choose from and you'd not need anything fancy at all.

A CRM system allows you to track every piece of communication, phone call, and actual in-person meetings so that you'd never lose sight of every interaction you have.

CRM tools also allow you to make special notes on every client, set up to-do tasks related to that lead, and mark the sales call as "hot", "warm", "cold", "converted", "deal", etc.

Using a CRM helps you keep a tight control on your lead data. It allows you to follow up thoroughly, and ensures that you have a system in place.

Follow up until you get a response

As Steli Efti of Close.io puts it, most people who have anything to do with sales and follow-ups give up after the initial calls and a few random follow-ups.

The key is to follow-up until you get a response – no matter what that response is. If it's a yes, you are in business. If it's a no, try to find out why (even if you don't get business, you'll get insights, referrals, or maybe just a friend you can chat with).

Keep in touch

All of us are busy, and have work to do. Life also comes in between. Your prospects can forget your pitch, end up doing something else that's high priority for them, and time can pass through a vacuum. It's important to keep in touch without being pushy or salesy about it.

Use social media if that's what you are comfortable with. Or maybe email marketing?

Which of these freelancing sales mistakes do you make?

Freelancing Basics: How To Negotiate Better With Clients

What's the first thing that comes to your mind when we say 'freelancing'?

For most people, it would be freedom from the torturous routine of doing that dreaded 9-5 shift.

But freelancing isn't exactly the answer if you are looking to escape work. In fact, it's the other way around. The harsh truth about freelancing is that it is challenging.

A full-time job guarantees you regular income, but if you are a freelancer, you are as good as your last project. Once you have delivered a project, finding a new client/project becomes essential.

Also, unlike full-time job-holders, freelancers have to haggle for price for individual project or client. And in the content writing industry, variation of prices are shocking enough to give you sleepless nights.

So, for surviving as a freelance writer, polishing your negotiation skills is essential. Here are some tricks you can use for negotiating with the client and earn more.

Highlight your expertise

Do you bid for a project by saying:

> "I specialize in all types of writing - web content, press releases, blogs, and whitepapers"?

Evaluate this pitch from your client's perspective. Every content writer specializes in different types of writing. So, what's your specialty and justification for demanding a higher price?

The first step for increasing your rate is to stress on the special skills you possess as a writer. Maybe you love researching and can pick out interesting info. Or maybe you are efficient in explaining technical terms in a simple language.

Find out your strengths and promote them aggressively.

Request your client to quote a price

It's crucial to understand how much your client can spend. A simple way of knowing this would be to request them to quote their rates. You'll be shocked to know that the rate they quote could be higher than what you were considering.

Or, it could be drastic. Where you are expecting to get paid at least for what you are worth, you'd receive a quote that can derail your ego. It's not uncommon for clients to send in quotes that are less than the minimum wage in El Salvador or Somalia.

Offer an alternative proposal

In case a client quotes a rate that is low, offer an alternative proposal. For strengthening your case, justify your higher rates.

Justifications could range from writing good quality content to doing background research or presenting the content in a unique style.

Also, if the deadline is short, it's ethical to demand higher rates.

Choose your clients wisely

The content writing industry is full of clients who need 'high quality content'. However, many of them possess vague notions about good content. We have come across clients who believe that writing a 'good' 500 words article should maximum take 15 minutes.

Since such clients do not understand the effort that goes into writing good quality content, the pay they offer is equally disastrous. If you want to increase your rates, avoid such clients.

Instead, choose clients who respect your effort and offer standard rates. Here's a wonderful article that elaborates this point.

Never "fix" prices before you know more

Some writers promote themselves by stating a fixed rate on their websites (such as $10 for 500 words article) or quote an hourly price. We know this is done to simplify the "pricing" problem. However we are against this strategy.

Once you have a quoted a fixed rate, you cannot get more than that.

Also, the time and effort you need to invest usually vary (even for 2 articles that have the same word count). So, avoid this strategy. Instead, quote a price after you have read the project brief.

Many freelancers avoid negotiating because they think that the client will reject the proposal. Unfortunately, if you stick to this attitude, it would be impossible for you to grow. For understanding the reality, coming out of your bubble is critical. Start by researching about current industry rates so that you know what other writers are charging. If you require more tips, click here.

How To Master Negotiation
For Better Freelancing Deals

We've all bee taught to be humble, nice, and forgiving. We've been taught to believe in others, work your hardest, and be the best you can be.

Things are rarely that nice in the real world, especially in business. When you deal with clients and vendors, you are literally out there on the street. You are working with a bunch of unknown parameters. You are in the thick of wilderness and operate around thousands of blind spots.

You key to freelancing success and to make sure you have a sustainable freelancing business is to negotiate and make more money for every hour spent.

As for most things in life, you can learn the art of negotiation skills for freelancing. You'd just have to start with the following:

Know what you want clearly

You can't enter any kind of negotiation if you don't know what you want out of that interaction. Meeting clients, vendors, or anyone else puts in various situations that you'd need to know how to get out of, in a way that works for you.

If you walk in unclear, you'd walk out with a deal where you don't win.

Get tough

If you were any degree more meek, needy, or hungry for the deal than the other party, the other guy would eat you for lunch. Don't be someone else's lunch or dinner.

Eat others alive, if you can, or stay clear.

Successful negotiation requires a certain mindset that stems from mental toughness, lessons from the street, and the ability to take risks.

Always negotiate from value standpoint

Never try to negotiate deals with your personal stories at stake. It doesn't matter if you've had sleepless nights, unpaid bills, and even if creditors were knocking on your door.

Also, don't negotiate based on price.

If you ever find yourself saying anything like:

"I am the cheapest in the market…"
"Show me another freelancer who charges less than I do…."

Stop it. Now. Negotiate on the value you provide—nothing more; nothing less.

Keep those numbers on your side

If the first step is to negotiate from a value standpoint, the second step is to know your numbers. You should know not what you do (which you do know), but how your contribution adds value.

If you were a web designer or developer, you'd say:

"My website design can easily bring about 350% more conversions and increase your ROI by…"

If you were a blogger, you'd say:

"A single, SEO optimized blog post stays on the web, getting you at least 400 visitors per day, growing at 20% each month, to get you sales equivalent to…"

Numbers are everything in business. Don't underestimate the confidence you get with numbers on your side.

Be willing to walk away

At the end of it all, you either win or lose in a negotiation. No act of negotiation is a zero-sum game. Lose if you have to. Or, be willing to walk away from the deal if you find yourself on the losing side.

With experience, you'll develop a sense for it when you are about slide into the losing side of the game. But whether you get it or not, you get an amazing sense of power when you are in a position to walk away from it all.

How do you negotiate? How has the negotiation skill help you with your freelancing?

How Freelancers Can Start With Marketing Automation

It's hard enough to run your business, the way it is. Any work beyond billable hours is time wasted. That's why it makes sense for freelancers to embrace Marketing Automation. Write out a simple step-by-step process for freelancers to start with marketing automation.

So, you freelance. You work at hours; you feel comfortable. You get paid for those hours. But nothing is infinite. Neither money nor hours. Anything beyond the billable target is sheer frustration. Now wasn't that the first reason why you went freelancing?

The coming of age of Marketing Automation has changed the way the world earns money. For freelancers, this is akin to manna from heaven. Technology has bridged the gap between work and life and none seems to be in balance anymore.

So what is marketing automation?

"Marketing automation is a category of software that streamlines, automates and measures marketing tasks and workflows so that companies like yours can increase operational efficiency and grow revenue faster." - Marketo via What Is Marketing Automation?

It means a software that would do your bidding when you are sleeping. Guess that was the whole idea behind free lancing. So how do we go about doing it:

Track your time

Before you automate your system, understand what you would need to automate. Un-junk your workload. Put in place the priorities that would allow you work more freely. Toggl.com provides free service for basic time tracking and extra features available with a $5 monthly membership. Moreover it is one of the easiest applications of this sort to use..

Create sub-categories

You have tracked your time and now know the broad categories you spend your time mostly in, namely: Accounting, Lead Generation, Customer Service and Project Management. Now go ahead and create sub-categories. So for example, Accounting ends up being broken into invoicing, accounts payable and receivable.

Similarly, Customer Service breaks into Retention, new Customers and so and so forth.

The stepping stone

I named it such because that is how drilling down to the most basic level would feel. Do a time-tracking exercise again. But now it will be with the basic steps of a large process.

So for example, when a large part of your task includes invoicing, note the total time down along with the steps.

You know that there will be a hundred invoices to be created daily each having a 5 step procedure. That is 500 steps in a day. How about automating it?

Software like Harvest does these kinds of jobs in the quickest of time with the best of quality.

The important feature of automating your business is not what software to look for but what items you would want to automate and gain extra billable hours.

Eliminate

And for a moment act as The Terminator. Eliminate lengthy steps, either totally or automate them. At times, simple repetitive steps can be overcome by creating fixed templates and at other technology. Harvest halves your time spent on repetitive tasks. All you would need now is to insert the line items, do a quick check and send. Now, glance at your checklist and note the time. You are winning, mate.

Checklist, ahoy

Nothing helps in the world of work management as much as a check list. It's the veritable mover and shaker here. Keep striking items you have overcome, eliminated and automated. Do a quick math. How much did you save? How did it help you to increase your activities? Ponder. Realise. Move on. You are now ready to live more, work less.

Select your armor

The advent of technology has been a boon for people who loveto declutter. The world is paring down on its papers. The desk is getting smaller, the hard-drives bigger.

Marketing Automation leader Infusionsoft and second in command Ontraport has taken the game far ahead. The long and short of it is that if you are a busy freelancer, Infusionsoft has the capability of managing, automating and tracking most of the tasks that you're currently performing manually.

Zapier at $20 a month and IFTTT are affordable alternatives too

For email management, look no further than SaneBox, for email follow up Boomerang for Gmail, Social Media updates rely on Hootsuite and email marketing MailChimp all the way.

Is there any other method to unclutter one's work and create more space?

Yes, there is. The way you go about doing your work is a primary source of clutter. Stop checking your email every 30 minutes. Use online payment options and saving receipts as pdf rather than manual invoicing and constantly innovate to move ahead. Clients want new stuff to play with and more money to get rewarded with. Guess, that's motivation enough to start grooving.

Go declutter.

How To Plan Your Content Marketing Strategy For Freelancing Business

One of the biggest challenges you face as a freelancer is to promote your own business. Given that most of your time is spent on actual, billable work for your clients, you'll find that the time you'd need to do to deploy content marketing for your freelancing business is at a premium.

Digital marketing is much like a car's engine: it has to be on, and it can't rest.

Without getting stuck into regular workdays for just working on your freelance work, you'd need to spend time (and/or money) to promote your freelance business. There's a way to do it, and you'd have to do it.

This is how:

Blog for your audience

If you are a freelance writer, you are primarily writing for other businesses, individuals strapped for time (or flair) to write for themselves, and more. You can choose to specialize and write for very specific work categories such as copywriting (mainly for small and medium sized businesses) or blogging (for businesses), etc. You can also discuss the topics with which you want work.

Once you identify your audience, prepare a content calendar and start writing at a particular frequency you choose (1 blog post a week or 5 blog posts a week). Remember that you should be writing posts that hold value for your audience and not simply telling of your skills.

Amplify your content, reach, and brand on social

Use social media networks to your advantage by amplifying the reach of your content. Every blog post you write has to be shared regularly on social media (not just once), and then you'd also do well to share others' content (but relevant to your audience). In the middle of this activity, find time to engage with others.

Ideally, you should follow the 50:30:20 rule for social media management where 50% of the time, you'd be sharing other content (not your own), 30% of the updates would have to be your own, and 20% of the updates are pure engagement.

You can also use social management tools such as HootSuite to help reduce the time and effort put toward social media.

Build and nurture your email list

Email has the real potential to get you business and long-term branding. For that, you first have to build your list. Today, it's not as easy as it once was but if you provide enough value up front, it's possible to build your list quickly.

Give away something of value first such as a free trial, white paper, a report, an eBook, etc. Build your list and then nurture this list of subscribers who've all opted in to receive communication from you.

Each of the three aspects of digital marketing is continuous, relentless, and unstoppable. You have to keep the engine running so it will take you plenty of conviction, dedication, and focus.

How do you run your digital marketing efforts? Are you missing out any of the important tasks above?

4 Ways Freelancers Can Highlight Their Skills

Liam Veitch, a successful freelancer, once said that client's won't hire you because you have some skills. Instead, they will hire you because you can help them with your skills. So, you need to have a really solid ground before you expect to have a lot of work in your hand. You need to show the world that you're good and can help them with your expertise. So what's important is that you tell clients why they need you for your skills. Rather than simply talking more and more about your skills, you should stress more on how helpful your skills are.

There is no way to tell the world how good you are at what you do except when you make your success and progress visible to them. Freelancers need to highlight their skills and achievements as much as they need to land good jobs. And which can be the best way to sell skills online? You can think of some ideas like these:

Write stories of your achievements and showcase

You need to talk about your accomplishments and your work. Information like what type of projects you've worked on, how they went, how did you successfully complete the tasks, how challenging the projects were, how did you address the challenges, how happy were your clients, etc. will be very helpful to your future clients. So when you put this information out there, you need to showcase how you used your skills to successfully end the projects. You need to show the application of your skills so that clients can relate their concerns to the information provided and see your potentials.

Have a successful website

Have an awesome website where you can write about your and other freelancer's successful career. If you've started your own side business, talk about that as well. Having a websites with lots of valuable information can be very helpful from all perspectives. Websites that share information on jobs in your niche, and interviews other freelancers who made a great career will do very well. Put lots of photos and videos on your site. But, they should be helpful and teach something. Try to inspire people through your skills. Clients will love that.

Write for others for free

Write guests posts for other remarkable websites. Don't take it lightly. There are dozens of amazing freelancing sites which will let you write about your niche. You need to build an audience through your guest posts. The more you write engaging posts, the more response you get from the interested readers. Also, this is where the people needing to hire freelancers will come. So, try to make a memorable impression. Show off your qualities, your fan base, and your skills and abilities via amazing guest posts.

Take help from sites that will let you showcase your profile

There are some sites which will let you build a profile and tell the target audience your story. You can highlight your skills on these sites. You can tell the world what you do and how you can help others. This is one amazing way to intimidate the prospective clients.

The point is, you need to find out the places where highlighting the skills will make a big difference. It can be your website or some very popular site of someone else. But above all, tell the world what makes you do what you do and how you can help clients with your talent and skill.

5 Easy Ways To Build Your Portfolio

You don't build a portfolio; you build your reputation. Through your hard work, your name becomes a brand. According to Jeff Bezos, the world renowned Amazon founder, a person tries to build a reputation by trying doing hard things well.

That's true. You start your freelancing career to help someone with business difficulties. You help businesses to improve performance and increase scope for growth and success. You help with critical designing, marketing, writing, promotions, or business development.

If your professional expertise is to help clients get prospective business leads, which you always efficiently do, how are you going to let the world know about that? That's why your portfolio should be a free marketing tool of your expertise. It should be a track record of your achievements. And you have to be as careful as you can when building portfolio over time.

As your portfolio is going to be the mirror image of your professional experience and expertise, how do you build it over the years? Are there any easy ways to build your portfolio?

Include professional skills and expertise

This is the first thing that you include in the portfolio. Be sure to include all relevant skills and expertise in your portfolio to help clients know how you can help them.

Correctly choose the skills and expertise to show in your portfolio. In this case, your portfolio is going to work like your biodata. A well-developed portfolio will help you get attention from the clients and bag the kind of projects you want.

Tell the world your biggest achievements

As you gradually start working on numbers of projects over the years, you should include them in your portfolio. One way to build an attractive portfolio is to work on different types of projects. Clients love to work with people with diversified experience. Take challenging work and showcase them on your portfolio.

While it's always hard working on challenges, it certainly improves our expertise, trains us to face problems, and deal with them. Your portfolio should tell the world what you've learned though the challenges and how they added to your experiences.

Include links to case studies

This is very important. How do you highlight your accomplishments? Develop few case studies, publish them on your website and include links in your portfolio. Ask your clients if they are comfortable enough to share their stories and your contributions.

Develop case studies of your most challenging and successful work and explain how you helped the client, or solved their problem. This will increase your credibility and market value.

Receive feedback and testimonials

One way to help clients understand your true worth is to share client testimonials and feedback. For example, when you buy a product online, don't you try to find and read customer reviews, if available? Client feedbacks and reviews work as assurance for a product or service. Likewise, client feedbacks and testimonials will ensure you and your service are what they expect. That's why you should add as much client feedback as you can to your portfolio.

Frequently update portfolio

Do you update your portfolio? If you don't, you should do it frequently to help clients know your latest accomplishments, jobs, projects, and improvements. When you update your portfolio with new skills and latest projects you're working on, you show your gradually improving abilities, expertise and experience.

How do you build your portfolio? It's in your hands. But, as you're free to develop it anyway you want, why not make it an astounding tool for career growth and development?

How To Really Make Your Portfolio Stand Out

You'll have to work hard to make your portfolio stand out. Nothing apart from experience can add value to your portfolio. What do clients want to know? Your client is most interested in your expertise and exposure. Your client would like to know if you really can use your expertise to help him/her accomplish their business goals.

You'll have to work hard to showcase your expertise and skills. You'll have to prove that you understand client's problem well, and can help with an adequate solution. So, what are the things that you will need to make your portfolio stand out? Below you'll find what professionals have to say about it:

Add success stories

Why would clients believe that you can do what they want? Scott Belsky is an entrepreneur, author, investor, and currently the vice president of Adobe.

He talks a lot about how to build a stunning portfolio which can help professionals outshine in the crowd. According to Scott, you'll have to make your portfolio like a story.

Add brief information about how did you become a freelancer, your vision, your goal and ambition to the portfolio to help client understand how serious you are about your profession. Also, don't forget to add your success stories. If you're a client and trying to find a suitable freelancer for your project, wouldn't you like to know if the applicant is experienced and an achiever?

Show case studies of successful projects

Only mentioning successful projects in the portfolio will not be enough. You will have to showcase how you helped clients with their projects. Clients would love to know your understanding of the problem, your problem- solving abilities and your approach to challenges. Being able to solve a problem is not always what clients look for.

But, as a recruiter, the client would like to see how good you're at putting your best foot forward. You will have to define your abilities to handle a project, deal with the time line of a project and provide the best possible solutions.

Show diversity of skills

Clients would like people who can manage several tasks so that he/she doesn't have to waste time finding people for each small job. For example, if you're a writer, but you also know some internet marketing best practices, it will increase the chance that the client will hire you.

Why, you ask? It's because clients will think that you can also help with some online marketing essentials, besides providing some writing work. Diversity of skills will give you competitive advantage.

Promote your blog and website

If you have a blog or a website, mention that in your portfolio. Although it will not ensure that the client is definitely going to hire you, it certainly adds value to your portfolio.

Yes, if you have an awesome blog or website that talks about your achievements and can show few client testimonials, that would be an added advantage. The client will get a practical idea about your work samples, your successful projects and what other clients say about you. You can also add your social media profiles for that.

Share your professional circle of influencers

The social media profiles, your connections on those profiles, followers, etc. will help client understand your professional credibility. This will give the client a ready idea about your professional engagement, type of people you're associated with, and your professionalism.

These are few of the ways to build a portfolio that can stand out from the rest. A portfolio with all these details will improve your credibility and your chances of getting hired.

Bold Ideas To Get More Clients For Your Freelancing Business

Apart from the fact that PeerHustle connects with you small and medium-sized businesses in the U.S., you always find the need to get as many clients as you can, and perhaps more than you can handle.

Since the churn rate is omnipresent, and because you can never be too sure of any client (or anything at all) you should always be on the lookout for new business.

But what exactly should you be doing to get new clients? How can you make sure you have your bases covered? Apart from doing basic marketing to get clients for your freelancing business, what else can you do?

You can do a lot more if you stop being boring by doing things everyone does. It's time to shake things up a bit. Drop red-hot coal into ice tea, so to speak.

Here are a few bold ideas to get more clients for your freelancing business:

Knock on virtual doors

If you are a freelancer in the modern context of work, you will more likely spend a lot of time online – be it work, recreation, or when just looking around or browsing about.

You will continue to do that, except this time, you won't lounge about but do it with intent.

First, what you'd look for depends on your area of freelancing. While browsing the Internet, for instance, a few possibilities could include:

- Freelance copywriters can look for copy on websites. When you see a possibility for improvement, you can reach out to the website owner.

- Graphic designers can keep an eye out for chances to improve web design quality.

- Translators can put up an offer to turn the existing English content into another language.

All you have to do is to reach out and make an offer your potential clients can't refuse.

Go offline

Given the ubiquitous nature of the web and the presence of so many sources of opportunities for freelancers, it's almost stupid to think of spending any time offline at all. But that's where you have opportunity.

What would happen if you were to spend a bit on business cards, business mailers, direct mail pieces, or even walk directly into your prospect's offices with or without appointment?

Here's what David LaMartina did and how he cracked over $11,000 worth of freelancing work with direct mail pieces.

Partnerships, channels, and joint ventures

There's a thing or two you can learn from the good old Internet marketing scam gurus or anyone from the "make-money-online" niche. The good thing about any of the forums there is that you will see a feverish energy around the possibilities of doing Joint Ventures with fellow marketers.

Go out and create new channels of business, form partnerships, and initiate joint ventures with non-competing businesses.

But it's not just them who do strategic partnerships. Some well-known companies also do it. Check out Moz Perks, for instance, or Unbounce Partners.

Whether you choose to go the usual route, or you choose to go bold, one thing is for sure: you'd always have to work to bring in the rain.

How are you going to do some bold marketing? How exactly are you going to step out of the way?

How To Use Social Media For Freelancing Better

Freelancers need every possible opportunity they can get as a channel for marketing. Nothing works to a freelancer's benefit in multiple ways than well-set up and well-managed social media accounts . While social media can't beat the power and longevity of email marketing, it's certainly an almost free (you are still spending effort and time) and noticeable way of marketing your freelancing business.

First things first: social media isn't for selling. It's not a place for you to pitch your products and services. It's not meant for you to be a hawker of sorts, peddle stuff, and come across as pushy.

As Jay Baer of Convince and Convert puts it:

"There's social in social media"

He can't be more apt than that.

With that out of the way, let's see how you can make social media work for your freelancing business:

Social profiles: Set them up right

It's the starting point, and it's often overlooked. Many freelancers start off with Twitter handles, Facebook Fan Pages, and LinkedIn accounts but they don't work to optimize each of those accounts. After you decide which social profiles you want to stay active on, you have to use what each of those social accounts gives you.

Make sure you fill up your information right, setup cover photos and profile images. Be sure that your logo is optimized for social media (usually smaller in size than your usual logo size), and more.

You don't want to start out half-baked and unprepared.

Hunt for the right people to follow

On the one hand, you want to follow people, companies, and online publications that have direct relevance to the niche you operate in. Whether you are a transcribing specialist, designer, developer, marketer, or writer, you usually have a set of publications, individuals and other social accounts you ought to follow.

Beyond this, from a marketing perspective, connect with clients, vendors, other freelancers, and potential clients.

Get into conversations

If you were to think from a purely business perspective, you'd wonder what random conversations have anything to do with business, ROI, revenue, and profits.

We, however, forget that it's people who finally buy from us. Your random conversations on social media are for those people. It's for them to like you, trust you, and then buy from you.

Have conversations, build up your network, and get to know as many people as you can.

Use hashtags

Every social account today runs on hashtags. These little #hashtags have the power to make your account be visible to many others (who aren't your fans or followers yet). You'd have the power to amplify every single update you make on social media.

If you think of social media as a loud room, hashtags are like a public addressing system.

How do you use social media for freelancing? Share your thoughts with us.

How To Use Twitter To Find Clients For Freelancing Business

We did write about how to use social media for your freelancing business, and also the right way to approach social media as a channel available for your marketing efforts. While we did write about how to use each of the digital marketing channels available to you to promote your freelancing business, we thought it'd be great to actually drill in and squeeze the most off every channel to which you have access.

Twitter happens to be one of the busiest, most active, and rewarding social media networks for you and it's time to squeeze it for your benefit.

Here's how to use Twitter to find clients for your freelancing business:

Build real relationships

On Twitter, it doesn't make any sense just to hoard up followers. What really matters is the quality of relationships you have. Follow influencers and your potential customers.

Follow the target audience you believe have the potential to use your services. If you were a freelance writer, for instance, you can follow individual bloggers, digital marketing agencies, web design/development companies, and many others.

Share content to win

You are known by the content, insights, tips, and everything else you share on Twitter. While you'll follow a methodical approach to sharing content, do share content the right way.

For instance, always give credit to the source of information you share. Mention magazines, online publications, startups, businesses, and people you can attribute the content to.

Get into twitter chats

Twitter chats are quick, easy, and they have the potential to change your business. Plus, you'll see your follower base growing exponentially while also letting you to get in touch with many Twitter users you would not be able to find otherwise. Twitter chats are also fun, apart from being amazing learning experiences.

Use hash tags to your advantage

On Twitter, the hash tags you use are everything. It's with hash tags that what you update on Twitter has the "amplification" potential. Using hash tags, you can search for news, information, tips, people, and companies. You can also use hash tags to find freelancing opportunities, jobs, and even make deals with other companies (depending on what you are looking for).

If you were a freelance writer, and if you were looking for jobs, you could use the following hash tags to get in touch with prospective clients.

#freelancewriter
#wanted
#Ineedafreelancewriter
#writing
#blogging
#bloggerswanted

Use visuals

Every now and then, use visuals while sharing updates on Twitter. Visual content performs better than traditional text on all social networks (including Twitter). You don't have to be (or use a) graphic design. Use simple and free tools like Canva to create the visuals you need.

How do you use Twitter to your advantage? Do you use Twitter to find new clients for your freelancing business?

Tell us all about your experiences.

How To Use Video To Manage, Hire, Or Build Your Virtual Team

Video is a great means to tell stories. It can also be used for a lot of other purposes such as explaining things, teaching, showing complicated workflows, and a lot more. Apart from everything else, for virtual teams, video is the closest you can get to being in person. Use videos to manage your virtual team full of freelancers, and you'd never even feel that you have a remote team or a virtual company.

As for managing your virtual team and to manage your freelancers, here are different ways you can use video effectively:

Communicate your brand, goals, and vision

You are an entrepreneur and you have a vision. You've set out on a journey all by yourself and you probably glide along alone. Yet, you can use video to communicate the essence of your brand.

It comes out best when you communicate with stories, your personal experiences, and your vision for your company. Use a video—or a series of related videos—to communicate your story.

This way, your team understands better. Your freelancers see you for real. They are likely to believe you when you show up.

Describe complicated workflows

If there are set ways on how you do things or if there are processes you'd need your freelancers to follow, use videos or screencasts to show how it's done.

Along with your voice and screen recordings, let your freelancers follow along as you complete tasks. It's faster and more effective to do a screencast or a video recording than it is to write up a brief with flow-charts, annotations, and more.

Teach, and do it well

Not every freelancer is trained. However, even experienced freelancers will find the need to understand your way of doing things.

Teaching or training your freelancers is best done over video. You could add annotations to videos, add cards, zoom in, zoom out, and highlight areas on your screen to point over to hard-to-explain concepts. You do this one time and it remains as a way for you to use these videos over and over for training and teaching.

Video to collaborate

Often, you need to get together with your team. A weekly huddle, a brief chat, or a really important strategic discussion about the project may be the topic at hand.

You can use anything from Skype or Google Hangouts to GotoMeeting.com and get your team together to collaborate, communicate, and discuss projects. Nothing goes better than a well-managed, focused, and intense team talk.

How do you use videos for your business? Do you think using video to manage your virtual team works great?

4 Communication Hacks To Score With Clients

Business coach and communication expert Skip Weisman believes, every aspiring businessman should develop expertise in three major communication skills - self-communication, one to one communication and public or group communication.

However, numerous studies have indicated that a person's listening skill plays the most important role in business success. When researchers followed the daily business communication pattern of the study participants, they found that participants spent around 45 per cent of their overall communication time listening.

Therefore, you'll have to design an effective communication channel to build long term business relationship with the clients. Here are few things you can do:

Understand what communication mode client would prefer

You need to contact client for regular project updates, feedback or recommendations, that's understood. But, you will also have to understand how your client will prefer to be contacted. You can contact client via phone, email, text message, etc.

But, in an ideal professional environment, you should approach a client only via the way he/she likes. You'll have to ask client how to contact him/her during the day to day business working hours. Remember to be respectful to client's preferences and privacy standards.

Be patient to listen to what client has to say

Listen carefully to client's requirements during the face to face meetings. Give attention to every spoken word so that you can develop a clear understanding of client's requirements and also frame your response carefully. When you listen attentively, you reduce the chance of misunderstandings.

According to Forbes, around 85 per cent of what we feel we've learned is through listening. A good listening skill makes the clients feel you care for his project, you're paying attention to his/her project needs, being empathetic and you are mindful.

Frame and ask the right questions before project kick off

Take time to frame questions that you think you're going to put in front of the client. Be absolutely sure about your own capabilities, skills and requirements when you communicate with the client.

Also, don't be hesitant to ask questions.

Before you even respond to client's requirement, you should ask questions to be sure of project requirements. Ask questions like what is the end vision of the client. You must not develop your own assumptions before having a clear conversation.

Be proactive to stay connected with clients

You should always be proactive to communicate with the client. Your client will not like it if he/she has to contact you repeatedly and ask for project updates every time. Instead, you should approach your client via email to send project details and ask for recommendations.

Frequent project updates via regular communication will help you figure out the mistakes and misunderstandings quickly. Clear communication and occasional feedbacks will ensure project success.

Here is another scenario where prompt and proactive communication helps. If you find out a breaking news pertaining to your industry one day, don't wait for your client's call to talk about that.

Instead, you call your client, share the news and be bold to express your opinion about the recent industry change. This helps clients understand that you're smart and very much aware of the latest industry events. This is how you gain client trust and confidence.

Clear and honest communication is most appreciated. Don't keep the client waiting for your response and answers. Do your part the best you can and help the client prosper. Certainly, this will also ensure your prosperity and business success.

Email Marketing: Why Freelancers Should Stick To It?

Social media is hot, glamorous, and sexy. It's what everyone talks about and most freelancers believe that it's the best way to get business.

It is. But maybe it also isn't.

Social media has "social" in it. What that means is that your social media account can give you exposure, branding, impressions, and help you build relationships. It might also get you an occasional sale.

Social media, however, isn't like a marketplace where you could pitch, sell, and sell some more.

If you had to depend on a marketing channel for sales on a consistent basis, plus everything social media could give you, trust email marketing.

Email marketing is the old workhorse. It's not hot but it works. For freelancers, using email marketing paves the perfect roads to inbound marketing.

Here's why you should learn to depend on email marketing for freelancing:

Email Marketing is the bridge for your marketing funnel

With email, you could do automation. You could set up full-blown marketing funnels or even micro-funnels and nurture leads that way. Automated emails using auto responders, for instance, can be completely hands free. A few email programs also offer behavior-based emails, transactional emails, and more.

With an ROI of 4300%, you can't ignore the real beast email marketing is.

Email marketing helps nurture your leads

Freelancing is basically into B2B. Say, if you are a freelance copywriter or blogger, your primary market comprises of other businesses (whether they are single personal businesses or major conglomerates).

B2B buyers typically take longer to close sales since the decision-making process involves plenty of stakeholders.

Nurturing leads for B2B segment can get real expensive with paid ads or traditional advertising. Meanwhile, the shelf life of your updates on social media is just about three hours or so.

That's where email shines its magic. Email messages stay longer in inboxes. Emails invoke more trust, and they are easier to manage.

Email has a huge ROI

According to Graham Charlton of Econsultancy, more than 68% of companies rate email as an excellent channel for digital marketing investment. In 2014, businesses attribute about 23% of their total sales to email marketing (which has grown by 28% since 2103.

Email marketing is affordable

Ever spent too much time trying to keep up those updates on social media? Ever tried writing blog posts each day?

Compared to the time and effort those activities take, email forces you to take a mean and lean approach. You spend way less effort, money, and time on email marketing to get whopping returns for what you spend.

If you started with MailChimp, for instance, you don't even have to spend on email marketing if you are just starting out. MailChimp offers you a free plan limited to 2000 emails and 500 subscribers.

Get to it.

Do you do email marketing? Tell us all about it.

Freelance Writers: How To Find More Marketing Channels

We've been talking about direct hustling for a while now and while it's the usual norm, there are many other ways to bring in business through intermediaries and channels. Business is as much (of not more) about hustle as it's about networking. Sometimes, it's in your best interest to reach out to agencies, intermediaries, brokers, and other businesses that don't directly compete with you.

By reaching out to these parties, you essentially bring in leverage to your freelance writing business. Here are marketing ideas for freelance writers and what you need to do with them you do find them:

Peer Hustle

Look no further than our very own Peerhustle to bring yourself a steady list of well-paying, carefully chosen clients for your freelance writing business.

Depending on the power of local communities, and the increasing demand for freelance writers, PeerHustle is perfectly positioned to be your freelance career boosting secret. Without having to advertise or market yourself from scratch, your freelance career goes where you go.

Freelance networks

While freelance networks such as Upwork, Elance, and others can give you a hard time when you go looking for the right clients and the right payout to work with, you do find good clients to work such platforms.

Pick a strong bunch of 2-3 networks just so that you'd have an alternative channel to source business from.

Most freelance writers wince at the thought of bidding on these networks. It could, however, be a great "bread-and-butter" strategy.

Job sites, communities, and forums

Apart from the freelance networks, there are plenty of job sites, private communities, and forums that you can leverage and tap opportunities from. It's a hard job since your direct and valuable contribution is required upfront but almost every other channel is like that.

Explore digital

Digital marketing – for most freelance writers would be limited to blogging, social media, and email. Almost no freelance writer ever tries the Pay Per Click route. Plus, there are tons of traffic buying sources, trackers, and other methods including mobile-only that are waiting to be explored.

Take your time and see how you can explore the vast world of online advertising.

Negotiate partnerships

Freelance writers can negotiate relationships with web design agencies, web development agencies, mobile app development agencies, content development brokerage houses, and many other intermediaries to form partnerships.

By thinking creatively, you can negotiate contracts where you could take up the bulk of copy, editing, writing, blogging, and other related works that you are good at.

Get into joint ventures

Joint ventures can be with practically anybody. Since you do freelance writing, you should aim to look for individuals or companies that provide something you don't, but the services or products are closely related.

You can joint venture not just with services and products but also for general marketing.

Create your own affiliate program

While it's a slightly more aggressive and a well-planned strategy, creating your own affiliate program can bring in thousands of eager, enthusiastic, committed, and focused affiliates who'd do all the marketing and promotion for you.

Only about 20% of affiliates will ever bring in results but it's well worth the move since affiliates rely on their own expertise, contacts, skills and knowledge to make those sales numbers move.

What are the different channels that you think you can build for your freelance writing business?

Simple Ways To Use Email Marketing To Grow Your Freelancing Business

Here's the thing about inbound marketing in general: your content begins to get traffic, you'd work hard engaging with potential customers on social media, and get your potential customers to read up, consume, and get excited about everything you do as a freelancer.

The bad news: you are not doing enough. Although you get traffic, get eyeballs, and probably a few leads, you need a consistent system to ensure that leads come in on a consistent basis.

For that, you need email marketing. Here's how you do it and a few ways you can use email marketing to nurture your leads:

Grow that list

The very process of growing your list puts you into the frame of "giving". In an earlier post, we wrote about how giving helps you get more business. To grow your email list, you'd need to provide considerable value upfront, and that's a good thing.

Create reports, eBooks, give away a free trial of your services, or provide actual services that you got paid for – no matter what you do, your list grows and that's a good start.

Touch Base

Selling all the time won't help. While sending out information regularly certainly helps, there's another great way to use email marketing: to touch base.

Send out an occasional email to your list to do surveys, ask questions, send out your thoughts, point them to something you found, or get them to engage with you in a real conversation.

Set up your RSS Campaigns

Since you are blogging and your blog sees regular blog posts on a weekly basis, there are chances that you'd receive regular traffic to your blog.

However, most people (especially your potential customers) don't remember your domain name to type in and visit directly. Some might remember, but life comes in between.

That's when setting up an RSS-to-email campaign makes perfect sense. The campaign works with RSS feed of your blog setup as an email digest that goes out to your list of subscribers – the perfect way to nurture your leads with more information.

Each week. Every week. Without you lifting a finger.

Broadcast emails

Giving offers, running contests, and sending out specials is an awesome way to boost your freelance business. Doing it every so often using the normal methods of marketing can be expensive.

Not if you use email marketing. With a big, growing list of subscribers who've opted in to hear from you, your broadcast messages can be your way for selling unapologetically.

How do you use email marketing to grow your freelancing business?

How Networking Skills Can Help Freelancing Career

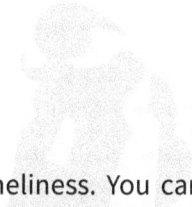

One major drawback to freelancing is loneliness. You can run out of ideas, or face challenges when trying brainstorming. Therefore, you will need to connect to many experienced industry people. Gallup Inc, which is an American management consulting company, does a lot of research and surveys on entrepreneurs and employees globally.

According to Gallup, no businessman can survive without an increasing focus on knowledge.

Networking is a very effective tool that you can use to gather information and knowledge. When you meet experienced people with an wide area of expertise and talent, you learn and absorb knowledge through information exchange. Hence, here you will find how networking skills can help your freelancing career.

Cambridge study shows importance of networking

According to a Cambridge University study, the benefits of networking can be noticed at various stages of a business. Networking can be very helpful even if a business is in the conceptual stage.

So, if you're a solopreneur or a freelancer, networking will help you build confidence. You will talk to many people, let them know about your work, get an idea what you're doing wrong and take suggestions. Networking will help you evaluate your own work. You will be able to know what others, pursuing the same professional aspirations, are doing for freelancing growth. So, networking is important for self-assessment and evaluation.

Networking helps in decision making

According to Gallup Inc, networking is actually a tool for relationship building. But, solopreneurs and freelancers can use this excellent relationship building tool to engage with their end clients. With networking you try to build a social group.

And when the time comes, you get help from this social group in terms of exchange of ideas, information, source of motivation, to raise funds and increase your popularity. Networking can help you make a well aware and conscious professional decision.

Networking with the target clients will help you connect to them at a personal level. And gradually over time, you build a sense of trust, optimism and personal integrity. Your knowledge, expertise and interests will help you build a group of like minded people. You will be able to grow your freelancing business by maintaining a mutually supportive relation with your connections.

Opportunity for partnerships

Networking can help you become a known face. You will be known among your social groups for your work and active participation in group matters. This is how you actually create your professional reputation. But besides that, you will also have opportunities for collaborations.

If a company or a small business likes your work, they can contact you for establishing business partnership. You can work as a freelancer for the business and help in business development, expansion and other things.

The more you try to build reputation among the interested audiences, the better for you. You have to develop very good interpersonal skills to be able to take advantage of networking. You will have to learn public speaking, get out of the comfort zone and ask your audience how you can help them. Your connections will love your productiveness.

And this is how you get to show your skills, expertise and emotional intelligence.

Things To Avoid

Top 4 Differences Between Successful And Struggling Freelancers

The basic difference between a successful and struggling freelancer is their mindset. Their mindset drives their actions, decisions, and hence, their success. Researchers investigated the two different types of professionals to find out what causes them to differ so extensively.

Carol Dweck, who is a professor of psychology at the Stanford University, believes that these two types of professionals have two different types of mindsets.

It can be said that successful freelancers prefer to keep trying to grow, even during extreme and odd situations. On the other hand, struggling or unsuccessful freelancers have a tendency to give up to complexities very easily.

This basic difference in their personality determines the scope of success and the chances of failures. Let's see the 4 major differences between successful and struggling freelancers:

The mindset

As mentioned earlier, the mindset of a struggling and successful freelancers differ distinctively. Professor Carol Dweck says that the mind of a successful professional is identified as a growth mindset, and the mind of an unsuccessful or average professional can be identified as a fixed mindset.

People with growth mindset always try to grow. They enjoy challenges and always try to find out solutions to problems. Their mindset helps them to grow and succeed. But, why struggling freelancers have to wait so long for success? Why they can't grow fast?

Science says it's because their fixed mindset doesn't allow them to work that way. The fixed mindset of these people leads them to think they don't have the abilities to be successful. They tend to give up to challenges very fast.

Motivation

Successful freelancers are motivated professionals. They don't need to be told to work hard. They love their work and try everything possible to prosper. This is why a freelancer who loves to work on complicated and challenging jobs doesn't mind to working beyond their comfort zone.

And this is just the opposite in case of a struggling freelancer. Struggling freelancers often suffer from lack of motivation. They don't feel the drive from within. It's hard for them to stay focused and maintain consistent hard work. After all, motivation is one of the key factors of professional and academic excellence.

Determination

Again, determination comes from your willpower. Do you love to freelance? Are you satisfied with the independent career choice? Or are you just doing it for the sake of earning some extra cash? The biggest difference between a successful and struggling freelancer is their passion and love for their work.

Successful freelancers are so much in love with their profession that they take it as one of the most integral part of their life. They are determined to face any challenge and find out solutions to every problem. They think freelancing is the only and the last thing they would like to do.

Never ending desire for self-development

Successful freelancers never stop learning. But this has lot do with their mindset again. Yes, because of their mindset and belief, successful freelancers love to thrive. They never think that they know everything.

On the contrary, struggling freelancers don't take much initiative for self growth and learnings. Their limited approach toward growth restricts their success scope.

3 Excuses That Can Kill Your Freelancing Career

Life gives us ample opportunities to do what we want. But our lame excuses tear things apart. Many of the successful entrepreneurs still recall how their childhood advice from their mentors have helped them get over excuses that could kill career opportunities they had.

Patty Lennon is a crowdfunding expert and a founder of a successful crowdfunding consulting firm. She says one of her school teachers used to tell her not to make excuses for wrong things in life; but rather, change the behavior in question.

This was a wonderful childhood lesson for her which helped her change her outlook for life. So now when things go wrong, or she fails to achieve a business goal, she doesn't try to find the reasons to back up her failure. Instead, she tries to change her behavior.

So, it's important to remember that excuses can never get you success. Let's see how you significantly lower your chances of freelancing success by making these worst excuses:

Excuse 1# You never had the opportunities

It sounds like a disastrous excuse. Life is never perfect. It's an absolutely silly thing to think that there will be a perfect moment to start something you love, or make the highest effort for your freelancing career. No, it's never going to happen. The only sure thing in life is that there will always be some ups and downs.

Read how some of the best entrepreneurs succeed. If you don't have money, there are many things that you can start without significant investments.

Being a freelancer, you always have the chance to start small, and then grow your business gradually. You need motivation, courage and determination to push your career ahead. Everything else comes after. So, don't wait for things to get settled. Don't wait for opportunities to come. Take things in your hand. Find your own opportunities and go for it.

Excuse 2# You don't have enough time

This is another lame excuse which can significantly ruin your freelancing career. A best selling author, business and data expert Bernard Marr, says most successful entrepreneurs like Richard Branson, Oprah Winfrey, and Bill Gates also have the same 24 hours in a day.

But, the biggest difference between us and those people, is that they know how to make the best use of their time. Most successful entrepreneurs are efficient time managers.

Work when you feel you're the most energetic and productive. Numbers of people have talked about time management tips and techniques. Keep yourself happy and inspired to reduce wasted time.

Be mindful to identify the present opportunities. You will have to leave behind the negativities of the past if you want to have enough time in your hand. The more you worry about the past and the future, the more time you waste. So, you don't have enough time is just an excuse that can only kill your freelancing career.

Excuse 3# You're not that talented

The moment you think so, you ruin all success possibilities. It's not talent you should be looking for. It's individuality that you should be after. All of us has an uniqueness that differentiates us.

You are known for your own style of work. Explore your strengths and unique abilities. Maybe, you write with an extremely affectionate tone that no one does. Or you are very good in people management. Maybe you can make friends very quickly.

So, in all, you should try to find out your strengths and weaknesses. Don't use excuses which will only delay your success.

Here's What You Absolutely Can't Afford To Do As A Freelancer

Freelancing is different. It's not exactly full-fledged business (as in with leverage) but it's a business nonetheless. It's self-employment. It's your own thing.

As such, it's a world apart from a regular day job (no matter which level of day job you'd like to compare it with).

In effect, freelancing isn't even comparable with the job of a CEO of a multi-national corporation. For the CEO, it's still a job. He or she gets paid at the end of the month.

For freelancers, there's no security like that. There's no fall back-cushion. There's nothing but you to rely on. We see some freelancers succeed and many fail miserably. Here's what you absolutely can't afford to do as a freelancer:

Comparing. Then comparing some more

What are you comparing with? Why do you need to compare apples and oranges? Many freelancers are often tempted to compare themselves with those who hold full-time jobs. They are often jealous of the fact that people with day jobs have a better life and a paycheck that arrives on time.

Here's what freelancers get:

- Freedom and flexibility
- No politics. No bullying from the boss.

- If you do it well, paychecks can arrive all week, every week.

- At least a better opportunity to make more than an average person with a day job.

- An opportunity to say "no" to jobs, projects, or clients you don't want to work with.

You have a good life. Stop comparing.

Unjustifiable pricing

Pricing is certainly an art. The secret to pricing is this: you'll always find a buyer at any price point.

However, your pricing needs to be justifiable. It has to be value-based. It has to accurately reflect your skills, experience, results, and more.

Some freelancers mistakenly think that "low price" or "high price" is good. No, it isn't.

It takes a lifetime of work to figure out what you should be worth. Balance your pricing, take cues from the market, ask your clients, and do your research.

Get lazy

If you get lazy, you lose opportunities. Getting lazy just because you have enough clients on the table and sufficient cash rolling in is the worst thing you can do. You'll never have enough clients or the money, ever. Plus, what you have today won't be there tomorrow. Clients come and go. Cash flow goes positive to negative and back.

Some freelancers get lazier when there are actually no projects or no work to do. It should be during times like these when the hustler in you wakes up.

Lying around doing nothing, watching television, and taking off anywhere you want to (just because you can) is just plain stupid.

Not managing yourself

The biggest stumbling block to freelancing is you – it's not the state of the economy, the market, the clients, or the falling dollar. You are the biggest reason you don't succeed.

Obviously, you are human. You go through mood swings, ups, downs, and you'd often drift into a state of limbo. That's fine. But managing yourself is your biggest and most important responsibility.

What are you doing to hold yourself back?

Freelancing Isn't For The Faint Hearted: How To Handle Uncertainty

Rachel L. Swarns of The New York Times writes about how freelancers in the gig economy find a mix of freedom and uncertainty.

She writes a story about Josh Springer – a New York City-based freelancer – a member of The Freelance Union, and one of those many freelance workers hoping to find gigs to support their fledgling freelance businesses.

When asked about handling uncertainty, this is what Josh has to say:

> *"It's great, it's scary, it's worrisome, it's stressful, it's exciting. It's every extreme adjective I can think of. You really don't know what to expect. Every day, you're hit with something new."*

Freelancers have anything in their lives, except certainty. You have no way to expect anything for sure by the end of the month. You have no recourse. You always walk along dangerous edges. You are perennially at the end of a cliff.

Freelancing isn't for the faint-hearted. Here's how handling Uncertainty in freelancing is done:

Accept and embrace uncertainty

It's irony, but it is what it is.

Every freelancer, small business owner, and even large corporations have to handle uncertainty. Although it might not seem like regular employees and everyone else do not face anything remotely similar to uncertainty, they all do.

Uncertainty is a part of human life. No one knows a thing about the next minute.

Just embrace uncertainty instead of fighting it, getting frustrated, or getting stressed.

Work with the numbers

You could be a writer, designer, illustrator, developer, or whatever else it is that you freelance on.

Your skill isn't as important as your ability to "market yourself" and get paying clients for the skillset you have to offer.

For that, you'd need to sell, pitch, apply, bid, network, and be on the constant lookout for projects. You'd need to be more of a marketer than what you really are or what you are an expert at.

Assuming an average conversion of about 10% (you'd land one project out of every 10 applications, pitches, queries, or cold emails), you'd need to set time aside everyday to go neck deep into this hustle.

The more you pitch and sell, the more clients you have. The more clients you have, the less you have to put up with uncertainty.

Build alternate sources of income

If you are making good money now, find out ways to make that money work for you in the form of regular savings, dividend paying stocks, returns from other investments, real estate, etc.

While doing freelancing, start other businesses on the side and build them to the point that each of those businesses makes you money.

If you are a designer or developer, for instance, build website templates and sell them on online marketplaces like Envato.

If you are a writer, write a book, go the self-publishing route, or create eBooks and reports to sell them using GumRoad, Amazon, or elsewhere.

If you've been a service provider, dabble with selling products online.

No matter what your skill set is, you can always build another business that has nothing to do with your core skills.

Sell on value. Go on the retainer mode

First, stop charging by the hour and don't compromise on your price. Pitch your value. Read *Breaking the Time Barrier: How to Unlock Your True Earning Potential* by Mike McDerment and Donald Cowper of Freshbooks.

While you are out selling, get away from one-time, low-value projects and focus on retainers and long-term contracts. This way, you get paid for a long-time and more consistently.

How do you handle uncertainty? What do you as a freelancer do to get away from your worry mode and into the productivity mode?

Freelancing Blues: What Should You Do When You Are Down?

Feeling down the dumps? Lost your mojo? Is the act of getting yourself-motivated an uphill task everyday? Have you lost the fire, the intensity, and the energy to wake up every morning because of a few instances of unpaid invoices, bad clients, or because no projects are showing up at your door?

Welcome to freelancing 101. You are now a part of a huge, growing group of independent contractors and what you are feeling now (or might feel later) is as common as a cold.

It could be so unsettling to work so hard and not get paid for it due to a client's vanishing act. It could be heartbreaking to not be respected for what you do and when there are instances of project scope creep.

But unlike most people, you have amazing choices to combat with your freelancing blues. Since, throwing your laptop away or yelling at your dog are not options that help, here's what you do:

Accept and embrace

This is freelancing. It's a business. Ups and downs are common in business. Entrepreneurs are special because embrace and accept this as reality. They work their mindset around uncertainty and challenges. Because things are the way they are in freelancing, the only way you can you keep yourself sane is through pure hustle.

There's no point in questioning the nature of freelancing, your life as a freelancer, or why things are the way they are.

Fire away

One advantage you have over most people who have day jobs is that you can "fire" at all. Fire your clients if you think they don't treat you well, pay you on time, or if they don't treat you with respect.

Don't entertain freeloaders. Don't do free samples. Don't go over the board for a prospective client, especially if they have a bad reputation or if you don't know any better.

Do this only if you can bring in new clients.

It is what you make of it

Just as it stands for most things, your freelancing career is what you make of it. How well you do freelancing depends on your skill level, ability to communicate, the pace at which you land new clients (while retaining the old ones), and how much value you provide.

Above all that, your freelancing career also depends on the strength of your character, your inner resilience, positive attitude, and more.

It's only the beginning

Freelancing is all you need if you wanted a better alternative to full-time jobs. It also makes sense if you are happy with what you do in terms of freelancing and if this is enough for you meet your goals (long-term and short-term). If you want to get truly rich (if that's what you want) or build a business that can scale and grow, freelancing only introduces you to the big world of business.

There's more that you have to do (if you intend to) than this.

So, why stop now?

4 Freelancer Types Who'll Never Make It, Ever

If you're unable to grow your freelancing career, there can be many well-justified reasons behind that. Freelancers, solopreneurs, entrepreneurs fail because they lack clarity, courage, determination and consistency.

Scientists and experts from the medical world, who study human brain and mental health, can differentiate the personalities of professionally successful and unsuccessful people. They say, a few personality attributes significantly contribute to the failures of people.

Based on years of research and close observations, scientists say that few types of professionals will never be able to make it unless they consider changing their mindset. Here are the types of freelancers who will never make it because of their personality and behavioral attributes.

Freelancers who complain

If you're only complaining about not having adequate resources or lack of support, you're not doing any good to yourself. Studies show that people who complain the most are the most unhappy people. Scientists say that people who only talk about their problems are more likely to develop depression and anxiety.

Complaining too much actually lowers self-esteem. When you only complain, you lose focus and hurt your self-esteem. And people don't like to work with a person with low self-esteem.

Besides, when you only pay attention to your problems, you actually forget to find solutions. This makes you more vulnerable to challenges. And thus, it makes you more stressed.

Freelancers who make excuses

You will never be able to make it if you like to rely on excuses. According to one of Bill Gates's most popular quotes, one should try to make the work look good if they can't make it good. Freelancers who always find out excuses for why something can't be done, or why something shouldn't be done will never be able to succeed. These types of people are not problem solvers.

Don't let your mind focus too much on uncertainties. When you face a problem, take it as a challenge, not a threat. Therefore, it's very important that you change your mindset. Learn to love solving problems. Only then you will refrain from making excuses.

Freelancers who don't value time

Sir Richard Branson says that a person will never be successful if he/she doesn't identify the fact that time is more valuable than money itself. So true, isn't it? If you're not good with time management, you will fail.

Similarly, if you're not good at deciding how much time to give to which work, you will end up using your time unproductively. Freelancers who can't dedicate time effectively toward their work goals will not prosper, or at least will take much longer time to succeed. You will have to learn time management, prioritize work and allot time to the priorities effectively.

Freelancers who only think of money, not adding value

Freelancers who only think of earning money without considering adding value to their work will never be able to make it. You will never achieve financial freedom if you only think of how to make money and don't take the importance of skills and knowledge improvisation into consideration.

People like Bill Gates and Mark Zuckerberg followed their passion before they even thought about earning money from it. This is how they are different from the average.

Your chance of success will depend on how you make efforts for it. If you feel you're making the above-mentioned mistakes, think over it and change yourself.

4 Mistakes Freelancers Commit Before Starting Up

Mistakes are good for us – they teach, they make us wiser, and they guide us towards what's right.

Some mistakes, however, are better avoided.

Since freelancing isn't easy, and because freelancing is a leap of faith, there are chances that you will walk into the big world of freelancing after having committed a few mistakes. Now, most of these mistakes aren't anything like the point of no return, but knowing about them in advance makes it so much easier for you to take the right path to freelancing success.

Here are a few top mistakes freelancers commit before starting their freelancing business:

Not starting freelancing part-time

Freelancing is hard. You have to get used to an entirely new mindset, situations, and everyday instances, especially if you are coming from the corporate world. Since freelancing calls for something new, demands your time, and you need time to grow into this business, it only makes sense to start freelancing part-time.

When you start freelancing while you have your day job, you don't take much of a risk. That's when you have a great possibility to shine.

Not keeping sufficient emergency cash

You won't get paid every day when you do freelancing. You won't know where that next paycheck is or when the next payday comes.

Given the nature of freelancing, you will need a pile of cash (it has to be at least 6 months to one year worth of your monthly salary) to bank in times of emergency or when your business is low. It's just freelancing cash-management basics.

Asking others for advice

Freelancing is a solo journey. It's entrepreneurship and all entrepreneurs walk alone. Of course, you'll work with may people but this journey is yours. The responsibility of the outcome of this journey is yours. The results of the journey also are yours.

So, asking people if "Freelancing is good or bad?" makes no sense unless you are actually on an online (or offline) community of freelancing professionals.

Stop asking. Just do it.

Taking it easy

So, you started part-time and you have the cushion your day job provides. You also have the emergency cash balance. Given that, can you see why most rookie freelancers don't succeed? The only trouble with this careful approach is that you'd tend to have a weak, no worry start.

It's good, and it's bad.

It's good because it's safe.

It's bad because you are not under pressure to perform. Eventually, without an increase in pressure, you may not perform.

What mistakes have you made?

How To Guard Your Time Against Common Time Killing Habits

All time killing habits can be managed. However, the most important thing is that you're aware of the influential factors. Do you know a wrong work attitude can become a serious time waster?

Start a day with a happy body and mind

Your mental and emotional condition can have a huge impact on your daily productivity level. According to mental health practitioners, overthinking as a habit is not good for your overall productivity levels. If you're in a creative field, like programming or writing, overthinking can actually kill your time and destroy your will power. You must get over this habit to increase your efficiency.

Set some deadlines for yourself and make yourself accountable for them. Don't hold yourself responsible for anything beyond your objectives. This is one way to increase happiness, and thus, the level of productivity.

Work as long as you can stay focused

It's a irreplaceable requirement. Most freelancers work from home. But, at home, if someone doesn't have a supporting environment, that can be a disaster. One of the common time killing habits found in freelancers is not being able to focus on work because of several reasons.

One way to stop this habit is training your mind to shift focus on possible opportunities and stay focused. Don't stick to any rule for time management. You can finish all assigned work for the day quickly if you can work with the highest level of concentration. Work when you feel you can concentrate.

However, from health and well-being perspective, it's recommended that you develop a habit of starting work early in the morning. After the long rest of night, the human brain works with the highest level of efficiency.

Prioritize work to meet targets

You must prioritize your work in order to set deadlines for each day. One time killing habit seen in most freelancers is not being able to prioritize personal and career goals. The biggest benefit of being able to work from home can turn into the biggest obstacle for growth if you don't know how to manage your priorities.

If you really want to work a lot within a smaller time frame, learn to prioritize and complete the most unpleasant tasks first. A study conducted on 500 almost participants found that people love to put the most difficult task aside until the last moment.

It's a serious work attitude mistake that you should try to avoid to improve your productivity. By completing the most unpleasant task first, you can concentrate on the rest of the task better and save time.

Don't limit yourself to fixed working hours

Who said that you'll have to start and finish work exactly at the same time daily? You'll be losing the biggest advantage of being in freelancing if you do that. Discipline is good. But, everyone's mind is different. Some people can't work for long stretches.

Divide your work in small length of times. Understand which tasks will take how much time. If you think a task can take around 1.5 hours, start the work and try to finish it within the deadline. After you complete the task, if you're not feeling like starting a new work immediately, don't do that. You can start the new task when you feel you can concentrate and finish without losing your focus in between.

Inhibit the Distractions

Working at home can be challenging if you don't know how to overcome the distractions. You'll have to be strong to be able to restrict all elements which can ruin your workflow.

You will have to figure out what's causing you to waste time. Is it lack of attention? Or, are you not able to safeguard yourself from human influence? Do you have to work in an environment that is too chaotic? Plan how to safeguard your time from unnecessary distractions based on your situation.

How To Handle Scope Creep In Freelancing

Every now and then, you'll work with clients who'll expect you to deliver more in terms of work than what you've agreed to in the first place. Freelancing Scope Creep is a huge drain on your resources, demands more from you without rewarding you in any way whatsoever, and is also a cause for strain, stress, and potentially debilitating relationship with clients.

As a freelancer, you'd do better without any scope creep at all. However, you won't know when it hits you. So, before it happens (and when it does), here's how you can manage scope creep in freelancing while working with your projects and clients:

Work with expectations and set your milestones clearly

The sheer excitement of a new project, the rush to start work, and the potential payoffs with a project are understandably evident. In fact, many freelancers dive deep into projects without setting up client expectations first and setting up milestones for projects.

Doing your due diligence is your responsibility. After you are briefed, handhold your client and run them through the expected work. Setup milestones immediately after so that both you and the client always know what's expected.

Always start with a contract

No matter how careful you are with step 1 above, you'll do well to start every project with a contract. Send out your quotes and proposals.

Once your client accepts the quote or the proposal, send out a legal contract along with other legalese such as NDA, service policies, and other documents and get them signed by your client.

A contract could save your life.

Stay calm and be assertive

Scope creep usually happens while working on the project well into the life of the project. Although you take steps and keep communication clear, you'll likely step into the big jungle of scope creep. When this happens, don't lose your cool. Instead, have a chat with your clients pointing them to a scope creep possibility.

Be firm, but polite. However, put your foot down and explain why the extra work the client requested cannot be managed with the existing budget.

Use scope creep to your advantage

If your client insists that the extra bit of work has to be done, try to use this to your advantage. Instead of risking a "no", accept extra work for extra cost.

You could say things like:

"Sure, I'll work on the SEO for every blog post for an extra $15 per post."
"I'd love to do it. I'll send out an invoice to accommodate this."

Send out a miscellaneous invoice to reflect the charges for the extra work your client demands of you.

Be willing to fire clients

Sometimes, despite everything you do, your client could very well insist that you accept the scope creep. You have two choices: go ahead and do it anyway in the interest of long-term work or fire the client.

Don't choose the first option because you'd be training the client to allow scope creep. If you can, choose the second option and fire the client.

How do you manage scope creep in your freelancing projects?

How To Manage Scope Creep

During your project management or freelancing career, you may experience the monster of "scope creep" at some point in time. Managing scope creep could be a challenging situation, since it affects deadlines, budget, and milestones. Some projects may extend beyond their scope, which may affect their budget, schedule, and even chances of success.

Every project has a set of deliverables, with fixed budget and agreed-upon tasks that must be completed before the project closure. The schedule and budget of a project may change with even the slightest amount of variation in its scope. This may happen once or several times during the life-cycle of a project.

What is scope creep?

Scope creep is any change, addition, or update in the whole or a part of the project when it is under way. It may occur when a client or customer that had requested the project changes their mind and wants something done in a different way. They may request a different outcome as opposed to what they had requested earlier. This may happen once or multiple times during the project.

A change in a client's business may also influence the scope of the project. A new stakeholder may be pulled into the project when you are almost 90% done with it. The development could have significant changes on the way you manage the same, affecting your morale, draining a project budget, or spinning your project out of control.

Even before a project begins, it is important to have clarity around the goals and objectives. What are the deliverables? How important is each stage of the project for the client?

Don't underestimate the complexity of a project when you begin working on it. It is important to take measures to ensure that the project goes as expected. Break the deliverables into short milestones. Of course, you do not want to face any problems, such as budget shortage or deadline delay.

Fortunately, you can follow a number of strategies to prevent scope creep from affecting your project submissions. Identify key milestones, divide tasks into priority, urgency, and importance, and put each of them on the timeline. It will help to keep reviewing milestones when the client requests any scope changes. The set deadlines will help keep the project on track.

When you meet a potential client in Peer Hustle or in any other on-demand marketplace, make it a point to review, plan, and prepare your plan of action and get it approved by the client, so you do not have any major hiccups during the project's lifecycle.

Horror story

I have witnessed scope struggles during the beginning of my freelancing career. Since I was the only one working on the project, besides the web developer at the client's end, I had to handle the work burden on my own. The project was a breeze in the beginning and I was able to complete it successfully. The happy client extended the project and didn't have any specific guidelines for me in the initial stages of the second project. But the client hired a new web developer, who demanded all sorts of changes at my end, making work really difficult for me.

Since I had happily worked with the client earlier, I prepared myself for the challenges, which sometimes were like a nightmare as I had to make changes to the project when I was already toward completion.

But I braced the challenges at every twist and turn and completed the job to the client's satisfaction despite the scope creep horror. Gladly I took it on a positive note and as a lesson to be always prepared for such challenges.

Scope control starts with the beginning of the project

Preparedness is indispensable to the success of a project. Controlling the scope of a project must begin even before the project starts. It will help to have a corresponding project plan or agreement before beginning the project. Documenting your efforts will have a positive impact on the outcome of the project.

Here are a few guidelines to help you set yourself up to control the scope of the project:

Project vision

Do you understand the vision of the project? Make sure you thoroughly understand the vision before you agree to go ahead with it. It is important to explain how you plan to approach the project to the project drivers. Delivering an overview of the project to those that can influence changes would help you be prepared for scope creep.

Priorities

What are your project priorities? Are your priorities the same as that of the project drivers? Make an ordered list of all critical items, including deadline, budget, employee satisfaction, feature delivery, for timely reviews throughout the project's lifecycle. Upon the commencement of the project, use the list to justify your scheduling decisions.

Deliverables

Set deliverables, that is, how you plan to go about the completion of the project. Get them approved by the project drivers. Break the approved deliverables into detailed work requirements, depending on the length of the project. A larger project would require more details. Break down the project into smaller deliverables and get everything in writing. This will ensure that everything is accounted for. Set a predetermined rate for additional tasks and be ready to do justice with them. You want each project to sail smoothly. You can discourage the client to avoid the higher price by sticking to the initial project guidelines. Make sure the client reviews your plan and understands your actions.

Critical path

When the schedule is ready, you may want to use a project evaluation and review technique (PERT) to determine your critical path, which may change over the course of your project. Proper evaluation of the critical path is a must before beginning the project.

Process for changing scope

Expect that you will face scope creep. Do not hesitate to implement change order forms early. It is important to educate project drivers early in the project, so you can easily assess cost and benefit before scheduling any requested scope changes. Define how you plan to manage the scope changes and who will handle them. You may want to set a price for accepting and implementing the requested changes. Or you may also want to let the client know that you are okay to accept the changes, but do not hesitate to inform them that you will need to spend extra time for the requested changes, which may affect submission or deadline of other projects. Your client may accept your terms or reject them. Satisfy your driver constraint and set off on a successful project.

Know when to say no:

Of course, sometimes there may be unreasonable requests. You cannot give the green light to every demand that comes all of a sudden from the client's side. You do not want to hold up other work in order to make the required changes to critical path elements. Such changes must be scrutinized carefully and made sparingly. This may discourage some future unreasonable requests.

Accept requests:

You cannot reject a client's request, especially if you have been instructed to do so. The best strategy is to accept the decision and move forward with the request. Constant negative reminders until the completion of the project will only reflect bad attitude. Review the request closely and then document the change. The document should spell out the exact requested change and its anticipated implications. Get all stakeholders to sign on it.

The initial steps of a well-thought-out project management process will help carve out a successful path. You have put in a lot of effort to design a plan and do not want all of it to go down the drain. Sure, the client may be keen to get the changes implemented mid-way, and it may help to argue the case for more time or cost in the event of a scope creep. In most cases, it helps to stick to the plan and base it as the road map to project completion.

Not something to be feared

Any change or new request in an ongoing project can invite stress. But if you are really caught up in such situation and have no other way out, it will help to use your due diligence and understand the scope. Remember, nobody wants their project derailed. But it certainly can get frustrating if a client suddenly wants to part ways with what they had requested earlier, requesting an altogether different change in the project.

However, scope creep is part of successful project management. It isn't something to be feared; rather, you will be in a better position to remove it altogether from the equation. In every project, there are trade-offs and compromises.

Once you have the control of the project in your hand, you would be in a better position to take it toward completion. When you cannot prevent the scope creep, you can manage it through proper planning and action plan. Informed planning and needs assessment will help prevent major hiccups over the course of the project.

Do not hesitate to calculate the additional hours of work when invoicing the client at the time of project completion. Your scope creep will become their cost creep. Are you ready?

How To Manage Freelance Pricing Blues

If knowing what to do is one thing, knowing how much to charge for what you do is something else, and not everyone gets it right.

Pricing your freelancing services is almost an art, and you'd have to go through multiple experiments with yourself, your work, and your clients.

Mastering the fine art of pricing, however, allows you to be well on your way to freelancing mastery. It allows you to earn more, and maybe even get away from the clutches of daily work lead yourself towards financial freedom.

Here are a few tips on how to manage the blues that come with freelance pricing:

Don't start with low pricing

Contrary to popular advice, which goes something like:

> *"Start with a low price, build your portfolio, and then slowly raise your prices…"*
> *"Always start low, because you have nothing much to show in terms of portfolio…"*

Stop, right there. If you don't have a portfolio, build one. If you never had a client or if you are just getting started, create a speculative portfolio with self-initialized work.

Whatever you do, don't start with "low" prices. Instead, start with prices that are justified for you. Look at your competition, take the average price, and mark your price at least at an average of the price your competition (fellow freelancers) charge.

Get away from hourly jobs

Hourly jobs are usually the norm. They are also convenient and give both the clients and freelancers a well-channeled and well-delegated work to achieve. Hourly jobs make no difference for a client (especially if they are looking for long-term, well-planned work). For a freelancer, however, hourly jobs are bad on several counts:

- Hourly projects punish freelancers for efficiency. If you can finish a job in 20 minutes, what do you do for another 40 minutes?
- There are only so many hourly projects you can pick in a day since you have limited time in a day.

Your prices are non-negotiable

Almost every other day that you spend hustling, pitching and working to get clients, you'll be expected to lower your prices. You'll hear something along thes lines:

- Other freelancers are charging so less. Why are you so expensive?
- Can you give us a discount?
- We'll give you work in bulk, can you give us a better rate?

Assuming you are good at what you do, and if you didn't know this earlier, we'll say it now: your prices are non-negotiable.

Take it or leave it

You decide your terms and conditions, work quality, and portfolio. Your general feeling about the client, clients' business, and the work itself, holds true for you and you don't need justification for that.

You determine your pricing too. Increase prices as much as you need to, as long as you can justify the price with the value you provide.

When you are freelancing, you are in business. The reason why you wanted to be on your own and freelance is because you wanted to be your own boss.

In your freelancing business, you call the shots. No one dictates terms for you.

Productive Freelancing: How To Ensure You Control Your Time

Time is money, and it's all right if it's clichéd or if you have heard that a million times.

Time is still money and hourly projects are a good testament to that. Productivity is important not because it's a measure of how effectively you use time to your benefit but also because productivity determines how much you get paid.

The more work you pack into an hour and the better you do it, the more you make. So here's how to do productive freelancing and how to make sure you can control your time:

Let those goals flash

You won't put in the commitment and dedication needed to get more productive if you don't know why you'd have to do it in the first place. Have goals? Make sure they flash, all day long, from where you sit.

Was it a home at an exotic location that you wanted? Was it to get out of debt? Did you want to travel the world?

Make sure you put up this on your desktop background or office walls (if allowed).

Wakeup early

Early risers are often more productive. There's just something about early mornings, in the eerie silence as the rest of the world sleeps, that makes that block of time extremely productive. Some freelancers we know reserve that precious time for the most important tasks of the day such as pitching, applying for new projects, or getting some brain-intensive work done such as writing, designing or coding.

Take breaks while you work

It might seem counterintuitive but taking breaks makes you more productive. It helps you get a breather, re-energizes you to get back to work again, and just gives you time to decompress. Sitting is the new smoking, in case you didn't know. Follow the Pomodoro Technique and take breaks of 5-10 minutes every hour or so. Now, for that one hour you put in, you pack a punch.

Pull away from Internet and phones

The fact that you are connected to the Internet while you work and that your smartphone is in your pocket makes you vulnerable for distraction. Once you drift and surf on those links, there's no coming back. Apart from research, and finding information related to the task at hand, do not use the Internet. Don't go reading blog posts or magazines. Also, avoid picking calls, chatting, and playing with the apps on your phone.

If you struggle with impulse control, don't worry. There's still hope for you. You can find numerous applications online, or in your app store, that will help you block distractions for set amounts of time. You'll find that when you cannot be distracted, your productivity skyrockets.

Don't let anyone barge in

You are lucky if you work alone. If you work with teams or if you sit at a co-working space or a shared office, chances are that your time will be prey to people who want your time for anything from opening doors (no access cards? to asking for help or opinions.

If success is more about saying "no" more than saying "yes", here's your chance to say no, now.

This also holds true for friends, visiting acquaintances, and family members as well. No one holds your time as precious as you do.

It's all in your hands.

3 Instances Of
Bad Freelancing Advice And What
You Should Do Instead

Look up the web and you'll find a sea of advice on freelancing across all genres and not all of that advice is good.

Thanks to the ease of putting up information and consuming it, it's easy for almost anyone to write up anything they like.

If thousands of freelancers do something, that doesn't necessarily mean it's a good thing to do.

A lot of freelancing advice you see on the web is all right. Some of that advice is terrible. Your job is to take stock of your own situation and carefully wade through that advice taking each snippet of advice with a pinch of salt.

We did some of the wading through the muck for you. Here are at least 3 instances of bad freelancing advice and what you should be doing instead:

Freelancing isn't stable or reliable

From the time you decide to do freelancing and through the time you actually do it, you will hear this from your family friends, acquaintances, and even fellow freelancers. There is a hint of truth in the "unreliable" and "unstable" parts.

However, you can make freelancing as stable as you like and make it a reliable source of income.

All you need to do is to hustle enough to make sure this happens. Build a pipeline of clients; keep those conversations going with potential clients, and work on developing a system to get projects regularly. Read more on how to handle uncertainty.

When a set number of projects flow in, thanks to your regular marketing, freelancing cannot be unreliable or unstable.

Freelancing is a business

Yes, freelancing is a business – a one-person, mostly service led, zero-inventory business. However, it could also feel like a fancy job if you just kept at it without doing anything else.

While it's up to you as to what you want to do really, freelancing is mostly a one-person business. If you want to call it "business", freelancing doesn't technically fit the bill because:

- You are the technician, offering services for cash.

- Scaling up this "business" is hard.

- You are trading your time and skills for cash. So, you only have a few productive hours a day.

Real businesses can scale up. They have built-in leverage. While freelancing is a business, it's not the "real" business.

You should note that.

It's too late to do freelancing

It's never too late to start freelancing. It's true that there are thousands of freelancers all over the world and there's stiff competition. But the cake is too big and you are sure to make a tidy living off the slice of the pie you seize.

New businesses sprout up everyday, clients move from one freelancer to another, and some freelancers go out of business. Also, a majority of freelancers aren't as good as you are. So, in a lot of ways you have an edge over your competition.

What are some of those pieces of bad advice you got? Or the "good advice" that you realized was bad for you? Tell us about them.

4 Mistakes You Should Never Do As A Freelancer

Freelancing is the single best non-capital intensive, location-independent, global business opportunity you may ever get your hands on. It's the best answer to be on your own and never have to sell your soul, mortgage your home, or go neck-deep in debt.

It's also disaster-prone.

If you don't get your marbles in the bag right from the start, you'll be spending a lot of time wading through the muck your mistakes will leave you in.

While making mistakes in freelancing isn't expensive money-wise, they can damage the energy, gusto, and the enthusiasm you started with (plus, a lot of time and a little money here and there).

Here are some freelancing mistakes you should avoid:

Not marketing yourself enough

Freelancing is less about your skills and more about marketing. Apple wouldn't have been what it is today especially in the thick of the dust clouds that its competition kicks up without brilliant marketing. That applies to Starbucks, Airbnb, and many others.

Freelancing unshackles you from the misery of a day job but it still pushes you to do something you've never done before: sell.

Marketing for a freelancer isn't about ramping up pitches, cold emails, cold calls, networking, bidding, and applying when the projects aren't there. It's about doing it all the time, no matter what.

Selling yourself short

"Thanks for your proposal. Please do this free trial for us to complete this application."

"You are too expensive for us. No one we are interviewing currently is charging the rates you do."

"Work with us for a week, for free, and we'll then consider your application."

Run for cover if you see (or hear) any of the above. Go hungry and wing it without projects if you have to but don't ever sell yourself short.

Consider this: if you were a writer, you'd have to work hard and produce "excellent", "impeccably-written", "original", "magazine-style" content anyway. You'd have to do that whether you are being paid $5 per article or $50.

You are better off doing the $50 post for that effort, right?

Learn to "fire" customers

Too many freelancers get "stuck" with deadbeat clients, low wages, and other obvious come-ons such as "scope creep", disrespect, and more. The reason why you chose freelancing is because you could be on your own, choose clients worth working for, call your shots, and be a boss.

Freelancing isn't slavery. Don't ever take any sign of disrespect from clients.

Strike one or strike three, learn to fire your clients at will. There's always another one around the corner.

Contracts, NDAs, and the Legal Stuff: Do it

Freelancing contracts are saviors. While providing you legal protection for not getting paid on time or not getting paid at all, they are also ways for you to protect your own craft—be it legal documents, NDAs, receipts, invoices, or credit notes.

Keep everything organized and handy. You never know when things will turn nasty. When you find yourself facing clients gone underground or when legal nastiness shows up, it's these boring documents and signatures that'll save your skin.

What mistakes are you making in your freelancing career? Share them with us.

4 Specific Instances
When You Should Say No

They say that success is more about you saying "no" than it's about saying yes. The saying "no" habit can bring efficiency, focus, and liberate you from pseudo-opportunities—the ones you thought were opportunities but really aren't.

When you are doing freelancing, you'll come across many instances where you may have to say no to. You'd be faced with tough decisions. Your decisions will make all the difference between your success and failure.

Here are a few specific instances when you'd have to say no:

Free work

Unless you want to do work contributing to charity, you should never have to do any work for free. Doing work for your portfolio is one thing; doing work for clients is totally something else. You'll often have clients asking for free trials, free work samples, and free whatever.

No matter what you feel about this, refuse to work for free. Period.

Giving more when you don't need to

One of the keys to success is to give more than what's expected of you. When you do that, you are on a path to provide value. You are creating value for your clients and in turn, you are increasing the worth of what you provide.

The key to this path, however, is this: you provide value when you want to. You do more than what's asked of you when you want to do so. Not when your clients ask.

Giving your time away

Today, distractions come in all shapes and sizes. There are also many different kinds of distractions that threaten to waste your time. This is one of those things you'd need to learn to be ruthless and say no to.

Did you know what the biggest vulnerability is with time management? It's you. People will try to take your time away. The Internet itself is a major distraction.

Your tendency may be to let go of your own time. You may slip. Others may force you to slip. Time is vulnerable. Begin to say no to anything related to your time that's not in your favor.

The wrong people to work with

You'll eventually begin to hire freelancers, full-timers, or vendors until you get a good team in place. But the hiring and onboarding process is an incredibly draining and time sapping process. Just finding someone worthwhile to work with is excruciating.

Every time you come across someone who isn't a good fit for your team, learn to say no. Refuse to accept team members without the hunger, passion, and the drive to work.

While your search will never end, you at least need learn to manage your time wisely.

4 Things Freelancers Should Do To Avoid Late Payments

According to recent market studies, the trend of late payment from clients seems to have increased significantly. Many authorized sources, like The Wall Street Journal, have confirmed that small businesses are going out of cash especially because the big clients are delaying their payments extensively.

According to the Wall Street Journal story, a small web development business owner had to postpone his business expansion and hiring plan because of cash crunch. One of his clients, which is a big online retailer, cleared his invoice of $6,600 after 404 days from the date of the invoice.

So, if you're a freelancer who looks forward to establishing an uninterrupted and smooth payment cycle with your client, you will have to make sure you're taking the invoicing system very seriously. Here's some mojo on how to avoid late payments:

Understand the late paying clients

Freelancers Union suggests the first thing a freelancer should do is understand the different types of late paying clients to better handle the situation. According to Freelancers Union, you'll find primarily 4 types late paying clients.

The first is the well-intentioned nonpaying clients who will always find plenty of reasonable explanations for being unable to pay on time. You will have to maintain 100 per cent clear and transparent communication to be able to handle this type of situation. Tell the client to make payments in small installments rather than paying all at once.

Then there will be unhappy nonpayers. In this case, the client would like to withhold or reduce the agreed payment as he is not happy with your work. You will have to figure out a mutually agreed term to fix the situation.

If the client is a serial nonpayer, it's better you simply don't work with them. These types of clients would like to keep their freelancers waiting for the payment with no justifiable reason.

There will be big corporation non payers who can keep you waiting for the payment for months. These types of clients usually have 90 to 120 days payment cycle. In this case, you should talk and plan a simple and short payment cycle before you start working with them.

Try FreshBook tips on how to handle late payments

FreshBook is an online billing service. According to the CMO of the company, freelancers should be very punctual about their invoicing system. They should prioritize and organize the invoicing system to delay the payments. Be polite to the clients and request the payments.

Establish an electronic payment system to fast track the system. Take your and your client's time seriously and try to be specific about the payment timeline.

Help client remember your invoicing cycle

According to ABFA Asset Based Finance Association, small businesses in the UK are suffering the most when it comes to late payments from clients.

Their study shows that businesses with less than 1 million annual turnover in the UK waits for average 72 days to get their payments from their clients.

So, you should not take the matter lightly. You should always send the client reminders to take a look at the invoice and clear the payment. Send clients automated reminder emails.

Develop a reward and penalty system

Design a reward system to encourage the client pay on time. Maybe, you can offer a bit of extra service for on time payment. On other hand, you can also build a strict payment policy. Like, you can retain the right to withhold the copyright of the work until the clients clear all the due payment.

So, this is how you ensure quick payments from your clients. Would you like to share what you think has worked the best for you?

5 Head Smacking Freelancing Realities You Ought To Know

For way too long now, thousands (if not millions) have been dreaming of making money online. You are especially susceptible to this since the online space is now full of scammers, fake "gurus", and all sorts of people claiming to be experts.

There are opportunities out there, it's just that you are never told the whole story. You are made to believe that "you can make millions" but no one tells what you'd have to go through or how many times you have to sell your soul over to get there.

Freelancing has always been a great opportunity to earn money part-time or full-time. But it helps if you know the full story.

You have to sell

Most people have a condescending view of sales. They think sales are only for those slick-haired, oil-selling charlatans who do nothing but keep knocking on doors and making pitches all day.

Here's the news: everyone is in sales. Yourself included. You just don't know it but you do it everyday — with spouses, kids, clients, partners, managers, fellow workers, strangers, merchants, and even dogs.

If you read the book *To Sell Is Human* by Dan H Pink, you'll realize that you are in the business of moving people.

You need to have skills

Next time you see a meet up on freelancing or if you intend to take up a course on freelancing, remember that you got to have those skills (whatever niche you want to work in). If you want to do freelance writing, you have to have the chops to write blog posts or articles.

No one is going to teach you how to write (because it's presumed that you already know). The same is true for design, developers, artists, caricaturists, and everyone else.

It's not easy

Let's be upfront here. If it were easy, my granny would be doing it some grannies do freelance, and that's not the point. When it comes to free-lancing, it's not just about the skills. It's also a lot to do with entrepre-neurial hustle.

It'll demand that you think, feel, work, and manage like a true busi-ness owner does. This is self-employment. It's ridiculously hard. Which leads us to:

You're going to sacrifice

If you had a day job, you'd have a 5-6 day work week, with at least one day off. You'd then have vacations, holidays, and what have you. Plus, you can afford to take leave of absence. Forget all that when you get into the world of freelancing. You'll probably work 12-16 hours a day, all week.

You have nothing, except truckloads of work. Work every single day, and work forever. As for getting out of this self-initiated rut, that's for later on.

You have to chase

As a freelancer, you have to chase your opportunities because they won't come to you. You have to chase your invoices since some clients don't pay and some others come straight from hell. You have to chase your partners, vendors, and pretty much everyone else if you are a free-lance project manager or if you run an agency.

Chasing is your everyday job. Period.

Client Relationships

How To Grow Indispensable For Your Clients

Clients come and go. You have this difficulty as a freelancer and it's not fun at all. As if the uncertainty wasn't enough, you also have to deal with scope creep, unpaid invoices, the hustle, and in some cases complete disrespect.

But it doesn't have to be that way. While there are several factors that will affect the degree of importance you have with your clients, you can grow your perceived value in the eyes of your client.

Here's how you grow indispensable for your clients:

Keep that relationship up

It's not just a client you are dealing with as a freelancer; it's real people. In the rush to meet deadlines, get paid, and then get more clients, we forget this. In fact, some freelancers only talk business. In the interest of efficiency, that's pardonable. However, people don't work this way. We aren't machines.

Your clients have problems just like you do. They'd often share their problems, mention family, or explain their life in the passing.

Acknowledge that. Talk about it. At least, lend your ears.

Deliver more. Promise less

When you have clients finalizing deals, we get eager. We get excited that a project is likely to take off and there's a possibility that you'll crack the deal. In this rush and excitement, it's natural that we overdo things, like promises.

"I'll do this in a day."

"Oh, that's easy."

"I could do more than just that, you know?"

We know you can do that and more. Just don't say it. Only do it. In fact, do more than what you promised. Over deliver all you want.

Work hard. Really hard

There's no substitute for hard work and we all know that. It's understandable that all this freelancing can take its toll on you. Yet, there's no looking back. There's no way you are going to under-deliver. There are no excuses for poor work and missed deadlines.

If you go wrong, admit it. If you don't know something, say it out aloud.

Only consistent and hard work can differentiate you from thousands of other freelancers who can take your place.

Consult, without expectations

So, there's a lot of talk that happens to and fro. Your clients will have questions that need answering. They'll have doubts, fears, and they need solutions. Often, you'll be asked. Take that opportunity and consult with your clients. Tell them what's right. Show them solutions. Solve their problems.

When you do this, you are already 99 percentile better than your competition.

Be a partner

You aren't just a vendor or a freelancer. You aren't "remote help". You are a partner (without any actual stake) in your clients' business. You are there to solve problems, to do magic, and to make your clients' lives – and/or businesses – better.

Talk like a partner. Behave like a partner. Speak up. Put your foot on the ground when you need to. Feel free to give out your two cents when needed.

How To Make Your Clients See Value In Your Work (Without Doing Much)

We all say that we want to help our clients achieve a goal or solve a problem. But, how do you ensure that client will love your work, or see value in your work? Albert Einstein once said, to be better at what you do, you will have to know the rules of the game, and then work harder than anyone else.

Therefore, to help client see value in your work, you'll have to work over and above the typical work delivery criteria. You'll have to work harder to add value to your work and help client by making a serious contribution. Here are few things that you can do to make your work incredibly meaningful:

Think from client's point of view

How do you make clients see value in your work? For that, you must think from the client's point of view. What would you have wanted if you had to hire someone to get a job done? The client is a person in need. You will have to help him/her out with your expertise and talent.

If we take the client's job with an open mind going beyond the thought that we are working to get a handsome amount of money, we will be able to deliver amazing work that the client will love. Your personal dedication toward the work and effortless contributions will make the client see value in your work.

Think out of the box and be creative

To be able to offer a work which can really help the client beyond his or her expectation, you will have to work a bit differently. Whatever the work is, you should always try to make it better with more creativity, analysis and a unique approach.

Talk to your clients clearly to understand what they expect. You can never deliver a valuable work without understanding client's real expectations and the scope of the project. You must try to think out of the box so that unique ideas and solutions can be added to the project. Also, take a creative approach to help client see value in your work.

Provide a bit more work than stipulated

Clients need help. If you want to work differently and make the clients happy, you will have to work more than what clients expect.

That's not to say that you have to sacrifice your personal hours to give some extra work to your client, but, you should learn to manage your time to offer the client an amazing work. Help your client with some great work that they may not have expected. Don't only do what you've been told to do. You have to add value to your work by offering extended help to the client.

Love your work to make a valuable contribution

Needless to say that you will be able to do a better job if you love your work. You will feel the drive to work harder and think of various possibilities to make the job excellent. Your work will look amazing to your client when you will help clients with various solutions they may never have thought about before.

To help clients see value in your work, you must try to take the job personally. You must perceive it as if it's your job and how you can get it done successfully.

How To Build Credibility As A Freelancer, The "Giver" Way

One of the most popular, untold secrets of the very successful has been this: they are all givers.

Takers, as opposed to givers, don't succeed in the long run. Never before has this little secret been exposed with so much potential. Multiple paths and ways now exist for "giving" – at least in terms of knowledge, wisdom, and insights. In case you were wondering, giving is also alive and well on the mentor front with crowdsourcing communities such as KickStarter.

Why are we talking about highbrow philosophical stuff like giving while we should be focusing on freelancing?

Success demands giving and as a freelancer, it's the best way for you to grow your credibility. More credibility leads to more business. Period.

How do you build credibility then? What exactly are you supposed to do?

Embrace giving

You might wonder – even before getting into the act – as to how "giving" helps. When you give, you get into the motions of dispensing knowledge. You become the source of knowledge, inspiration, motivation, and advice. You get into the beautifully selfserving act of helping others solve problems.

People will look up to you (including your clients).

You drive, instead of being driven.

You lead, instead of others leading you.

You set the course; others tread the path you create.

Spread your wings

Once you determine your customer persona – that is, you find out exactly who your customer is – that's just step one. You have to figure out exactly where they are, what they do, the demographics, the geographic locations, and even get down to details such as their interests, what keeps them up at night, and more.

Online, this translates to forums, communities, and social zones where conversations take place around the services you provide as a freelancer.

Get communal

Now that you've found your communities and you know that they are all probably looking for your services, you might be tempted to jump right in and pitch your services.

Not yet. In fact, you don't ever hustle directly when you are either on social media or when you are participating in social conversations.

While you are here, it's time to get communal. Talk, respond to questions, quell doubts, motivate, inspire, and give out your two cents.

Be generous

Apart from your communal participation, a growing presence on social media, and all the conversations you are a part of, you also have clients initiating business deals. In comes a client, and out goes a pitch or a proposal. Or so business practices would make you believe.

That's a shortsighted practice that gets you money today but puts you back on the street for more.

Instead, offer things of value to your clients. If they asked for a blog post, work on Meta information too. If they asked for a logo, provide extra source files for offline uses such as signboards and print advertising.

You get the drift?

Do you practice going at freelancing the giver way? Are you generous? Do you go out of the way for clients? Share your experiences with us.

Power Of Community. Build One For Your Freelancing Business

As freelancers or business owners, we are always looking to "market", "pitch", and "advertise". That's how it's been for a long time, and we are afraid it's going to be like that for a while.

But there have been many smart businesses in the recent years that are worth millions of dollars not because they advertised, but because they are a community around their products and services.

Here's why you should leverage the power of community for your freelancing business:

Embrace the power of communities

What's common between the following companies? CopyBlogger, Kiss-Metrics, Unbounce.com, LeadPages, The New RainMaker, and Studio Press?

Answer: they all focused on building communities.

By building a community, the focus is automatically on "delivering the goods". The emphasis is on providing value, and there's barely a pitch or a marketing message anywhere.

Let others do the heavy lifting

In a community, the interactions are all between complete strangers (who'd later get to know each other). With minimal interference or moderation from you, users or members of your community will help each other and keep the conversation going. They generate content all on their own.

Plus, they point to, help others with, or even evangelize your products or services as if they work for you (but they don't).

Gain from an immersive branding experience

Pick any forum or community that a business manages and it'll be easy to see how many people keep talking, discussing, and even sharing tips and ideas on how to use your products and services better.

If you were a real estate attorney, for instance, all those members of your community could be your potential clients and you could be giving away free tips and knowledge to solve their problems.

You might keep your service offer open, and you'll be contacted soon enough.

Get feedback in real-time

In a moderated community (or not), you may often have many people discussing your services or products. In due course, you'll also hear plenty of user-generated, unsolicited, and unbiased feedback.

That's pure gold. If you had your ear to the ground and were truly listening, you can improve your products and services just the way your community wants it.

That's real feedback – the kind you can't buy.

Line up your buyers

Once you build your community, your followers, audience, or members always look forward to what you do next. Your new services or product release could be lapped up pre-release. Launching something new? Prepare for your servers to be crashed.

The larger and more passionate the community is, the bigger impact it has on your marketing (without you actually doing anything directly related to marketing).

Are you focusing on building your community as a freelancer?

Managing Clients: How To Pick And Choose The Dream Clients To Work With

Clients make you money. You might as well say, you have a tacit understanding with yourself that you will do everything you can to serve your clients well, deliver promptly, give your work the best chance to shine through, and maybe even go out of your way to serve them.

Apart from the act of "getting clients", the only thing that determines how sustainable your freelancing business is how you manage your clients. The better your relationship is with them, better off you'll be.

Not everyone you work with will turn out to be a dream client though. In fact, before you know it, you'll soon end up with a few clients from hell under your belt.

While you can't completely avoid such clients, you can do a lot to minimize the presence of such clients. Here are a few tips on managing clients:

Screen clients as they screen you

You see a brief, you send out a pitch, and you wait for a response. It's a delight to see replies to your proposals. However, don't get too carried away. You know you are in the limelight when clients consider your proposal or ask you for a quote. Similarly, you should use the initial emails, calls, or meetings to screen clients too.

Most freelancers freeze at the thought of "screening clients" (that's not normal, is it?), but it's the best way to avoid clients from hell.

Pick up cues and red flags

In the normal course of a pre-sale communication, you'd normally be able to pick red flags, little red herrings, and tons of clues about a client. First, you'd get to know their business and your clients' approach to their business. Is your client asking for discounts? Are they taking too long to reply your messages for seemingly simple questions?

Are they clear about the scope of work? Are their expectations realistic? Do they want the moon and still want to pay you peanuts? Do they bargain too much on the price?

Think about it.

The ball? Whose court, exactly?

Here's a great way to make sure you get what you want and your client just gives in: put the ball in their court.

What do we mean by that? On the very first call (or any form of communication you use), screen your client. Look for the clues. If they pass the first two tests, then throw in a bunch of rules that are to be mutually acceptable by both parties. A few examples could be:

- Pricing, terms and conditions, frequency of payments, and form of payments
- Deadlines, delivery, and how exactly you should work.
- Whether you would work hourly, for a fixed price, or on a retainer?

If your potential clients see enough value in your offering, if you are reasonable enough, and if your potential client is serious about doing business, you should get a "yes" at best or a series of "negotiations" at worst.

If you flinch or if your heart tugs at you for any of the points above, you are likely to be heading straight for trouble.

As you work the numbers, spend your soul on the hustle, and work hard to build your freelancing career; bad clients are not worth your time and effort. They aren't even worth the money they pay.

How do you handle bad clients?

5 Ways To Make Clients Love You More

Basics of client management are simple. If you want to gain a client's trust and confidence, you have to prove that you are worthwhile. But that's not all. Just a few mistakes can ruin your months of hard work and relationships with clients. World's most successful freelancers suggest you need to expertise client relationship management early in your career.

Expertise and skills are necessary for accomplishing a task. But, how do you manage client expectation? How do you deal with a hard to please client?

How do you ensure your personal life is not compromised because of wrong professional commitments? These 5 tips can help you make clients love you, build long-term business relationships, and make clients love you more.

Choose clients wisely

It's the first rule of successful client relationship building. You really need to be sure who you're working with, at least, in the beginning of your career. A successful long term professional relationship depends on mutual support and collaboration. It's equally important for you to know if you will be comfortable working with the client.

Do background or company research before you put your proposal before the client. It will also help you understand the client's general relation with other freelance workers. Two out of ten failed professional relations is acceptable. But, if the ratio is more than 50 percent, that's a suspicious scenario.

Be bold to set a right expectation

Remember to set a right client expectation in the very beginning of the project. Communicate clearly and request the client to let you know about his expectation from the project. Be bold to clearly communicate and inform the client about all possibilities. Make sure your client knows the deliverables before you start working.

Set a right client expectation to keep your professional relation healthy. If you can't provide something, don't hesitate to say no.

Do not over-promise

Be sure of your own abilities. Will you be able to deliver what you promise? Your relationship with your client will likely come to ruin if you can't provide what you guaranteed. Be professional. The success of your freelancing career and long term relation with client will depend on trust and belief.

So you'll have to make sure clients trust your words and promises. If you promise to over deliver, but can't do that, it will gradually affect your professional credibility. Better, promise less and try to over deliver.

Be polite during the tough times

You can't expect to have smooth business times always. There will be some rough times when you have to be patient, sit with the client and talk about the problems. Never lose your temper, or be rude to client during the meetings or interactions.

A clash of opinion will always be there. But when you handle a difficult time responsibly, try to be patient and provide solution, client's trust on your ability increases. Maintain your dignity. Respectfully deal with your clients, no matter how difficult is the situation.

Learn to deal with criticism

It will be hard to satisfy a difficult client. Some clients will have greater propensity to criticize. But, you have to learn to deal with them. Try to stay calm and professional. Rather than taking the bait, address your client's complaints politely. Respond to their concerns and explain.

There will be moments when you will feel lost and impatient. But, if you love what you do, you will definitely figure out ways to resolve those concerns. Clients are normal people. They also have emotions and understanding ability like you. You just have to be honest and clear to them, and gain their trust gradually. And soon you'll have many happy clients to brag about.

4 Small Things You Can Do To Keep Clients For Life

It's not easy, doing this freelancing thing. Look for clients, work, and then look for more clients. The cycle never ends, and there's a never a day you can call off really. If only clients could last longer! If only you could somehow make them work with you on a continuous basis, sign up contracts that last for years, and have a steady flow of income coming in, no matter what.

Guess what? Even with something as volatile as freelancing, you can make it happen. Here's how you keep clients forever:

Go beyond business sometimes

It's easy to get stuck in a rut with conversations, meetings, and calls centered on business and nothing much else. We forget that we are people and we connect with other people.

Instead, we take a bunch of instructions and work to get an output. We deliver and we move on. People don't operate this way.

Take your time out to see what your clients are up to. What kind of updates do they put up on social media? What's that little something you can talk about that's common to you and your client?

Communicate regularly

It's so simple and it stares right at your face. For some reason, we just don't do this enough. In the normal scheme of things, communicating clearly, regularly, and precisely is already paramount.

Since freelancing would mean telecommuting, all of this work happens remotely. Clients don't get to see you and you don't get to see your clients. Hence, the case for communicating regularly is even stronger for remote work or freelancing.

Do more than what you think you should do

If you've been hired to do something, do that. But don't stop there and look for ways to do more. So, if you are a designer and your client hires you for getting a basic website done. Go ahead, and add a blog page although your client didn't mention it. If you are a writer, publish your clients' blog posts and share it on social media networks.

Doing more always puts you in good books. Being there is almost like having a chance to work with the client forever.

Always seek to provide value

Clients are in business just as you are. In business, there's a need for accountability and to know the return on investment for every dollar spent. Since clients are investing in your services, it's their right to know what they are getting for it. Meanwhile, it's smart to over deliver in terms of value on your end.

Can you pass on information that can make your clients' job easier? Do you have any recommendations for making that project better?

What do you do to keep your clients for long? What's your secret? Want to share?

6 Things Freelancers Can Do
To Enrich Their Customer Service

Customers are like babies. They need coddling more often than not. They want to be in your thoughts all the time. And providing them with awesome services is what every freelancer aspires to do. At the end of the day, what basically matters is the payment, your "baby" provides to you. So what does Nanny McPhee do to assuage the money spewing toddler?

No, we have nothing to do with your dog but we will provide you with awesome, crisp articles of your pet and your love for it. People will look up to you for inspiration or for; let's say, something as usual as "How to clean dog poo?" Let's just say, we will create a memorabilia for you, which you can be proud of, minus the funeral casket. And an epitaph.

I am a freelancer and I want a happy client. Someone who will recommend me for more work. But that isn't happening if I deliver your work an age after I had promised I will. And even after I have, I may not hear from you ever again. Manage time and meet deadlines. That's what they keep saying. I wonder why? I thought being a freelancer meant more "Me" time? But, now I realize money remains the same everywhere and clients too. So, being punctual works.

Customer Service can never be quantified. You cannot put any numbers to it. You know you have screwed up, if your mailbox oozes with customer abuse or no customer at all. More often than not, customers just don't care. They will move away to the next option. And in the world of freelancing, options are a plenty. This is the age of the freelancer so if you think you are unique. Great. So does everyone else.

Be Honest and Be Yourself. Know your limitations and bid accordingly. Be frank to your client about what you can and what you intend to do. Also, give them ideas. Clients, except the ones from hell, are very receptive to new ideas. This will also help you gauge the intent of the client. I addition, it can form a sort of camaraderie.

Communication is an art. The better you are at it, the more smoother the road becomes. Keep your customer posted on every move you make regarding his project. Generally smaller projects do not require such diligence, but once you start going north on the success scale, the picture gets bigger. When it involves a decent sum of money, going incommunicado is self defeating. Exercise some empathy and understand the pain of having to deal with an invisible freelancer.

Planning a project has its own importance. In fact the role of planning cannot be more emphasized than the fact that freelancing involves just you. So if you mess up later, you really cannot look for anyone else to blame. Hence, you chalk up the road map and get it authenticated by the client. A project outline helps you understand the complexity of the work as well establish the time line. The customer too will get an idea about the project challenges and think accordingly. This helps to avoid a lot of stress later.

I did my research - and paid attention to the competition. Do you think here any other way? Well-researched articles are those which have successfully stood the test of information. The world lives and thrives on information. It is by nature an extension of communication. You will also get a hint of your competition. Well informed freelancers are those who look at the bigger picture while not losing sight of the fine print. As they say, the devil lies in the details.

Value added service. Now how many times have we heard that before? While freelancing, remember, qualitative values are also considered as tangible. For example you can throw in a couple of free features into your project and then explain it to the customer. As the name suggests, adding value to the service provided. Care should be taken not to go overboard, or let the client take advantage of you.

Enriching your clients with superior customer service is an intriguing affair. And a winsome one. Happy Customers offer more. Happy Customers also talk about you more. They are your ready made advertising. Use them.

Merry freelancing and let the mirth of a happy customer be with you.

How To Get Creative With The Act Of "Looking Out"

You are always looking out. The information is always there. It's just that you have to continue bridging what you have and what's out there.

If you've ever wondered about what else you could do to maximize your own opportunities to find jobs, gigs, and land lucrative projects, the Internet is a blessing and the fact that you are reading this puts you at an advantage.

There are job boards, job listings, and advertising opportunities. There are hidden opportunities too.

Jen Hubley Luckwaldt of Payscale points out that more than 80% of job openings aren't advertised. While you let that sink in, Peter Cappelli of Harvard Business Review explains why employers aren't filling up open jobs.

Clearly, there's impetus to getting creative with "opportunity seeking" for freelancers. The competition is understandably high for every opportunity. So, here are a few ideas to kick-start your opportunity patrolling and how to look for freelancing jobs:

Find channel partners

Don't just lounge on communities like LinkedIn Groups and answer/ask questions on Quora. Send out a customized emails to relevant people out there to see if you can partner with them. If you are a writer, find designers and developers.

If you are a designer or developer, find content writers. Virtual assistants could team up with anyone. You get the drift, don't you?

Lash out with relevance

Let's say you are a freelance designer. You come across a website that should win the "Most Pathetic Designs in 2013 People Choice Award"—send out an email to the owner explaining why it needs improvement and make an offer.

Same tactic go for freelance graphic designers, developers (code that sucks, anyone?), and freelance writers.

Be everywhere with your mettle

Creative types should showcase – that's a given. Peer Hustle is already a great way to show your mettle and put up a remarkably impressive online presence.

Additionally, if you are a designer, showcase work on Behance, Carbonmade, and Dribble. Kelvon Yeezy of Hongkiat.com has even more places where you can showcase your work.

If you are a content developer, you could guest-post, create slide decks, upload content on Slide Share, give away free content, etc.

Brent Weaver of Hotpressweb.com actually built bcgurus.com as a community site that helps him get loads of credibility, trust, and visibility. Daniel Larsson of RightInbox.com chronicles how Brent Weaver manages to do it.

Do we have lessons to learn or what?

What other ways can you think of?

Hiring Or Working
With Other Freelancers

How To Hire A Freelancer:
10 Tips On Finding A Freelancer

The shared economy has created a buzz all around. With the market flooded with professionals, who are willing to let go off their stable jobs to grab a share of the freelance pie, it is time for freelancers to take charge. When it comes to finding a freelancer, you are looking for one in a million – someone who takes charge of things, makes quality work, and is reliable enough to be picked for both short-term and long-term assignments.

10 Tips on Finding a Freelancer

As more and more professionals are showing willingness to take their skills off the road and choosing to work from home, here are some tips to find a perfect solution to your freelancing needs:

1. Posting your job

When you are looking for the right fit for your vacant job position, you want to make sure that you do all things right at your end. Posting a job is one of the most crucial elements of finding a qualified candidate. Be as specific as possible about the vacancy requirements. Making things clear at your end before you sign up a freelancer is critical to a satisfactory client-contractor relationship and also to the future of your project.

Your work doesn't end at posting the job. Find time to invite the most befitting candidates to submit their proposals.

2. Identify skill requirements

Are you looking for an industry expert? Do you seek solid English skills? Do you want someone with a marketing? Are you willing to work with fresh talent or need an experienced hand to do the job for you? When you are clear with your skill requirements and know what exactly to get your hands on, you can easily wade through mediocrity in the freelance field so that you find only true talent.

3. Networking and hiring channels

There are a number of traditional hiring platforms that can lead you to some of the best candidates out there. When you are in search for real talent, it may help to spend some time in traditional job platforms. Social networks are a valuable resource when you seek talent. You might be lucky enough to locate a hidden gem. These networking platforms are a hub of professionals, and many are always looking for the right opportunity. When that opportunity knocks at their doors, they are willing to jump instantly! Who knows they might just be waiting for you!

4. Freelance marketplaces

On-demand platforms, such as Peer Hustle, are a hub of freelancers and independent professionals. These mobile talent marketplaces make it easy to find and connect with freelancers. By using such a resource, you can easily tap into a global pool of freelance talent and find the right fit. An increasing number of professionals use these platforms to share their unique skills and talent to make money. One advantage of using these freelance networks is that you get to find reliable and real talent. Using these platforms is as easy as searching for a specific skill set, short-listing a few candidates with relevant skills, getting in touch with them in real time, and agreeing on a price and job terms and ultimately hiring them for the job.

5. Previous connections or referrals

There are friends, relatives, and co-workers that you can trust. Drop an email to your connections, spreading the word about your requirement. If they know of someone who fits, they will let you know. If they have recently used a freelancer and found their services worthy enough of referring to others, they wouldn't waste a second before recommending them to you. If they can help, it will save you time. We all are aware that *time saved is money!* The more insights and information you can get from connections, the more quickly your business can grow.

6. Cheap isn't the best always

When you are trying to find a freelancer, you want the best talent for your job. Try to avoid going the "cheap" route. Though you may feel tempted into hiring the freelancer willing to work for a meager price, it may not be the best decision. Remember, you get what you pay for! You may not get the right fit for your job at a lowly budget. Cost is a big motivation for workers, including freelancers. Offer them the best price and they will be willing to go an extra mile to provide you with the best value for your money. So it won't hurt to be little flexible with your budget.

7. Match skills with requirements

You cannot compromise on the quality of work submitted by the freelancer. So in order to get the best quality submissions, you ought to look for the best talent. When it comes to finding a freelancer, make sure you check their portfolio, work experience, and samples of work done. You want to ensure that they have experience doing the same kind of work and have proven expertise in the industry. Who would want to waste time on a person that is new to the industry and can hardly move a foot without your guidance? Experience matters and it does count when it comes to choosing the right fit. The right person will be interested in spending some time to understand your business vision and goals.

Work samples are a kind of proof that they have handled similar tasks in the past. It gives you an idea about their style of work and commitment to their craft. Do not hesitate to ask for a small paid trial assignment if you aren't sure about the candidate's range of skills. It will help you determine whether they're a good fit for your work.

8. Flexible payment options

Freelancers want flexible payment ways so that they can get paid without much hassle, whether you choose to pay by cash or check or wire transfer. While traditional banking involves too many intermediaries, freelancers may not be happy to work for a client that is not open to other payment options. After all, they are working for money and want to ensure that they do not end up paying extra to intermediaries. Make sure you work with platforms with flexible payment options.

It is natural for clients to be skeptical when freelancers ask for up-front payments. However, it is a common practice in the freelancing world and contractors want to ensure that they will get paid for their time and efforts. To be on the safer side, you could create short project milestones for bigger projects so that you don't have to pay in lump sum upfront.

9. Determine workstation needs

Are you looking for a location-specific freelancer? Do you need the free-lancer to report to your office regularly? Employing someone remotely gives you a greater choice, with a deeper pool of applicants.

If you expect an independent contractor to work on-site, it is your responsibility to provide them with necessary hardware and software. For offsite contractors, you may need to ensure that they get remote access to specialized software and network drives so that they can seam-lessly carry on with your work.

10. Efficient and organized communication

When looking for a freelancer, you want to make sure you get a pro-fessional who communicates efficiently. You do not want someone who takes days to respond to your queries. Working with such professionals can be really frustrating. Simultaneously, it is important that you com-municate your requirements and messages clearly. You must be respon-sive to their questions so that they are clear with what you want and can produce the desired quality of work.

Your email communications must be organized. Sending different emails with bits of information scattered all over will result in confusion and frustration for the freelancer. No person wants to work with a client who is unclear of their expectations and not organized.

Create documents to organize invoices, assignments, projects, and pricing models. Be clear about deadlines and work schedule. Staying organized will save both of you time and keep the freelancer motivated to make timely submissions. Make sure you understand that your freelancer works for other clients and may be under contract. Do not forget to ask how much time they can devote to your assignments.

It's equally important for both sides to respect each other – while they respect your project goals and deadlines, you should respect their efforts and contribution.

Bottom line on hiring a freelancer

Remember, great freelancers are like cherished commodities in the freelancer industry. So you want to get your hands on them. It is up to you to determine how you can convince them to work for you. What extra are you offering to make them work for you?

Last but not least, make sure you draw up a legal agreement with your expectations about important items, including confidentiality, deadlines, deliverables, reimbursement, termination, and compensation.

Finding the right talent requires time and effort. While you are looking for the best freelancer, they are also looking to work with a client that can promise a lasting relationship and respect their efforts. When you find one, treasure them like your most cherished asset so that you can keep them. Pay them on time, respect their prior commitments and you can expect to enjoy a fruitful relationship with them.

How Finding Freelancers
Is Never A One-Shot Process

You decided to get external help for your business. Perhaps you decided to go completely virtual and have robust team of freelancers. Either way, you'll be out there looking for the best freelancers your money can find.

Most entrepreneurs think that finding freelancers is just about putting up a project brief and finding the best freelancer(s) possible from the list of applications.

It's not that easy; it's also not a one-time affair. Here's why:

No hiring without testing

You can't just go with a portfolio or a proposal to pick your freelancer – each of those instances only give you part of the story. That's why it's a smart thing to start with small tasks (as paid trials) and then take it forward.

To do that kind of testing, and that too with multiple freelancers, you'd take a considerable amount of time. Testing your potential freelancers, however, is a great way to make sure you only take in the best of the lot.

It's never permanent

You could do everything you could to find your team of freelancers, but just like it is in the offline world, no one stays with you forever. If you haven't stopped working with a freelancer already, they might choose not to work with you and there could be many reasons for that.

Since it's never permanent, you'd have to be on the constant look-out for freelancers.

Scaling or growing is imminent

Freelancers don't work like full-timers. For them, you are a client and your work takes up a chunk of their time or available bandwidth. Typically, freelancers manage multiple projects at the same time and they manage their time during a day or week to accommodate your project.

Since they can only do so much for you, there could be a time when you'd have to look for more help especially when you grow your business or scale up.

It's smart to play safe

With virtual projects, remote freelancers, and vague business scenarios, it always makes sense to play it safe. The more options you have in terms of potential freelancers you can hire (all tested, vetted, and eligible), the better off you are.

If this were true, it'd make sense to setup a continuous and systematic approach to hiring freelancers.

How do you find your freelancers? What's your approach?

Going Beyond The Resume: How To Find Real Talent In Your Freelancers

A brief is all that thats between you (the employer) and your freelancers. For most cases, a well-written brief is more than enough and can still get you freelancers as long as you do your due diligence and test your freelancers well before taking them in, all out. But there are times when you need to know more about your freelancers. Who knows? There could be a writer hidden inside a developer or a strategist behind the graphic designer?

Here are ways to go beyond the usual persona and how to find the real talent in your freelancers, if you'd want to:

Surprise them

Let's say you have a team of writers on your team: take a detour on the usual tasks you give your writers and make them do something else. You'd get to know a couple of things this way: first, you'll know if your writers are flexible enough to accept other kinds of work (of course, this work is still related).

Second, you'll know if they have any hidden talent.

Third, this is one of the few ways left to see how adaptable your team is and how they perform when you clip their wings off.

Social activity, the great revealer

Pick out on any random social stream of one of your existing or potential freelancers and you'll see a great deal of information behind every tweet and update. People automatically tend to skew towards brands they like, post updates on topics they find interesting, and you'll also know a lot about them by the updates they do. LinkedIn could show you their professional inclinations while Twitter can tell you what keeps them on their toes.

Get on Facebook if you want to get personal.

Talk to them

We've been spoilt by the fact that we don't really have to call up or meet anyone anymore. Since it's a virtual team that you are likely to be managing, you'd never have to take the effort to call. But that's exactly why you should. Just by taking the effort to place a single call (or skype meeting) you get to know so much more about your freelancers than you ever thought possible.

People open up much more when you talk to them or when you meet them (even better). Taking this step strengthens the bond.

What do you do to get to know your freelancers better? Share your ideas here.

How To Manage Freelancers Effectively

It's one thing looking for the right team of freelancers; it's something else to ensure smooth flow of projects. Collaboration with remote teams is usually a hard thing to come by. It's because it calls for a new kind of leadership; it calls for complete trust, and it requires you to be meticulously organized.

Managing with freelancers requires clearly defined roles, tasks, and project delivery planning. Here are a few project collaboration tools that work really well to manage your remote teams and projects:

Use project collaboration tools

The first thing you'd need when it comes to managing your team of freelancers and your projects is a project management tool or a project collaboration tool.

You'd need a way to delegate projects, assign team members, assign delivery dates, and manage work along with attachments, files, and documents that relate to your projects. You have plenty of options with project collaboration tools such as Asana, BaseCamp, and many others.

This is a critical first step. Find a project management tool that works for you.

Develop the process beforehand

You need your freelancers to be on the same page. You need a way to ensure that whatever is being worked on follows a process that can be followed by absolutely anyone on your team.

You can't expect freelancers to understand your vision or follow your way of working by just briefing them up with a one pager. Make a recording of the exact process or create workflows and document them.

Provide feedback constantly

Without feedback, your freelancers will be trudging along in a dark tunnel. Your constant feedback – when given well – works to improve your freelancers' work and gets them aligned to your projects and vision.

With a two-way communication early on, you'd not only open up more to your freelancers, but also get a great feedback mechanism in place.

Train your freelancers

Mostly, the freelancers who'll end up being a part of your team are already experienced. Yet, no business is built equal. Every business is unique and this means that your freelancers will need more than casual briefing. In some cases, they'd need all out training.

Use many of the available video training services to engage in regular training before-hand. Doing so helps your freelancers improve on their own skills, give you exactly what you need, and add value to your organization.

How To Hire A Graphic Designer: 4 Tips On Finding The Best Graphic Designer For Your Job

The role of a graphic designer is going to be extremely important as he/she is going to build the visual look of your brand in the eyes of your target customers. You will need someone who has relevant experience. This means, the professional should have skills and expertise needed for the job.

You will have to choose someone, who either has experience in a broad range of tasks, or has niche expertise only in the task you need to be done. The question is, how to find the best graphic designer? Who will be ideal for the job that you want to be done with utmost care? Here are few things that you should take care of when hiring a graphic designer for your job:

Screening the best graphic designer

When you hire a professional, make sure that you look for some essential qualities in them. You need to hire someone who can be ready to take your feedback, criticisms on work and can make changes to the work accordingly. Hire someone who knows how to get inspired. Graphic designers are creative people. A good designer should always be curious to know about new designs and innovations.

The best designer should not hesitate to take challenges and should always be ready to get out of their comfort zone to learn. They should be ready for any challenge to make a difference. So, never hire someone who seems only to stick to their niche expertise and seems reluctant to try hand on new opportunities.

Be flexible with your budget to hire the best designer

You can't be too conservative about your project budget if you're really looking forward to working with a talented professional. Some designers, who are experienced and confident about their abilities, might ask for a higher price. Will you immediately back out at that time? Instead, you should take a bit of time to analyze the potential of the candidate, and then decide whether it will be fair to pay a higher price.

If you can trust your gut feeling and are convinced that the designer understands your requirement completely and seems to have the abilities to perform the task, you should try to expand the budget a bit so that you don't lose someone eligible just because of budget restriction. It won't be an ideal thing to do if you want to hire the best graphic designer for your job.

Correctly identify and communicate the project goal to the designer

You have to be very specific about your project goal. Before you hire a graphic designer, you should be able to correctly identify what you want to achieve. After that, you should clearly communicate your project expectations to the designer. The designer won't be able to align the work with your visions if you can't explain him/her what you want to achieve. Therefore, you must communicate well with the designer.

Look for a person always ready to learn

In addition, a good designer should always be open to learn new things that come his/her way during the work tenure. You would like to work with a person who is open to hear what you have to say and learn new things from you, right? So, look for a professional who is humble and teachable.

These were the most important criteria that you should try to stick to when hiring the best graphic designer. A significant portion of your project and brand success will depend on this professional. So, be patient and research the qualities of best graphic designers to hire someone truly talented.

How To Hire A Photographer: 3 Tips On Finding The Best Photographer For Your Job

If you can find out how freelance photographers market and advertise their experience, skills, and expertise, you will know how and where to find the best professionals. You can find blogs about photography where freelance photographers write or put examples of their work. You may also look for websites that host photography competitions to find the best photographers.

However, there are several other things that you'll need to consider. After you find out and screen quite a few professional photographers, you will need to hire a photographer based on style he/she is best at, and also some other essential criteria. Below you will find the tips on finding the best photographer for your job.

Make sure you reach the right place

Learn where and how the freelance photographers advertise and promote their work. However, whether you will find some really good photographers or not that will depend on where you go to find them. Some of the places where you can find good photographers could be photography groups on social networking sites. Joining groups on social networking sites should be a part of the good photographer's marketing strategy.

You can check with good blogs to find the best photographers. Good photographers must be showing their work via guest posts or on their own blog. You must not ignore the important photo sharing sites like Flickr to find a good professional. The American Society of Media Photographers have their own platform where you can find some of the best photographers. They have a free service that will let you search their database of professionals by photographic specialty and geographic location.

How you should judge they are really professional?

Don't entirely rely on advertising and marketing platforms to find the best photographers. You will have to see if the photographers showcasing their work are really professionals as they claim. You may stumble upon many photographers who will have no real professional photography certification. So, how you can be assured your photographer is a professional?

If a photographer is associated with a professional organization like the Royal Photographic Society or the Master of Photographers Association, it indicates that the photographer's technical skills and abilities have been tested and are impressive enough to be accepted as a part of the professional association. So, look for professions who are member of a professional associations.

Do they have the qualities to be successful photographer?

How will you choose a photographer if you don't know the photography qualities that can turn a project into a successful one? When you plan to hire the best photographer, look for the essential photography qualities which make them great professionals. Ambitious and aspiring freelance professionals work hard, network like crazy and try to be part of an association which help them to learn.

To be successful, a photographer must know how to get better with time, face fierce competition and find out ways to showcase their work. Serious photographers should have a creative and amazing website. They should be interested in providing some extra work that you may not be expected.

Check on Google to find the local freelance photographers. Almost all professionals try to take advantage of SEO nowadays. So you may find few amazing professionals online. But before you select a professional, try to increase your knowledge and ideas about your photography project.

How To Hire A Software Developer: 3 Tips On Finding The Best Software Developer For Your Job

When hiring the best independent software developer for your job, you will need to consider both the pros and cons of hiring a freelance software professional. From many perspectives, it seems absolutely feasible to hire someone reliable and responsible. But, the process of recruitment is not going to be as simple if you want to hire an independent professional.

Why does it makes sense to hire an independent contractor? The reason is that this process saves a lot of time and also the money that you might had to give to a middleman or a recruitment agency otherwise. So, when you hire a freelancer software developer, you'll have to make sure you can trust the professional with quality work and timely delivery to make your overall project successful. Here are some great tips on finding the best software developers for your job -

Make sure you know all the costs involved

When you decide to hire an independent developer, you have to make sure you understand different types of costs involved in the process. You will have to know how much the contractor would like to get paid. One important thing to note that most freelance developers would like to get paid hourly. But, you've to make sure that you pay only for the mutually agreed fixed working hours for the job.

You will have to calculate and figure out the number of hours that the developer will need to dedicate to the project in advance. If you don't sort out the hourly payment well in advance, it might cost you much more than your budget permits. Therefore, speak clearly and let the contractor know how much you would like to spend for the project before you hire the professional.

Make sure the contractor understands your project expectations

Another important thing that you would like to talk clearly with the prospective professionals is that if they understand what you want to achieve. One difficulty many recruiters experience when working with an offshore developer is that the lack of communication and misunderstandings.

This might happen because of language differences or many others things. You have to make sure that you let the contractor know your project goal clearly so that they can align the work with your interests appropriately. For this, you will need to speak frankly to the contractor who you want to hire and let them know your project expectations.

Be willing to pay more for quality

This is one thing which will help you hire a great software developer. Sometimes, you need to be a little flexible in terms of the hourly cost you pay to the contractor. Some freelance developers really work great. But, they may charge above the average pay. If you think that you've found one who has the ability and skill to make your project successful, you should be little flexible to pay a bit more. It will inspire the professional to provide much better work and will also help you build a long term work relationship with this talented person.

It will be much easier for you if you communicate with the freelance developer and let them know your expectations. Only hire someone who can assure regular updates and seems willing to maintain communication throughout the project tenure. Right and timely communication will keep things on track.

How To Hire A Writer: 4 Tips On Finding The Best Writer For Your Job

To hire and add some great freelance writers to your team, you just have to make sure you choose the diamond from the mine. There are really good writers who can inspire readers with their enchanting thoughts and the art of storytelling. However, finding and hiring the best of them is the most important task.

Of course, you probably would like to start by seeking help from people in your circle who know some good writers. But, there are many other places that you should try. Below you will find tips for finding and hiring the best writers for your job:

Guest bloggers in great blogs

You want to find and hire the best writers for your job? Why not try the great blogs that talk about content marketing and writing overall? The aim is to get a person who understands your need and possesses the skill you're looking for. You will find out several talented people in such blogs who can work for your project and can make your project successful. Successful blogs welcome guest posts from other writers who like to write for that site and link back to their own blog or website. So, you will find several such writers who write guest blog posts for other blogs to promote their own skills and services.

Try LinkedIn and Twitter

Social media platforms are such places where you will surely find talented writers for your job. Most professionals would like to be in the network of marketers and other entrepreneurs.

So, if you research on social media sites like LinkedIn and Twitter, you will find profiles of great writers. You can connect with them and develop a great group of writers.

Find writers in writing forums

Writing forums are also great places to find the best writers. Most writers like to be part of a group or network with other like minded professionals. If you go to the forums and research a bit, you will surely find few great writers as per your project need.

Ideally, you should try to screen and carefully observe the various discussion threads to understand the writer's point of view, their writing style and subject knowledge. And gradually over time, you will get to know who fits your project goals the most effective way.

Hire a niche writer

Writers have different writing styles and subject interests. If a writer says they can write about almost anything, the work of the writer is going to be average. To write a great article, you need to have good amount of information and analysis. A writer will study, analyze, and link logic and thoughts to create a new story for the readers. Unless you don't want to waste your money, you shouldn't hire a writer who doesn't have expertise in couple of specific subjects.

A professional can be a great story creator for children, or a nonfiction writer, or a business content strategist. You have to decide who will fit your goal and can work best for your project. Therefore, invest in a writer who has niche expertise.

These are some of the best ways to head start your recruitment journey. It may take some time to select few really talented people. But, once you have them, you can build a long term professional relationship.

How To Manage Your Time Better While Working With Freelancers

Virtual teams are good to have but just like any other managerial work, getting things done through your team can take a lot of time.

Since projects are usually time and deadline driven, and also because a few of your freelancers may require you to pay them by the hour, managing your time is your prerogative. How you use your time and how you train your team to use time is a function of how profitable your business is going to be.

Here are a few ways you can manage your time better when you work with freelancers:

Train Freelancers and set expectations

Soon after bringing in a freelancer, take time out to set clear expectations from the projects. What exactly did you hire the freelancer for? What are the delivery schedules? What's the workflow like?

Apart from project specifics, also spend time explaining how it's going to be like while working for you. Insist that you want the team to be productive and that there's a huge emphasis on making good of the time available for you, together.

Let someone else do systematic hiring

You are an entrepreneur, and every hour you have today counts. Hiring good freelancers is a long and continuous process. Once you develop a system to hire the right freelancers, hire a virtual assistant or a human resources manager to do all the hiring for you.

Typically, you will enter the scene only after a freelancer is now a part of your team.

Time (not just days) as deadlines

Many project collaboration tools also allow you to fix time-based deadlines (and not just dates on a calendar) – there's a reason why time-based deadlines exist: fixing time-based deliveries brings in a sense of importance to each task and also allows for a lot more accountability.

If you are working on hourly projects, have a way to track every hour worked. Use an independent tool like Hubstaff which tracks time along with screenshots to show you exactly what your team is working on.

Set aside separate time for meetings

Avoid meetings at all costs. If you are meeting virtually, find time like Friday evenings or other days, at fixed time slots, to talk to your freelancers.

Don't get on a call for every single thing you thought you wanted to discuss. Instead, make note of things you need to talk or communicate with a respective freelancer, and hold a weekly meet to take on each of those points, all in one go.

How do you manage time when you work with freelancers?

How To Outsource Your Job: 4 Tips On Outsourcing Your Job To A Freelancer

According to Harvard Business Review, corporations are hiring independent and reputed workers as huge pool of talent who want to work dedicatedly and stay away from useless corporate politics is available nowadays. These people are graduates from top tier schools and universities. Still they want to work on independent and project based temporary jobs.

Also, companies are happy to be able to reduce their overhead costs, excessive money spent on training and work space. They enjoy the flexibility of choosing talents from any part of the world. Most companies love the fact that they can recruit the independent professionals according to the demand of projects. So, it's a mutually beneficial work agreement. If you're starting a business and want a helping hand to get some critical work done, here is how you should hire a freelancer and outsource the job:

Hire freelancers via online platforms or web apps

If you're eager to hire a freelancer, try to hire someone online first. Most freelancers will be registered to recognised freelancing platforms where they will have their portfolio and work experiences highlighted. You will need to look carefully at their portfolio to understand their skills, experiences and capabilities.

Also, the online platforms will help you understand the reputation of the contractor. Of course, a serious and professional freelancer will have consistent and progressive portfolio and jobs to show to you.

Look for freelancers looking to build long term work relation

It will be better if you look for freelancers who are serious and can commit to long term work responsibilities. This will help you have a serious and professional freelancer in your network who you can approach during the challenging requirements.

If you can build a solid team of freelancers with diversified skills and expertise, it will help you quickly hire someone without needing you to look for and screen freelancers every time.

Carefully analyze a freelancer's skills and expertize

Hiring a freelancer has its own pros and cons. When you hire a freelancer, you've no direct control over them. A freelancer is a person who will be working on flexible terms and off-site in most of the cases. Therefore, you will need to make sure the freelancer has strong work ethics and strictly adheres to their professionalism.

Ambitious and serious freelancers will stick to their commitments. They will communicate well and try to adhere to all promises and assurances provided. After all, you would also like to have a highly professional and sincere contractor by your side, right?

Keep legal terms ready

When you wish to get your work done by outsourcing your work to a freelancer, keeping things clear in legal term will be great step. This is just to make sure that you can keep the company's private informations and assets free of any dispute.

This is kind of a precautionary step where you keep your company's interests safe. However, when you hire a very reputed and talented independent worker, the chances of this type of dispute and issue realistically don't exist.

Hiring a freelancer is definitely a smart choice if you can build a long term relationship with an honest and committed independent worker. You don't have to worry about things like not having any direct control over the worker. An ambitious and truly committed freelancer will only concentrate on hard work and increasing their personal reputation.

Why You Should Test Freelancers Before Hiring Long-Term?

Telecommuting is a dream come true for not just freelancers but also for entrepreneurs. Human resources is no more a risky endeavor with blind hiring based on static resumes. You now have access to incredible talent locally, nationwide, or even internationally. Projects get done faster even if there's a difference in time zones, and you – as an entrepreneur – have almost zero overheads.

Freelancers can jump right in, without any need for training or onboarding, and get down to working on your projects. Their presence is not needed and their skills obviously get your project moving forward.

But it's not all roses when you go looking for freelancers to work on your projects. Here's why you should test your freelancers before hiring them long-term:

The choice is perplexing

If you were to just put up a brief for potential freelancers, you'll receive applications in hundreds, in less than a couple of hours. Just going through proposals won't do you justice, plus it's a drain on your time and resources. Instead, shortlist a couple of freelancers and bring them into a testing zone to separate the wheat from the chaff.

This way, you'll be able to quick whittle down your choices and make your own freelancer recruiting more systematic.

Testing tells you what you get for your money

Resumes are static. They are often misleading. Irrespective of the skill set you are after, there's bound to be evidence of previous work done. Designers, writers, and developers – the serious, experienced, and professional ones – usually have portfolios for you to take a look at.

Despite that, testing freelancers with a small task or a series of small tasks usually lets you know what you get for your money.

Everyone makes claims

For freelancers, there's low barrier to entry. They are in business with nothing more than skill sets and a laptop with an Internet connection. It's easy for almost anyone to claim anything. Without due diligence built into your freelance hiring process, you are likely to sign freelancers who might not meet your requirements.

You need to test those claims. You have to see the proof.

Testing leads to confirmed hires

Services are intangible. As such, buyers (you) don't have anything to touch, feel, or know anything before services are rendered. That's why it makes sense to test your freelancers with mini-projects or simple tasks to begin with. Write your brief clearly mentioning that it's a paid trial and that the simple task that you are asking for is a test.

Only freelancers with mettle, commitment, real skills, and great communication will survive.

How do you hire freelancers? Do you have a testing mechanism in place?

5 Social Traits That You Should Look Out For In Freelancers

They say the people are one of the most important part of the business in fact the quality of your team determines how far your business goes. however finding freelancers is easier said than done. Not every freelancer you talk to Is going to work out for you. Assuming you do find freelancers as part of your team, you won't go too far with just drones working for you. You'll need freelancers who are social, active, and easy to get along with.

Here are a few social traits you need to look for in a freelancer:

The initiation talk

Remember the first time we were talking to your freelancer how are your first impressions did you have a feeling that the relaxer easy to get along with do you think freelancer can be fun when not working does a fine line between being professional and being boring.

Go with your first impressions.

Social activity

Are the freelancers you're looking to hire active socially? Are they present on some of the most popular networks like Twitter, LinkedIn, and Facebook? If yes, what do they talk about? What do they tweet about? What do they share that they are passionate about? Who do they link with? Who do they network with? What topics do they feel strongly about? The more social they are on social networks, the stronger is their proclivity towards a community.

Ongoing communication

Often, you'd have taken the opportunity to talk to your freelancers maybe once a week or twice a week. How does it feel like while they talk to you? Do you believe that they understand the project requirements well? Do you walk away from these regular meetings feeling good about them?

Socially inclined freelancers are fun to be on the team. They are also creative, and more likely to be approachable.

How social are the freelancers on your team?

Resources

5 Awesome Books Written
Just For Freelancers

Countless numbers of scientific studies have indicated that regular reading habit helps improve cognitive functions, boosts mental health, improves leadership skills and increases the chances of success. According to Harvard Business Review, professionals, who aspire to build leadership qualities, must develop a steady reading habit.

A lifelong reading habit improves mental performance and helps develop a sharp brain. If you're a freelancer, you're going to have much bigger responsibility and accountability toward your own profession and career goals.

Therefore, it's important that you read books which can help develop new skills. Not to forget, reading habit is also helpful in developing a creative mind. A steady long term reading habit:

- Improves analytical skills.
- Increases creativity.
- Increases verbal intelligence.
- Elevates emotional intelligence.
- Reduces stress, improves concentration and productivity.

So, try to read books written on great leaders, influencers, personal development, self help, marketing skills, etc. The list below represent 5 awesome books written for freelancers.

The 7 Habits Of Highly Effective People - Steven Covey

This book will help you learn how to solve personal and professional life problems, find and take advantage of promising opportunities, and thus, achieve success.

Getting Things Done: How to Achieve Stress-Free Productivity - David Allen

You can't afford to miss this amazing book. This book will help you improve clarity of thoughts, learn how to relax during the most critical business days and increase productivity.

The 4-Hour Work Week: Escape the 9-5, Live Anywhere and Join the New Rich - Timothy Ferris

Another inspirational masterpiece. This book talks about how one can increase productivity to be rich and also follow their passion. This will give a boost to your career.

Brilliant Selling: What the Best Salespeople Know, Do and Say (Brilliant Business) - Tom Bird, Jeremy Cassell

This book has received numerous appreciative reviews for amazing thoughts on how to improve one's selling skills. Not to forget, you have to learn to sell your skills if you want to grow your business.

The Ultimate Small Business Marketing Book - Dee Blick

This book includes powerful case studies and tips on how to get started, build an attractive profile, and grow your small business or freelancing career.

These are incredible information sources and knowledge building tools. Read these books to hone your thoughts and challenge your weaknesses. Gradually over time, you will see how you become one of the most talked about industry performers.

5 Solutions To Build
Your Website Without Help

We've always believed that a website is your primary gateway to your freelancing business. It's your way to ensure that you are found in search, that you have a portfolio to show, that your blog can be your voice, and your social presence is justified.

Earlier, the very act of having to look for a designer or a developer was a painful process. Thankfully, today you have access to incredible tools that make a website just a few clicks away. Here are a few solutions to build your website without help from developers or designers:

Wordpress

The self-hosted Wordpress option is one of the most popular options out there for the entire world to get pampered with a website. If you have a hosting account, chances are that you can be up and running with the self-hosted Wordpress version (this is different from Wordpress.com – the managed and free option from Automattic).

Wordpress has an impossibly huge range of themes for you to choose from, not to mention plugins and the humongous community of people to help you.

Wix

Register, login, pick a template, tweak the template, and you are ready with a website. Wix is one of the easiest website builders out there and if you are not in the least technically inclined, Wix was built for you.

Last time we checked, they even have a template specific for free-lancers but the templates do not limit you in any way. You can literally pick and work with any template. Wix also lets you connect various apps to give extended functionality, work on SEO, social media, and more.

Weebly

Weebly recently released Carbon, bringing it to the same level as Wix. You can now sign up and build awesome websites that are lightweight, SEO ready, and completely responsive (great to look at across devices).

Just like Wix, Weebly also lets you to connect with apps that give you extended functionality – all the way from booking appointments to going e-commerce.

Mozello

Mozello is touted as the world's cheapest and yet still efficient website builder. The interface is by far the simplest among all the other options on this list. You have plenty of mobile responsive templates to choose from and you can also edit your website right there on the browser.

You can start for free and pay when you are ready. Hosting comes included in a single monthly price you pay.

SquareSpace

While SquareSpace isn't as open as the other options out here, there's really no need to be. SquareSpace is a slightly closed ecosystem but it can help you create websites that are really slick and advanced. SquareSpace also allows you to build a logo right off the bat and your website creation off a template is just a matter of few clicks and some content.

SquareSpace also lets you go e-commerce quickly with its simple to use interface.

Which of these options would you go with?

3 Brain Empowering Techniques Freelancers Should Use In Free Time

Don't take your hobbies lightly. Science says that your hobby can actually make you smarter. Studies have found that a human brain responds differently depending on the environment where a person lives in. During a study when a group of prisoners were placed in solitary confinement, where they were only allowed to think, they were found to develop uncommon cognitive abilities.

For example, one prisoner was able to recall all of his kindergarten memories. Another prisoner was able to multiply big numbers by big numbers accurately, which he was never able to do before.

There was another prisoner, who developed a house design in his mind when he was in the solitary confinement. And he actually built the house exactly the same way when he got out. So, many scientific evidences clearly say that if you involve your brain with specific types of exercises, and control distractions, you can actually use more of your brain's capacity.

So, by using your free time effectively, you can give your mind the essential, required time to relax, reduce stress, and increase brain capacity. Here are top 3 tips to use free time effectively and the Brain Empowering Techniques for freelancers as we promised:

Playing a musical instrument

It will be much more relaxing for you if you like music. Music not only helps to de-stress, but actually helps a person improve their analytical skills, motor skills, math skills, and creativity. Well, it's not hard for science to understand how the different parts of a human brain react to certain activities like reading or listening to musics.

Neuroscientists say that playing an instrument engages many areas of the brain all at once. It's exactly like a full body workout.

According to science, the corpus callosum, which links the two halves of the brain, gets stronger when someone plays a musical instrument. This means, it can improve your memory, problem solving ability, planning skills and the ability to pay attention to details. So, do you think you will like to play a musical instrument? After all, it's gong to make you more intelligent.

Doing regular exercise

Regular exercise is more effective than occasional exercise. You need to do exercise. And it's not only that you need to increase heart rate or improve heart health. When you exercise, your brain cells actually get a very important protein, the Brain-Derived Nerotrophic Factor (BDNF).

This element is excellent as it nourishes the brain cells and improves the brain's ability. The most noticeable results of increased BDNF are improved memory, learning ability and accuracy.

You need to exercise regularly because it's good for your brain and mental health. The point here is that why not use the time in a way which actually improves mental health? So, if you can develop a sport hobby or a habit of a physical activity, you may actually become smarter.

Doing meditation half an hour daily

If you can develop this as your free time hobby, there is absolutely nothing better than this. Yes, it's hard to begin. That's why start with the basic meditation method where you just need to concentrate on your breathing. You can start with just 2 minutes a day. Experts can do meditation for many hours a day. But that's certainly not possible for the beginners.

But, meditation works amazingly because it directly influences the brain waves. Long term practice of meditation can actually improve your cognitive abilities, will let you have better control on your emotions, increases happiness, peace, focus, attention, concentration, and memory.

All this can make you smarter and more creative. Find out what else can you do in your free time to be a happy and more productive professional.

3 Ways Freelancing Is Bad And Ways To Counter These

Freelancing is not for you if you don't have an independent and self driven work attitude. Freelancing might prompt many unpleasant challenges. Are you ready for them? If you're a person who gives up on problems too easily, this is definitely not the career for you.

Before you start freelancing, make sure if you are ready to become a risk taker, an excellent money manager, and a self driven person who doesn't need to be told or instructed when to do what.

Are you responsible enough to choose this independent career? There will be no one to guide you, create work pressure for you, or yell at you for your poor performance. It will be just the opposite of a regular fixed-hours working job. Therefore, you will have to figure out what sorts of plans will help you move forward and grow. It will not be an easy journey. Below you will find how these 3 ways freelancing is bad for you and how to overcome those challenges -

Freelancing doesn't provide regular income

Freelancing is bad for you if you want the assurance of regular fixed income. No, there will no assurance that you will earn a fixed amount every month. Freelancing is your business. not a job. The outcome of freelancing will depend on your consistent effort, quality of work, reputation, management and resilience.

Ways to Overcome: As freelancing is not going to assure fixed monthly income, you will have to very good at business planning and managing finances. You must not let go any opportunities that comes your way. When there is too much work to do, be ready to work over time to earn more than your usual target. You should always be proactive and ready to work hard.

Freelancing doesn't allow fixed off on weekends or holidays

There will be nothing like fixed days off on weekends. Yes, you have your personal work priorities, but, you must not expect to take days off on every weekend as you might have to work on those two days many times for the sake of client relations and project urgencies. So, if you're too particular about not working on the weekends, freelancing full-time is not for you.

Ways to Overcome: You can choose to work overtime on the weekdays to be able to take take some time off on weekends. But, you should be flexible enough to address urgent project needs. If you know how to prioritize tasks, it will be easier for you.

Freelancing will demand unconditional dedication

Freelancing can be bad in the way that it will need your time and more effort than you may want to give. You may have to sacrifice many friend and family gatherings to be able to do justice to this profession. It's your business. And no one is there to help you grow your business. So, you'll have to walk the road alone and be ready to give it whatever it takes to be successful.

Ways to Overcome: You must not give to the demanding situations. If you feel de-motivated, think about the numerous advantages it offers. You've the freedom to choose your own working hours. You can work on things that you're passionate about.

Freelancing is not bad in the real sense. It's hard and challenging. So, if you're a person who loves to grow amidst uncertainties and know how to find solutions to every problem, you will thrive in this profession.

4 Best Resources For Freelancers

If you ask successful freelancers to share their opinion on how to grow in freelancing, their first advice will be developing some focused expertize and sticking to it. Your growth as a freelancer will be too slow if you fail to understand and identify which markets are promising, and locate prospective clients.

So, you need to have an access to number of resources which can help you develop an understanding of how to use your skills and which one is your target market. You can't grow with a too generalized approach. You must be able to develop a solid marketing strategy and should be able to improvise it and continue it for a long period of time. Below you will find the best resources for freelancers that can help you get a clear picture of the future:

A platform that talks about freelancing success tips and tricks

Would like to get more freelance work this year? If so, then learn new things to increase your value. In freelancing, learning is going to be a consistent process. You should read regularly and try to find out more about how the freelancing industry is growing, or where it's going in a few years.

You should always read blogs and follow websites which can tell how to grow a freelancing business in simple and cost effective ways. Some of the very useful sites are Guerrilla Marketing and Zen Habits. These are some awesome, up to date sites that talk about excellent business strategies and personal development tips for the freelancers.

A place to learn new freelancing skills

You can't think of winning more jobs without developing yourself as a highly competitive candidate. According to successful freelancers, you must not think that jobs and opportunities are going to come to you without your efforts and strategised approach.

So, always be open to learn new skills. Any web resources which can tell you about the most popular courses and can offer training sessions will be very usable. For example, you will get to know about some amazing resources to learn and improve your freelancing skills. There are many very good web resources which can train you for your respective niche.

A place to read freelancing success stories

Another thing which is very important for your success as a freelancer is reading more success stories. You should read more about how successful freelancers achieved growth and success over the years. Every professional have their own unique success strategy. Read about them to get inspiration and motivation. Who knows? You may also find out your winning strategy and realize your mistakes after reading their stories?

Successful freelancers talk about what types of mistakes freelancers make when starting out. Maybe you can figure out what's holding your success back after reading these posts?

Good blogs to know more about freelancing

Read more blogs about freelancing. Anything about freelancing, like the freelancing industry overall, the change in trend, tools for improving productivity, tools for improving skills and expertise, developing successful habits, etc. can be of great use.

Select web resources carefully to speed up your career growth. You'll have to improve and become more competitive to stay ahead in this large market of highly talented professionals.

Top 10 Books
All Freelancers Should Read

When you have chosen to be a freelancer, it may help to read a few books to learn new skills and educate yourself. After all, you want to make sure you stay ahead of the crowd and clients keep knocking at your doors. It is important that you do not stop learning, so reading books for freelancers will enhance your learning prowess and help develop skills that matter in the freelance industry. As a freelancer, the zeal to learn should keep you up and running all the time. A great book will inspire you, teach you new skills, and expose you to a heap of new ideas that will help you get the better of your weaknesses and tread ahead in your freelance journey.

Here are a few top books all freelancers should read:

1. Rework

A book that clearly throws out key business rules for success, *Rework* is by Jason Fried and David Heinemeier Hansson. It delivers a powerful message and lays out freelance success tips and tricks clearly, suggesting that fluff tasks that don't bring you income should not be your focus area. Instead, the book outlines highly productive tips on money making that are designed to streamline success in freelance business.

Though there is nothing spectacular about this book, it is packed with advice, insight and information to help you make a successful freelance career. This interesting book shows how you can learn to be a rockstar freelancer and make good income from the industry. It shows you a better and faster way to be successful in this business.

2. Creative Inc.: The Ultimate Guide to Running a Successful Freelance Business

An excellent place to learn all the tips of freelancing, this book can prove to be a goldmine for learning tricks to find work for freelancers. Written by two successful freelancers themselves, Meg Mateo Ilasco and Joy Deangdeelert Cho, *Creative Inc.* gives you a good overview of what needs to be done to get started in the freelance industry. You will also find proven tips to balance your professional and personal life and set your freelance rates. If you are looking to start your online or freelance business, this book will teach freelancers from different industries how to establish a flourishing business.

3. The Freelance Business Funnel

For freelancers still struggling to find the best paying gigs, this book by Skellie can come in handy. With tried and tested hacks and actionable advice, The Freelance Business Funnel is a must-have book for every freelance professional looking to augment the flow of their work.

The book outlines how blogging can prove to be a blessing to market your freelancing business and connect with potential clients. Learn proven tips on how to market your freelancing skills, improve your career, and earn passive income. You will also learn how to create a popular blog, optimize your business, sell your services to blog visitors, turn readers into clients, funnel clients, charge your dream rates, and scale your freelance business.

4. Starting Your Career as a Freelance Writer

As its name suggests, this best-selling book is all about being a successful freelancer. If you've always dreamed of tasting success as a freelancer, this is the book you should get your hands on immediately. Written by Moira Anderson Allen, the top-selling book on freelancing gives aspiring writers the proven tools to become successful in the business, so you can start earning a healthy income.

The second edition dedicates a section to the "online writer," outlining how to start a blog, website. It also explains the importance of social media in today's marketplace and how to participate in social networking sites. Get all the information you need on electronic publishing and how to secure new writing opportunities as a freelancer.

5. My So-Called Freelance Life

Starting out as a freelancer may not be a hassle-free experience. However, Michelle Goodman in her book explicitly shares how it is possible to get a start in the freelance industry and keep the dollars coming. The book outlines how you can pursue a fulfilling career as per your terms and work schedule while simultaneously making a name and living in the process.

This how-to-guide book is a must read for women or stay at home moms, who seek work from home opportunities to watch their kids grow while making a living sitting within the confines of their home.

My So-Called Freelance Life has all the tips, advice, and suggestions to help you get started and pursue a successful career in the freelance industry. Learn how to transform your freelance dream into reality in this easy-to-read book that shares anecdotes from successful freelancers. Whether you are just starting out or are a seasoned freelancer, this is one of those books all freelancers should read.

6. Internet Marketing: 8 Key Concepts Every Business Must Know

Internet marketing is the most effective form of marketing today. This is exactly what you will learn in this book. Learn key concepts of marketing that will make you a successful Internet marketer.

A rich resource for Internet marketers, this is an excellent marketing book that makes an easy read. Short but concise, *Internet Marketing* by Jon Leland lays down tips and suggestions that every freelancing professional should know. The book doesn't promise dramatic results, but clearly mentions that the tricks will come in handy to succeed in the marketing business.

7. Think And Grow Rich

Whether your mission behind kicking your 9 to 5 job is to be your own boss as a freelancer or get rich, the book *Think And Grow Rich* will surely come in handy. The book is a goldmine for those seeking avenues to become successful and get rich. With inspirational notes and success secrets taken from the richest men of their time, this book is a must have on every business owner's book shelf.

Written by Napoleon Hill, *Think And Grow Rich* will inspire the entrepreneur within you and instill the confidence to take up the challenges that freelancing throws at you.

8. David and Goliath

A bestselling book for freelancers, *David and Goliath* covers a fascinating range of topics and suggestions for creative freelancers. Malcolm Gladwell's masterpiece, this is a valuable book for creative professionals to read, helping you see clearly what will work for and against your chances of success. If you seek a freelance film editing career, this book will offer you exciting new possibilities. Any Gladwell fan won't be disappointed with this fascinating book that makes a pleasant read and offers valuable advice.

9. Onward

Onward – How Starbucks Fought For Its Life without Losing Its Soul makes a decent read. Written by Howard Schultz, this book shares how a giant business that has lost its way can resurface and revive. It also presents a rough account of the difficulties a person may face in running a global franchise. It shows that the rewards of entrepreneurship can be thrilling as well as fulfilling while the lows can be heartbreaking.

The book points to the importance of passion for pursuing the entrepreneurial journey, which may require some sacrifices, hardships, and pain. It inspires you to bravely face the hardships for a better reward.

10. Different – Escaping The Competitive Herd

When it comes to choosing the best books for freelancers, *Different - Escaping the Competitive Herd* is a must read for anyone interested to learn freelance marketing or business strategy. Written by Youngme Moon, this book is more in the form of an interesting story than a jargon touting business academic.

Learn what it takes you to set yourself apart from the competition. The exhaustive book on freelancing will motivate you to be willing to take risks and do things differently that give you an edge over the competition.

The choice is yours

Freelancing is a charming career, which has become the preferred choice for a number of professionals. The freedom to set your work hours and be your own boss is one of the biggest attractions for people looking to give themselves the opportunity to make money as an independent contractor. There are benefits galore if you are aware of the nuances of the industry. The aforementioned books will certainly offer you the insight and information that you need for success in the field.

With so many bestsellers to choose from, you may be hard pressed to choose. While there are books for freelance professionals from different industry backgrounds, there are a few others that are specifically written for specialists in a field, but they certainly offer you adequate support and suggestions to start your own freelancing business. Packed with valuable information, these books for freelancers can prove to be the guiding force to take you to the next level of your freelance journey and get an edge over your competitors.

On-demand marketplaces

Additionally, when you are looking for work in the freelance industry, you may want to use on-demand freelance marketplaces, such as Peer Hustle. This intuitive mobile platform provides you the best resources to connect with prospective clients. Collaborate and work together with clients and tap into the sharing economy and use your skills to make quick money.

Top Website Builders
For Your Freelancing Business

If you are a freelancer who isn't a designer or developer, you will need websites to showcase your work, let the world know about your business, and actually get traffic.

If you are a freelance designer or developer, the world has moved on and you'd need to incorporate faster work flows and maybe embrace some of these website builders below.

Getting professionals to design might just be out of your budget for now (you can always do this later).

So, how do you go about getting a website? Use a DIY website builder.

So, here's how website builders (drag and drop platforms) can save you money, and we'll pick the best of the lot:

Webflow

By far, webflow is the only modern website builder that requires a slightly advanced user level to use its interface. While it's as close to hand-coding to build a website, it's still intuitive and retains drag and drop features. You can also opt to "clone" existing websites on their platform or to work off beautifully designed, marketing-centric templates.

After you complete your website, you can also export HTML5 and CSS3 code straight out and use it anywhere you like.

For all the fuss about bad designs, messy code, and "not the real thing" rallies that designers love to shout out, Webflow is the answer for DIY coding, without touching code.

Price: Free and paid plans start from $16 per month (Hosting extra)
Time to go live on average: 3 days

Wix

Wix is popular, and it has millions of users – small business owners – building websites off templates and cutting costs and time to im-
plementation down to a minimum. Wix is best used for simple websites
with a couple of pages and a contact form.

Building mobile responsive websites needs a few more tweaks but
it can be done by picking up a revelant template, making changes to it,
adding copy, and adding images.

You also have an option to go e-commerce but Wix isn't really built
for that. Yet, it's an option.

Price: Free and paid plans start from $4 for cheapest plan
Time to go live on average: 1 day

SquareSpace

Much like Apple and iOS, SquareSpace operates in a silo. You are boxed
into their platform but we don't see why you should not. Driven by existing, slick templates, SquareSpace allows for quick website, e-commerce
site, or landing page setup in a matter of minutes.

Hosting comes with any package you choose and you have pretty
much everything you need as long as it's about responsive and contem-
porary design.

Price:
Starts from $8 per month (includes hosting)
E-commerce plans start from $26 per month
Time to go live on average: 1 day

Webydo

Featuring a developer and user friendly website builder interface, Webydo also allows for template-driven design but allows for complete cus-
tomization without putting your finger into any kind of code. Yet, you
can always export the code and customize it to your liking.

Webydo allows for cross-browser build, as you go along, and gives you the flexibility you need to design your website the way you want it.

Price: Starts from $25 per month

Time to go live on average: 3 days

Weebly

Weebly has been around, just like Wix, and the new "Carbon" interface makes it incredibly simple to use. You can literally setup an e-commerce site within a day thanks to the existing templates and the ease of drag and drop.

Price: Free and paid plans start from $8 per month

Time to go live on average: 1 day

Which of these have you used yet? Tell us all about it.

14 Tools To Effectively Work From Home

More and more professionals are jumping onto the freelancing band-wagon and quitting their 9 to 5 jobs to kick-start their freelance career. To facilitate this transition, an increasing number of tools are available that will help you launch your dream career, control your work hours, and spend valuable time with family while making a good income.

1. Work space

If you choose to work from home, you need some isolated space, which can feel like a professional workspace. Of course, you do not want to mix work and personal lives and end up ruining both. The need for a separate and peaceful workspace cannot be denied. Creating your work space is as easy as cordoning off a part of your desk for work. This is especially useful if you don't have enough room for setting up a home office. Whether it's a nook above the kitchen or a spare room above the garage, you want a space that will fit in well as your home office, where you can receive clients or have video conferencing in Skype. The best part about having your own home office is that it will keep you disciplined and kicking.

2. Right equipment

Of course, you do not want to make major investments when setting up your workspace at home, but you still need a few essentials that would make a crucial component of your home office. Get an ergonomically designed desk and chair to set up an office-like environment, where you are comfortable working. When you have chosen to work remotely, it should be comfortable enough to sit for longer hours, so your investment should be in the right kind of furniture to ensure your body is relaxed and happy!

It may help to invest in a wireless mouse and keyboard to keep your space clutter free and make your work days much more comfortable.

3. Quality internet service

This is one critically important work-from-home tool that you cannot ignore at any cost. After all, your entire freelancing business depends on how quickly and efficiently you are able to connect with clients and customers. When shopping for an Internet connection, look for one that guarantees assured bandwidth, speed, uptime, download, quick response time, and a static IP address. You do not want your business to suffer due to poor network connectivity.

4. Business phone

Yes, you are working from home. But that does not mean you should choose your home phone for communicating with clients. You need a dedicated business phone line so that when a prospect or client calls in, your lines are open and can easily connect with you. Keeping a client waiting over phone could mean losing a client forever.

A separate phone will work as a rational choice for your business and ensure that you can answer calls immediately when a client calls in. This is a mobile-crazy world, but a true desk phone is what you need for office work, with guaranteed call quality. Having a smartphone will ensure that you stay on top of what's going on even when you are on the go, helping you respond to client calls and queries quickly. Pick a smartphone that handles email seamlessly. When you wish to start a freelancing career and aren't sure how to go about it, on-demand marketplaces, such as Peer Hustle, can come to your rescue. With a smartphone, you can easily set up a professional profile there and get set to connecting with clients from all over the globe anywhere anytime.

5. Web conferencing tools

These days we have virtual meeting places, including Skype or Gmail's inbuilt video chat messenger, to communicate freely over the Internet. If you don't have a web cam, Google Talk or AIM can come in handy. You can work as a team using group chat tools to stay in touch and collaborate seamlessly with your co-workers in a virtual space. Web conferencing solutions are some of the key freelancing tools you cannot ignore for a successful business.

6. Laptop/notebook

True, a powerful desktop machine is what you need for a home office, but you also need an equally robust mobile machine that can replace desktop when you are away on the road. This will ensure you can work anywhere anytime you aren't present at your work space.

7. Power protection

Working from home means you need to invest in a power backup system, so that you keep working even when there is an outage. Some projects are urgent and cannot wait for power restoration in your area. It is critically important to invest in a good line conditioning UPS so you can protect your digital equipment from power spikes and work seamlessly even when there is no electricity supply in your region due to reasons beyond control. This investment will ensure that a power outage doesn't wipe out your productivity.

8. Great lighting

Dim lighting cannot compare to bright light when working on a PC. Your eyes tend to get tired easily under dim lights. Installing bright lighting is a great investment for your work from home business, so your eyes are treated well. Great lighting work as a stress buster for your eyes and help keep you focused, raising your concentration level. With ambient lighting, you can work more productively and get your work done more efficiently.

9. All-in-one printer/scanner

A scanner that can take care of scanning, copying, printing, and faxing, is a handy tool for your home office. The printer may be long dead, but the machine can come to your rescue if you need to sign and submit a document immediately to a client. Isn't it more convenient than visiting a local printing shop? It does not make sense to lose your valuable time going to the shop to get the job done. Invest in your own laser printer that can do the job well and efficiently connect via WiFi and print directly from your smartphone.

If you want to keep your workspace clutter free, you may want to invest in a handheld digital scanner that scans all kinds of small and large papers and stores them digitally, where they are easily accessible.

10. Document collaboration

As a work from home professional, you need to be smart enough to use collaboration tools, which can come in handy when a client wants to share documents, slide shows, or spreadsheets. These tools allow you to make changes in real time to any document as and when required. What's more, you can access the documents stored in these applications wherever you go. DropBox and Google Drive are the most widely used document sharing tools used worldwide that make you more productive and efficient.

11. Customer relationship management

When you are working remotely as a freelancing professional, a reliable CRM tool will come in handy to store all of your database contacts, accounts, and documents. The best thing about a CRM system is that it integrates all communications, contacts, schedules, sales efforts, and project progress. Some of the more robust CRM applications come complete with compelling features, such as lead and opportunity tracking, which can play a big role in taking your freelancing career to the next level.

12. Redundancy, backup

As a freelance professional, you are online most of the time. In fact, you work remotely for clients from different parts of the globe. You cannot take the risk of losing all of your valuable work to a system breakdown or failure. Imagine a situation in which your desktop crashes and you are left with a blank computer! Sends shivers down the spine, right?

So why wait for such a terrible moment to strike and lose your data. Invest in an offsite and on-site backup system that can keep your data safe and secure all the time and quickly restore your desktop in the event of a failure. Offsite backup systems are designed to back up your data in times of a catastrophe or natural calamity.

Available through an online service provider, these seamless systems will backup your entire computer, saving thousands of crucial documents, files, videos, and pictures online. By investing in an offline backup system, you will thank yourself in the future when the inevitable happens.

13. Productivity monitoring software

Of course, you want to keep a tab on your progress. It would help to invest in a productivity-tracking solution to monitor daily work activities and run analytics on data. It was never so easy to keep a tab on your progress as with some innovative online applications available today. An efficient project management software can help boost efficiency while ensuring you are right on track.

14. Screen sharing software

As the industry evolves, an increasing number of businesses are interested to harness the power of this remote workforce and enjoy cost benefits. Since you plan to work from home, you cannot ignore a screen sharing software system that allows you to share screen with prospects and clients. These tools ensure easy collaboration and are quite handy when working remotely.

Working remotely is a dream for many professionals, and with the right work from home tools, you can give your freelancing career the heads up.

4 Productivity Apps
Freelancers Should Use

If an app can become an excellent reminder and can tell us which task to complete on priority, that will be amazing. Well, it's not an imagination anymore. Technology has turned our imagination into reality. According to numbers released by renowned sources, use of business applications has been the highest in 2014.

Users have been downloading and using the business apps more than anything. And why not? What if an app can help us improve our memory? Organizations have been trying to find out if the time management apps really work for employees. It's time to find out what ways an app can help us improve our productivity.

Apps to reduce your stress

You overburden yourself with huge targets, ambition and responsibilities, and then stress out. Is there something which can tell you that your mental health is at a risk so that you can immediately take precautionary measures? Yes, there is an app called GPS for the Soul.

How does GPS for the Soul work? Ariana Huffington, who is the founder of Huffington Post, has launched this new app. This app will help you calm your mind immediately when you're in a high stressful situation.

This is a tool to divert your mind from the point of worry. Of course, this will help you relax amidst a stressful working day so that you can use your time with a more focused and peaceful mind.

App to train the brain

You will require to do a whole lot of things to become an amazing solorpreneur. You've to be smart in building new skills, a fast learner and good with time management. You will have to ensure that you keep yourself focused all the time. Can there be something which can train the brain and improve its abilities?

Yes, there are few amazing apps which can improve your brainpower. With the help of these apps, you can put your brain to the test and improve your cognitive abilities. You can challenge your brain and improve your problem solving abilities. These apps will also help you to reduce anxiety and shift focus to positivity.

An app for tracking emails

Would you like to know who really read the emails you send? There is an app called MailTracker. If you can know if people really read the emails you send, it can save your lot of time. MailTracker is a very helpful app which can do this job.

This is an iOS app which can synchronize well with the iPhone's email box and let you know if the other person really read the email, or when they read the emails you send. This app can help you get a clear idea of whether it's really meaningful to send the emails, or if the receiver is really interested in your business or services.

Apps to improve time management

Apps like Focus Booster, Evernote, Dropbox, and Toggle can help you manage your time wisely. There are also many apps and tools for organization. They can help you manage your to do list. There are also apps for password management.

Although time management, work prioritization and organization will need huge amount of offline efforts and brainstorming, these apps can provide some sorts of help and can help you get started.

4 Reasons Why CoWorking Spaces Are Awesome For Freelancers

The idea of CoWorking is not new. It started way back in 1995 when a non profit organization named C-base first incorporated the idea.

You can book a coworking space or buy monthly membership to work independently and with many other professionals who are doing the same thing. Here, people with different backgrounds come to work and become a part of the community.

Deskmag is a coworking magazine. It does a lot of research on this concept and its benefits. According to Deskmag, the popularity of coworking spaces have increased among freelancers, entrepreneurs, and other independent professionals. Indeed, you can enjoy many benefits of sharing this community working place. Below you will find 4 reasons why coworking spaces are awesome.

Coworking spaces reduce boredom of loneliness

The idea of coworking makes professionals feel they are part of a community. Freelancers and independent professionals were interviewed to know why they prefer to work in a coworking space. Most of them responded that they don't like to work alone, and most importantly, they like the freedom of socialization that a coworking space offers.

Unlike an organization, professionals who work in a coworking space enjoy the freedom to decided how and when they want to interact with others.

Coworking spaces offer great networking opportunities as they arrange and organize networking events, training programs and other social events throughout the year to help people connect to others beyond their own company or professional circle.

Coworking spaces save time

A coworking space gives better and faster opportunities to find solutions to problems. People working there are likely to face similar challenges like you. This is why the chances will be there that you will be able to quickly know a solution that someone has already thought about. There will be more minds thinking creatively. So, you will get to know about new things, like a new apps, new resources, best practices, etc.

You will be able to save time by knowing solutions to many problems. You will find answers to your questions quickly. This will help you deal with any lack of ideas you may experience.

Coworking spaces are cheaper options

Don't you think so? Booking a coworking space is much cheaper than finding a commercial space to rent. Even if you have a team, you can book a space according to your need and on the basis of membership facilities. Also, these types of facilities don't rob the professionals by enforcing rigorous membership plans.

The coworking spaces are generally found to offer very flexible and short-length membership options where you don't have to block a huge amount of money by buying an annual membership plan. You can take monthly or quarterly memberships and can cancel a booking with prior intimation. Your money will be refunded. So, a coworking space gives you an excellent environment to work with an attractive and flexible terms and conditions.

Coworking spaces can give you better control on a job

Harvard University researchers decided to do a study in order to know why the coworking spaces help people work more effectively and succeed.

During their research they found out that people utilizing coworking spaces had more freedom in respect to deciding whether they wanted to work in a quite environment, could take a long break to go to gym in between the working hours, or they needed a very long day to complete a serious deadline.

Coworking spaces are excellent for solorpeneurs and entrepreneurs. Even organizations are employing the idea of coworking spaces nowadays to help employees improve their productivity.

6 Blogs Every Freelancer Should Read

A Reuters article revealed that almost one in three Americans are freelancing in America now. The study conducted by independent research firm Edelman Berland indicated some very interesting numbers regarding the growing popularity for this independent career choice.

Clearly, there will be more competition in the near future. You've to work harder, be proactive, get great at relationship building, networking, finding, converting leads, and creating demand for your skill.

For that, you need to stay connected to the industry. And when you work from home, you've to be an avid reader to know the latest updates on freelancing career. Blogs can be excellent sources for relevant information and effective platforms for networking.

But you have to choose blogs which publish fresh, and very informative content, and have impressive number of followers. Below you'll find 6 such blogs that every freelancer should read.

Time Management Ninja: Blog that teaches time management techniques

When working from home as a freelancer, one of the biggest challenges could be time management. A Forbes article pointed out that one of the biggest barriers to time management, for most professionals is lack of organization, focus, and attention. Many have a propensity to be easily distracted by unimportant things, lack motivation, or become lonely.

Time Management Ninja shares tips and advises on organization, how to save time and finish tasks within the deadlines.

The Freelancer's Union: A great way to stay connected with the industry

The Freelancer's Union Blog is a popular reading resource for ambitious freelancers. You will learn about the freelancing industry overall. You will find posts about how this industry is doing, what can be the future prospects for aspiring freelancers looks like, tips on how to grow your business and credibility as a freelancer, etc.

Plus, this blog is fun. It has a pleasing graphic design and a large range of posts. Want to know how to be a happy freelancer? You will also get it here.

Addicted2Success: Blog on personal development

You will need a huge amount of positive energy and attitude to stay motivated in your freelancing career till the time when you ultimately build your brand. You won't be successful in getting what you want, all the time. So, that's asking for a different mindset altogether.

The Addicted2Success Blog shares incredible tips and advises on how to face a crisis and achieve success.

Seth Godin: Amazing blog for knowledge building

Heard about Seth Godin? He is a best selling author, a motivational speaker, and also a world-renowned marketer. Want any advice on marketing, selling, brand building, or business intelligence? You should bookmark Seth's blog and take home his byte-sized information and insights.

Check out his blog and read his posts.

Buffer: Excellent social media marketing blog

Once you opt for a freelancing career, you'll always have to stay in touch with latest digital marketing trends and developments.

And for that, the Buffer blog will be the most beneficial choice. You'd learn everything you need to about social media management and how you'd be able to use social media for your business.

Inc: A great reading source for small business owners

Inc shares very interesting posts on small business growth strategies, tips to get over obstacles, failures, productivity hacks, reputation management, dealing with work stress, business management, innovations, technology, and many more things you'd absolutely need for your business.

These are some of the blogs you should always peruse, if you're trying to build a freelancing career. Follow these blogs to get helpful content related to your niche and professional aspirations.

What do you read?

4 Tools Freelancers Should Bet On For Productivity

Freelancers need to do huge amount of business work alone.

Why not use the latest techs and apps to reduce your work burden? Depending on the size of your business, you can try options for managing emails, tools for prioritizing work, availing cheaper calls, setting reminders and calendars, tools for arranging conference calls, etc. You can also try analytical tools to check the overall performance of your business website.

Thankfully, solopreneurs and freelancers today have plenty of options to take care of their daily tasks and ensure well-being of business. Below you will find some amazing tools for improving productivity.

Evernote

Ever tried Evernote for your work? Amazing features and smooth integration of functions have made this app very popular worldwide. Evernote is widely known as an online note taking app.

This popular app is extremely easy to use and excellent across platform support. Yes, you can use Evernote in Windows, Mac, iOS, Android, BlackBerry, Windows phone, etc.

You can use Evernote to make a to do list, to maintain record of reference information, as a digital scrapbook, etc. You can make a good use of the Evernote camera.

Another great advantage of using Evernote is that you can share the content stored in Evernote. Smartphones support Evernote's features. This is why it becomes another potential tool for busy freelancers. However, not all features of the app is available in all phones.

Wake up with Wakie

It's so amazing to think that how some great minds think unconventionally. Are you too lazy to wake up early? Do you often fail to meet business targets and deadlines because you're too reluctant to leave your bed early?

In an independent business like freelancing, this can cause a lot of problems. But, you can use Wakie to get some help.

What is Wakie? Well, this is an alarm clock app that will help you wake up with a stranger's voice.

Wondering what does that mean? If you're not a morning person, this app will help you make the daily process easier. This app has a community of users. All of the members of the community are anonymous. If you become a member of the community, this app will send you notification, in terms of an anonymous voice, to wake you up at the time you want. This is how you can avoid oversleeping and be on time to finish an important project.

Basecamp for project management

Basecamp can be used in your browser for efficient project collaboration. If you're working as a team, it will help you amazingly. This is mainly a project management tool which will help your team collaborate with each other when working remotely.

Explore the app more to know the attractive features.

Pocket is great if you love to read

This is mainly a reader service. It will help you read long articles that you would like to read later at your convenience. This is an application that will let you conveniently save the articles to the cloud.

Pocket can be used on vast range of smart devices like iOS and Android platforms. You can even use it on the Safari browser. Pocket will help you add the web addresses that you would like to read later to its list of popular readings.

Pocket is an excellent application which makes reading easier and helps you arrange and manage the content faster.

5 Free Tools Every Freelancer Must Use

Technology is a savior. Thanks to that, small businesses including freelancers are on the same playing field as the big boys. In fact, while really large companies are stuck with old time technology, others such as startups and freelancers have all the advantage of using the best technology has to provide.

Since "there's an app" for almost everything, you can use some of the best technology out there for your freelancing business. With tons of tools, solutions, and web-based applications to choose from, you'll only have to spend time doing research in what solution works best for your freelancing business.

Here are some of those freelancing tools and solutions for you:

Get Base

Given that you'd be reaching out to many prospects during the day and that you'd also follow up regularly, you'd need something more reliable than excel sheets.

In fact, you'd need a CRM (Customer Relationship Management) like Get Base so that you'd know exactly who each of your potential customers are, information about them, to-do lists for each lead, follow the status of each lead, etc.

MailChimp

We wrote about why every freelancer should use email marketing and MailChimp is one of those popular email service providers that lets you send out about 2000 emails and to 500 subscribers for free.

It puts you on a straight-line path to email marketing – the one digital marketing channel that's guaranteed to make you money and nurture your leads for the long term.

Unbounce

Put up a landing page for every offer you'd ever have to make and every campaign you'd ever run to promote your freelancing offers.

A landing page puts a tremendous amount of focus into the equation and doesn't dilute the attention of your buyers. It's also easy to track conversions on a landing page compared to a full-fledged website.

Normally, you have to hire developers or get IT help each time you'd need a landing page. Instead, sign up for a free Unbounce.com account and start creating landing pages for each offer you make.

Asana

Asana is free to use and it brings the best of project management to your freelancing business. Use it for managing your projects, assign yourself work, or even work with other team members you might have.

Asana helps you organize your projects by client and allows you to set deadlines, milestones, projects, tasks, and sub-tasks. The tool also integrates with Google drive to complete your workflow.

Due.com

You have to track time for hourly projects, send professional looking invoices, and keep track of your payments, receivables, etc.

Depending on where you are working from, you also have to keep books and maintain records of your business transactions. A solution like Due helps you do all that and more.

Other alternatives to invoicing are, Xero and Freshbooks.

What are your favorite tools? What kind of technology do you use for your freelancing business? Share your best tools with us.

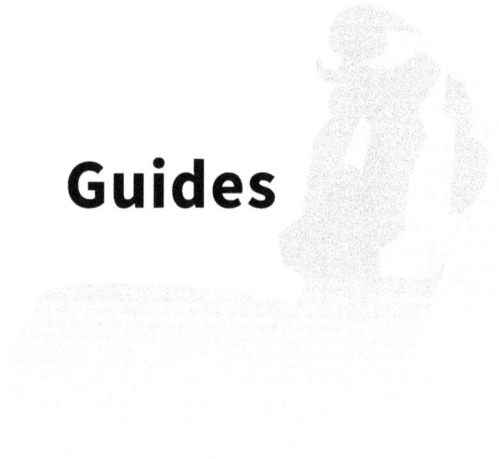

Guides

How To Become A Photographer: 10 Tips On Starting A Photography Career

A photography career has a charm of its own. If you yearn to become a professional photographer, you are already aware that this is a highly competitive industry. But does that stop you from living your dream freelance photography career? If you have the right skills, consumers will trust their time and money to you, hoping that you can produce a visually appealing image that tells a story. There is nothing better than making money doing what you are passionate about. Isn't it? When your clicks leave the world awe-struck, could you ask for more?

Yes, freelance photography gives you the opportunity to earn a reputation across the globe!

Photography is a huge world

All of us appreciate the ability of a camera to capture moments dear to us and freeze them in time, leaving us with beautiful memories to cherish all our lives. If photography is a passion, it can pay you rich dividends as a career. Starting a photography career isn't that difficult.

Here's how you can get started:

1. Build a portfolio

A strong portfolio is the first thing you would need to start a freelance photography career. It should include samples of your work and show potential clients that you have the skills and experience demanded by their photography project.

If you are just starting out, make sure you have something impressive to show clients. Show them your shots of your friend's marriage. Of course, you have covered a cute baby's birthday bash, capturing sweetest moments that would bring a big smile to anybody's face. Include them in your portfolio.

All such photos can decorate your portfolio and convince potential clients of your abilities and skills in using the camera to capture moments in real time. You may want to choose a theme for your portfolio and include an appealing statement outlining your experience and feelings about the subject matter. It would help to include relevant certifications in your portfolio.

However, it is important to assess the strengths and weaknesses of a picture before including it in your profile.

2. Choose your field

Do you have a passion for a specific field? Does nature inspire and motivate you more than anything else? Do you love to capture sporting events or find taking clicks of architectural buildings more interesting? Do you wish to be a military photographer or plan to capture lifetime events?

You may want to market yourself as a specialist in the freelance photography industry, with core skills in a specific field. Choose your field and get started with your camera.

3. Only buy necessary equipment

Don't feel tempted to buy unnecessary gear and equipment to "help your business." You don't need all the photography equipment that a competitor uses. Chances are you won't ever use all that you have invested in. It would only amount to wasting money by investing in gear that you don't need.

You can always convince yourself to be thoughtful about purchases. If you already own photography gear that creates the images you want, you have just the right equipment to frame shots and create memories for clients. So why waste money on something that you don't need?

But this doesn't mean you should buy a low-quality camera. The most important equipment you need is a single-lens reflex camera with a built-in light meter. Second, you need some editing software to edit images and organize photos. Buy a camera, lights, and lenses you can comfortably use and wait for your business to generate more money for investment in advanced camera equipment.

4. Encourage referrals

Word-of-mouth marketing continues to get people business. Prospective clients are more likely to trust recommendations of friends than magazine advertisements. Is there a relative or friend that has used your services? You can always spread out the word about your services to those around you, so they can bring you business whenever someone needs a photographer for an event.

When you have started with your freelance photography career, it would help to set up a formal referral program to reward clients for referring your services to others. It may help to hand out a stack of your business cards to happy clients and encourage them to tell their friends about you. A business card with a professional logo is a significant marketing tool to present yourself as a serious freelance photographer.

5. Market yourself

Starting a photography career may seem like a daunting task initially. However, once you understand the nuances of the business, everything will fall into place. To start with, you need to build a client base. Try leaving your marketing material with local businesses that attract customers. You may have the best photography skills in the world, but you may not see any success until potential clients know about you. Show potential customers that what you are doing is interesting and valuable. Go out of the way to impress clients and get business.

Leverage the power of social media to market your services. Engage with potential audiences and start a discussion.

6. Connect with potential clients

When you are wondering how to become a photographer, it may help to join online freelancing marketplaces and forums. Connect with your target audience through mobile, on-demand platforms that have become a hub for freelancers. Peer Hustle is one such freelance marketplace where you can connect with potential customers and impress them with your portfolio and skills and get started.

When you are already a professional in the industry and are looking to expand your freelancing business, the feature-rich mobile application can connect you with an entire team of videographers, photographers, actors, models, stylists, or makeup artists for a client's photo shoot.

7. Get a website

As a freelancer, you want the world to know about your skills. A website is one self-promotion tool that you may want to use to showcase your skills to potential clients. In fact, by having your own website, it's easier to establish your credibility among prospective customers and show them that you mean business.

- Include your best photos that instantly click with the audience and display creativity and experience.

- Keep the site updated almost every day with fresh photographs. This will enhance the popularity of your website and keep it fresh in the search engines.

It may also help to start your own blog and talk about photography. A blog would be a window to your photography knowledge and establish you as an expert in the industry. People will look up to you for advice and inspiration.

8. Shoot a lot

When you are starting a photography career, make it a point to take pictures wherever you go. By doing so, you will become more familiar with your camera and learn it better. Practicing photo shoots in different modes every time will improve your understanding and knowledge and give you a better idea of standing behind the camera. The more you spend time taking pictures, the better you'll get at using the lens.

9. Stay organized and disciplined

It's important to be disciplined and organized when you start out as a freelance photographer. Catalogue all of your projects and make sure you are able to easily trace any specific file that you may need later.

It's equally important to figure out what makes you stand apart from the competition. Use it to your advantage. The goal is to get work on the basis of your skills, not what is trending. It's your unique selling point that will outshine the present trends and establish you as a professional in the industry that clients can trust with their work.

Try to imitate the work of your heroes. By doing so, you will gain deeper insight into process and production and also learn more about your personal tastes.

10. Set your goals high and stay updated

See the big picture and remain professional at all times. Set high goals and never undervalue yourself. Bidding low on projects may create a wrong impression of your competence to clients. Underbidding reduces your value as a professional.

When you set yourself big goals, it will be easier to accomplish things and stay focused. However, it is not necessary to beat yourself up if things aren't going as planned. Initially it may be hard but if you have faith in yourself and continue to make efforts, your hard work will pay off.

Your goal is to portray a picture of yourself that you want clients to see. Remain professional to the core and always be updated with the trends of photography so you are never caught unaware by the demands of a client. As photography is an art, you need to show your creative skills and experiment on your own shots. Photographic websites and magazines are your best recourse to getting the latest updates in the industry.

Freelance photography is a lucrative career these days. With the right skills and work approach, you can carve out a niche for yourself in the industry and get your photography business running. True, starting a photography career and earning a name for yourself may not be a smooth ride, but you can outshine the competition with a dedicated approach to work and setting the correct budget. If it's a passion to photograph others, turning it into a profession is a great idea! Get started with a freelance photography career today!

How To Become A Model: 10 Tips On Starting A Modeling Career

Modeling is an enchanting career. It captivates and attracts young aspiring minds. An increasing number of hopefuls are choosing freelance modeling as a career. The modeling industry lends itself to a freelance lifestyle, since you may not be required to remain loyal to just one employer and are free to pursue as many freelance modeling assignments as you can manage. Who knows you might just be hired to become the 'face' of a brand!

With the freedom to choose the projects you want to work on, freelance modeling offers you the flexibility to design your career around whatever you like doing best, while paying equal attention to personal commitments. Of course, you hold the key to managing your time. As a freelance model, you have the advantage of grabbing opportunities to increase your earnings by seeking out clients directly, without having to pay agency commission.

How to become a freelance model

Modeling is a competitive industry, and aspiring models may have a bit of a struggle to find work. However, in the freelancing world, a good place to host your portfolio is your own website.

1. Online portfolio

Having a website of your own would give you the best platform to list details of your experience and background and promote yourself to potential clients. Having your profile in social networks will boost your online credentials. By doing so, you can launch yourself on a global level and promote your services through existing contacts while making new ones. It would help to have an online copy of flyers and business cards that could be linked to your website and used for promotional activities.

2. Marketing collateral

You can always leave your marketing collateral at places where they might be spotted by industry professionals. There isn't anything better than getting a call from potential clients that they are impressed with your portfolio.

3. Do not limit yourself

When starting your freelance modeling career, you may come across different gigs. Have an appropriate portfolio, with your best photos that instantly click with potential clients. There are many clients that do not hesitate to hire a "shorter" fashion model or a "taller" print model.

For models pursuing more than one modeling category, it will help to have the right images for each type so you have the right portfolio to show the right clients. When you submit your portfolio to freelance gigs, do not limit yourself to one category; rather, expand your horizon and submit to freelance castings for different categories, including swimwear, fitness and sports, and fashion/runway models, among others. Stick with genres that suit your taste as well as body type.

4. Cherry pick

Do not submit yourself to castings that don't interest you. In fact, the real beauty of being a freelance model lies in the ability to control your own schedule, career, and earnings. As a freelance model, you are free to cherry pick the modeling assignments you want and not what an agency forces on you.

5. Competitive pricing

When it comes to finding work as a freelance model, your competition is a big consideration. The number of competitors that can you do what you do is an important factor to decide your pricing strategy to stay competitive and in the race. If there are many models in your area that do amazing standard glamour shots, you are up against stiff competition. It may help to keep your price low. Contrarily, if you have a unique skill that a handful of models possess, there is nothing bad in using it to your advantage. After all, rare talent is more valuable!

When you enter the freelance modeling industry, explore the prices that others are willing to work for. Since you are new, it may not hurt to charge a little less than the average price. However, if offers are starting to flood you, you may choose to raise your rates by a fraction. Lower your rates if you aren't getting any offers and re-assess your portfolio.

When you have a few assignments lined up, give top priority to gigs offering monetary compensation and next in line should be clients offering tearsheets from the actual publication. You may want to try any other modeling gig that does not offer any pay or tearsheets if the client's work interests you. Rarely do clients share a CD of your images for your personal use. If a client agrees to do so, you may want to go for their modeling assignment.

Since you are not working with any agency, it is important to maintain your list of contact with clients and photographers and keep your portfolio up to date to be eligible for any upcoming modeling opportunities.

6. On-demand marketplace for freelance models

As a freelancing model, you are responsible for handling your own marketing and finding work independently. Modeling communities, including networking events, offer a platform for freelancing models to source work easily by establishing direct contact with companies and clients. On-demand marketplaces can come to your rescue when you are looking for freelance modeling gigs.

Peer Hustle is one such on-demand mobile app for the shared economy that simplifies the process of becoming a freelance model. By creating an account in this online platform, you can easily spread the word about your skills and harness the power of the sharing economy app to run a full-fledged freelance modeling business.

The mobile platform makes it seamless for professionals and clients to connect and run a successful independent business on their phones. As a freelance model, you are running yourself as a business, which requires great amount of work and dedication. These mobile platforms can prove to be the holy grail for freelance success.

7. Professional demeanor

It is important that you treat and carry yourself professionally and do not let a client push you around. Of course, you would not want a potential client to talk you into a situation where you are uncomfortable. This could happen if you show any doubt in your abilities.

Stand your ground and do it with grace and professionalism, without an iota of doubt about your abilities or skills. Stay cool even in a negative environment, never badmouth anyone, or do not exchange heated words with a client when things are getting out of control and walk away with your head held high. Gently let "problem" clients know that you are a professional model and if they cannot work with you on the same level, they are free to look for someone else.

8. Networking networking networking

A small thank-you note for the people you have worked with would be enough to remind them that they can rely on you for future projects. It might help to send out brief emails to the photographer and casting director with whom you have worked with, conveying your happiness that you have had a great experience working with them.

Impressing one client in the modeling industry could open the flood gates to success for your modeling career. Who knows a happy client might refer you to others!

After every shoot, shake hands with each person involved in the project and hand out your modeling business card. Sending out a follow-up email to each one of them, letting them know about your experience, might do wonders for your career.

9. Discipline

Discipline rules the roost in every industry. Always arrive on time, reply to all emails in a timely manner, and answer every phone call. Your positive and fun attitude would be welcome by clients and photographers that choose to work with you.

Clients automatically start associating you with being disciplined, punctual, and dependable. What more could you ask for when you are just starting out? Remember, everybody wants to be associated with people that are a joy to work with.

Showing up early makes a great impression on clients and can work magic for your freelance career. Imagine clients remembering you as a model "that shows up before the rest of us do!" Discipline is one weapon that can enhance your marketability in addition to your looks and hair/makeup and help you create a lasting impression on clients.

10. Be easy to work with

State what you will and will not do before you are roped into a specific assignment. Clearly state your expectations when you are starting a modeling career. Put time in perfecting your craft. Doing so would save you and the client time, and they may be willing to pay you more for that reason. Clients love to work with such models that read their mind before they can utter a word.

Remember, beauty alone does not make you a great model. Clients look for beauty with brains that simply flows with their expectations. Unless you are a perfectionist in your industry, avoid attempting to coach the photographer or else you may end up on their black list. Of course, you do not want to be counted as time wasted for clients.

Professionals do not mind paying a higher price for a beauty with brains, because they will get exactly the shots they expect. If you have the skills and qualities they can appreciate and are amazing at what you do, you can launch a prosperous freelance modeling career.

www.ingramcontent.com/pod-product-compliance
Lightning Source LLC
Chambersburg PA
CBHW022109210326
41521CB00028B/170